THE ILLUMINATI 666

Compiled by
William Josiah Sutton

Introduction by
Roy Allan Anderson, D.D.

TEACH Services, Inc.
Brushton, New York

Copyright © 1983 The Institute of Religious Knowledge
Copyright © 1995 TEACH Services, Inc.

ISBN 1-57258-014-3
Library of Congress Catalog Card No. 96-60014

Published by

TEACH Services, Inc.
R.R. 1, Box 182
Brushton, New York 12916

DEDICATION

"Although ministers have always been aware of the presence of evil powers, this book of about three hundred pages puts the teacher/preacher in possession of astonishing materials that will, when rightly used, make his ministry more powerful and effective. It sets forth in vivid language some issues too little understood." Kenneth L. Vine, Dean of Religion, Loma Linda University

CONTENTS

Introduction

Is there such a thing as The Illuminati? Does this fit into our sophisticated age? Some ridicule the very idea, but in these chapters a fascinating portrayal is uncovered.

Are such words as *Illuminism* or *The Illuminati* new to you? That is not strange, for today these expressions are unknown to millions, even among many well educated people. This results from the plan to keep that giant Conspiracy under cover, to always remain secret.

"The great strength of our order lies in its concealment," declared Adam Weishaupt, founder of the new order in 1776. "Let it never appear in any place in its own name, but always covered by another name and another occupation." (Quoted in Robison's *Proofs of a Conspiracy*, p. 195.)

This world-wide cover-up has been so cleverly conducted through the centuries, even milleniums, that most folk are entirely unaware of its existence.

This Conspiracy goes back to the time of Nimrod, that evil genius who began that ancient apostasy in Mesopotamia.

While every Sunday School teacher knows something about the Tower of Babel, yet few realize that the principles and philosophies of that ancient movement are right now playing a tremendous role in both our political and religious life.

In this book, *The Illuminati 666*, we bring together many startling, almost unbelievable, facts. Before getting into the depths of our story, let us note briefly some of our sources. How thankful we are for books, even those with which we do not agree, for they show us the thinking of other writers. But some, like that century-old classic, Alexander Hislop's *The Two Babylons*, open a vast area of thought and knowledge.

We are quite aware of how some scholars regard Hislop's work. Their attitude, however, only reveals how sadly ignorant they are of the real issues. Others, like Neal Wilgus' *The Illuminoids*, throw much modern light on the subject, although he does not go much on the idea.

Of course we could not expect Hislop to know many things we know today. They had not been discovered at the time he wrote, which leads us to wonder what he would write were he living today. His most valuable contribution has always been what history he opens up for a real researcher. I have in my hand the author's personally autographed copy of the third edition, 1857, to London's great preacher, C. H. Spurgeon. This was picked up in a London used book store, more than 50 years ago. Hislop presented it to Spurgeon after he had dedicated it to Lord John Scott, a contemporary who is regarded as an authority on "Primeval Antiquity."

The most reliable book of all we possess is, of course, "the book of books" — *The Bible*. While we will be quoting from many authors, yet we will regard God's Word as the final light of truth. In both the Old and New Testaments much has been brought to light to clearly identify the Conspiracy, which is the purpose of this present work. In two of the Apostle Paul's strongest letters to the church he speaks of two great mysteries. The "Mystery of Godliness," which in his words is "God manifest in the flesh," is without question the Lord Jesus Christ (I Timothy 3:16). In his second letter to the Thessalonian believers he describes the "Mystery of Iniquity" whom he calls, "The Man of Sin," "*who opposeth and exalteth himself above all that is called God or that is worshipped; so that he as God sitteth in the temple of God, shewing himself that he is God* (II Thessalonians 2:7, 3 and 4)."

At the time the apostle was writing he said, "The mystery of iniquity doth already work." It was working in his day. But he foretold a greater demonstration of Satanic power that was to come. It would be backed up by "*all power and signs and lying wonders*" (verse 9).

Shortly after the apostle's death, the church, which for decades had given such a powerful witness to the power of God through miracles and especially through the conversion of thousands to the simple gospel, began to "fall away" just as Paul had foretold in II Thessalonians 2:2. The elements of deception were already evident, especially while Philip was doing a mighty work in Samaria. The story of this is in Acts 8:5-21, where we are told, "*the people with one accord gave heed unto those things which Philip spake, hearing and seeing the miracles which he did* (verse 6)." Then there comes "*a certain man, called Simon, which beforetime in the same city used sorcery and bewitched the people of Samaria*" with sorceries. This man was also baptized and the scripture says, "*he continued with Philip, and wondered, beholding the miracles and signs which were done.*" It is evident this man was more interested in the miracles than he was with the marvelous conversions.

When news reached the headquarters at Jerusalem, they sent Peter and John who prayed for these young converts that they might also receive the baptism of the Spirit of God, for as yet it had fallen on none of them. After the apostles prayed for them and laid their hands on them they, too, received the Holy Spirit in power.

This man Simon was watching closely what was being done. Then, coming to Peter and John he said, "Give me also this power, that on whomsoever I lay hands, he may receive the Holy Spirit." But there was something lacking in his life which the apostles discerned. And this brought perhaps the sharpest rebuke recorded in Scripture: *"Thy money perish with thee,"* or as Phillips' translation reads, "To hell with you and your money!" to which the translator adds this note, "(These words are exactly what the Greek means.)" *You can have no share or place in this ministry, for your heart is not honest before God.* Acts 8:20-21.

Now who was this Simon? The Scriptures make clear he was a Samaritan deceiver who practiced divination. He *"used sorcery, and bewitched the people ... giving out that he himself was some great one, and the people from the least to the greatest were so bewitched that they proclaimed him to be the great power of God* (Acts 8:9-11)."

The Samaritans were not Israelites, they were Babylonians placed there by the King of Assyria (II Kings 17:24-25). They were placed in the cities of Samaria instead of the children of Israel; and they possessed Samaria and dwelt in the cities thereof, but *"they feared not the Lord."* These folk were pagans in every way. In Hastings' *Dictionary of the Apostolic Church*, we read, "The amalgam of paganism and Christianity ... was especially obvious in the Simonian system (p. 496)." Simon Magus evidently became the leader of a retrograde sect, using some Christian terminology, but in reality anti-Christian (*ibid.*). The author of this baptised heathenism ... was Simon Magus. He unquestionably adulterated Christianity with pagan ideas and practices (see *Apostolic Christianity*, Vol. 2, p. 566).

This paganized Christianity was already having its effect while the apostles were living, for in II Corinthians 11:3,4 we read Paul's concern in these words, "I am afraid that your minds may be seduced from a single-hearted devotion to him (Christ) by the same subtle means the serpent used towards Eve for apparently you cheerfully accept a man who comes to you preaching a different Jesus from the one we told you about, and you readily accept a spirit and a gospel quite different from the one you originally accepted (Phillips translation)."

Under the influence of Satan's ministers, Christians were being transformed into the ministers of unrighteousness and many were being led astray. The mystery of iniquity was already working, and later it blossomed into a full and diabolical apostasy.

Simon is never spoken of as a member of the true church - the body of Christ. He took the name of Christ and espoused a few of His teachings. These he mingled with his Babylonian mystery religion. "Thus he became the leader of a retrograde sect, perhaps nominally Christian ... but in reality anti-Christian, and exalting Simon himself to the central position which Christianity was giving to Jesus Christ (Hastings' *Dictionary of the Apostolic Church*, Vol. 1, p. 497)."

Simon's influence had reached as far as Rome, according to Justin Martyr. When he wrote his Apology in A.D. 152, he mentions Simon four times as the founder of a formidable movement. He "came to Rome in the day of Claudius Caesar and made such an impression by his magical powers, that he was honored as a god, a statue being erected to him on the Tiber, between the two bridges, bearing the inscription: *Simon's deosancto* (i.e., 'the Holy god Simon')." Quoted in *Dictionary Of Christian Biology*, Vol. 4, p. 682.

When we become more familiar with the origin and history of the Babylonian Mystery Religions it will open up areas of understanding, throwing light on the world's present situation. It is not generally known that pagan deities were known as "Peters" or "Patres" and that the special gods, or the *Hierophantae*, in the majority of their temples had particular priests who were constantly "occupied in the celebration of mysteries (see *Ancient Mythology*, Vol. 1, p. 354)." Even more interesting is the fact that the consonantal word P-T-R, indicating Peter, means "to interpret." They were "interpreters" of the mystery religions or the pagan mysteries of ancient Babylon. It is not surprising then that Simon Magus the bewitcher from Samaria became known as Simon Peter or Simon the interpreter.

Moses evidently knew this when he wrote the Pentateuch, for we read in Deuteronomy 23:4 that Balaam the son of Beor of Pathor of Mesopotamia was hired to curse Israel. We read in Numbers 22:4, 5 and 7, that Balak the son of Zippor, king of the Moabites, sent messengers to Balaam the son of Beor to Pethor and "the elders of Moab ... departed with the rewards of divination in their hand." Then follows the account of the ass that refused to pass the angel and who later spoke to Balaam.

Mesopotamia was the very home of idolatory or the Babylonian mysteries. The name Balaam in Semitic language means "Conqueror of the People" and definitely links us with "*Nimrod the mighty hunter before the Lord* (Genesis 10:9)." We read in verse 8 that this Nimrod, the son of Cush, began to be a mighty one in the earth. He was the great grandson of Noah and "*the beginning of his kingdom was Babel* (verse 10)." He built other cities like Ashur and Nineveh, which later became the capital of the Assyrian Empire. Nimrod is styled "the mighty hunter before the Lord," or as Dr. Strong renders it, "against the Lord." He shows that the Hebrew word *paniym* is more correctly translated "against" rather than "before." Nimrod was a great leader and he and his cohorts "*changed the glory of the incorruptible God into an image liken to corruptible* man, and to birds and fourfooted beasts and creeping things (Romans 1:23)." The following verses of this Roman Epistle are upon the whole diabolical practice of homosexuality among both men and women, which is becoming so popular these days even among certain religious groups.

Nimrod was certainly "against" the Lord in all he planned and did. "The mighty hunter against the Lord" led multitudes away from the Creator and laid plans for a world-wide Conspiracy against God. That was the reason behind the Babylonian Mystery cults. Nicholaus was the name he was known by in Greece and that also means "Conqueror of the People."

Some claim that Balaam was the chief of a college of priests at Pethor, a sacred high place in Mesopotamia. From that old location near the site of the tower of Babel he organized what he thought was a complete cover-up destined to become one universal religion. And his plan almost succeeded. By the end of the fourth century, real Christianity was almost dead and in its place, but under the name of Christianity was, to use the words of Griffen, "a corrupt hierarchy controlling the nations of Europe, making the Church a veritable cesspool of iniquity, spiritual corruption, heathen philosophy, and whoredoms ... a closely-knit group of Satan-inspired, power-hungry and lust-filled rebels masquerading under a 'Christian' label but embracing all the Satanic rottenness of pagan Babylon (*Fourth Reich of the Rich*, 1978, Des Griffen, p. 38)."

In the year 323 A.D. the Emperor Constantine officially adopted this Simonized Christianity, which was nothing more than "baptized heathenism," and made it the official religion of Rome. Thus was the church led into a period of degeneration, often styled the "Dark Ages." A subline in his *History of the Reformation* on page 17 says, "The nations of Christendom no longer looked to a holy and living God, but had recourse to all the means that a superstitious, fearful and alarmed imagination could devise." And that condition prevailed for over a thousand years, at least until the Renaissance, beginning in the 14th century, which revived interest in science and literature, followed by the Reformation in the 16th century. Then things began to happen. Part 1 of Chapter I and the following chapters of this book plunge us into the background of the great apostasy showing its results and the Divine call back to the apostolic faith found in the Holy Scriptures.

Roy Allan Anderson, D.D.

CHAPTER I

Part 1

1. The Origin of False Religions Began with Lucifer.

2. The Rebellion in Heaven Against God.

3. The Rebellion on Earth Against God.

4. Lucifer Was and Is Today Worshipped As the Sun-god.

5. The Doctrine of the Immortal Soul, Basic Foundation of Witchcraft.

6. Astrology, the Origin of All Pagan Sciences.

Chapter I

In the last book of the Bible, Jesus Christ gives His Last warning before He returns the second time. This Last Day warning is found in chapters 13, 14, 16, 17 and 18 of the Book of Revelation. Jesus warns His people about how the whole world will be deceived into worshipping Satan, symbolized as the *Seven Headed Dragon* attacking a woman, a symbol of the True Faith.[1]

In Revelation 13:4, 8, 9 Jesus' prediction about the worship of Satan throughout this world may be read: *"And they WORSHIPPED THE DRAGON which gave power unto the beast: and they worshipped the beast, saying, Who is like unto the beast? Who is able to make war with him? ... And all that dwell upon the earth SHALL WORSHIP HIM, WHOSE NAMES ARE NOT WRITTEN IN THE BOOK OF LIFE OF THE LAMB SLAIN FROM THE FOUNDATION OF THE WORLD. If any man have an ear, let him hear."*

The Apostle John wrote: *"Little children, it is the last time: and as ye have heard that antichrist shall come, even now are there many antichrists; whereby we know that it is the last time."* I John 2:18.

The Apostle Paul warned: *"Let no man deceive you by any means: for that day shall not come, except there come a falling away first, and that man of sin be revealed, the son of perdition; Who opposeth and exalteth himself above all that is called God, or that is*

1. The symbolical language that pictures Satan as a Seven Headed Dragon can be seen in Revelation 12:3,9.

worshipped: *so that he as God sitteth in the temple of God, shewing himself that he is God."* II Thessalonians 2:3,4. There are various ways our Lord has made known to His followers how to detect Satan who is the invisible head of a partly religious and partly political movement. Revelation 13:18 warns it would be branded with the number 666. In Revelation 17:5 our Lord describes this satanic movement that is antichrist in a symbol of a lewd beautiful woman. *And upon her forehead was a name written,* "MYSTERY, BABYLON THE GREAT, MOTHER OF HARLOTS AND ABOMINATIONS OF THE EARTH."

The very last warning our Lord is now giving the deceived world is found in Revelation 18:4 — *"And I heard another voice from heaven, saying, COME OUT OF HER, MY PEOPLE, THAT YE BE NOT PARTAKERS OF HER SINS, AND THAT YE RECEIVE NOT OF HER PLAGUES."*

There are three distinct messages symbolized as three angels in Revelation 14. Revelation 14:6,7 is calling the world away from the worship of the Dragon, to worship God who created the heaven, earth, and the sea, and the fountains of waters. In Revelation 14:8 it tells how Babylon the Great is fallen and how she has made all nations to drink of the wine of the wrath of her fornication. However, in Revelation 14:9,10 we read *the most solemn warning ever given to the world, of which most are completely ignorant.* Satan is hardly ever mentioned in many Christian circles, much less how he is predicted in Scripture to lead most to lose their salvation.

"And the third angel followed them, saying with a loud voice, If any man worship the beast and his image, and receive his MARK in his forehead, or in his

hand, the same shall drink of the wine of the wrath of God, which is poured out without mixture into the cup of his indignation; and he shall be tormented with fire and brimstone in the presence of the holy angels, and in the presence of the Lamb." Revelation 14:9,10.

God reveals that all nations have already been deceived by "Babylon the Great, The Mother of Harlots and Abominations of the Earth." And our Lord is calling His people out of Babylon. But, the question to most is, what is Babylon? This is the whole purpose of this book. It is to lay wide open for all to see what the sins of Babylon the Great are, and who she is, and who this mysterious scarlet colored beast is that she is riding on, as described in Revelation 17:1-8.

While we study the history and the nature of "Babylon the Great (and of the Beast that is carrying her)," we will learn that there was, is, and always shall be in this world, avowed worshippers of Lucifer. Some will be shocked to learn that Luciferians have lived and died in promoting the worship of Lucifer through Babylonian, Egyptian and Druid Witchcraft, and are determined to overthrow all religions and governments. Their goal is to unite the world into a One World Government, and exalt Lucifer as the only god of this world!

As we continue to study the nature of "Babylon the Great," we will study the philosophies of "Wicca." Wicca is the modern version of Babylonian, Egyptian, and Druid Witchcraft with millions of both male and female members. We will learn how apostles of Lucifer in the past and present are using Secret Societies, Communism, International Banking, Christian fronts, social issues to further their plans. We will learn how these modern day witches

are ever determined to overthrow the worship of
Jesus Christ and Christianity by using *subliminal
warfare* (Mind Sciences), and physical force. This
Luciferian plot to destroy all religions and all governments, so that a One World Luciferian Government
may be established, is coming today, in what is
known as "The Aquarian Age," or "The New Age
Movement." In Latin it is called *Novus Ordo
Seclorum* (New Order for the Ages). But its real, concealed name is *The Illuminati*. And, it will be shown
that it was from the Secret Order of The Illuminati,
that Communism was derived!

   We will study the origin of the number 666,
and who today is branded with it. We will study the
Mark of the Beast with whom no true follower of
Jesus will identify. We will take a journey through
documentive history starting with Lucifer's rebellion
in Heaven, and continue to expose through history
how Lucifer was worshipped, both ignorantly and
openly, through the astrological systems of Sun worship. After the camouflages have been removed from
paganism that reveal it was in reality Satan who was
worshipped as the Sun-god, then we shall remove all
the camouflages Lucifer is hiding behind today,
through false systems of Christianity, and through an
international political movement for a One World
Government.

   These two symbols, "Babylon the Great" and
the Beast that ascendeth out of the Bottomless Pit,
will be carefully studied and understood later on in
the book. However, before the ordinary reader can
comprehend any of these things, we must go back into history to the time of Adam and Eve, and to the
time of Noah and Nimrod.

   The origin of lies traces to Lucifer (Genesis
3:4). And the origin of false religion also began with

Lucifer. In Isaiah 14:12-15 we read:

"How art thou fallen from heaven, O Lucifer, son of the morning! How art thou cut down to the ground, which didst weaken the nations! For thou hast said in thine heart, I will ascend into heaven, I will exalt my throne above the stars of God: I will sit also upon the mount of the congregation, in the sides of the north: I will ascend above the heights of the clouds: I will be like the most High. Yet thou shalt be brought down to hell to the sides of the pit."

It has been Lucifer's plan from ancient times to gradually unite this entire world into a One World Government that would reject its Creator and worship Lucifer instead.

Lucifer before his fall was the most exalted angel next to Christ. The "son of the morning" stood in the presence of God with Christ. He was the covering Cherub, the light bearer for God. However, Lucifer began to think of himself as equal in splendor and wisdom to God. He began to think he also deserved worship from the Lord's servants, and began to plot against the Lord of Heaven. Lucifer, the covering Cherub, did set his face to overthrow the worship of God. Lucifer did not at once reveal his covetousness. If he had exposed all of his plans to the Universe, where sin and rebellion at that time were not known, he would not have gained much following. Lucifer's plot to overthrow the government of Heaven would take long and careful planning. Little by little, Lucifer began to find others whose sympathy he could gain by criticizing how the Lord managed the affairs of the Universe. Lucifer tried to make the God of Love, the Lord of the Sabbath, appear to be a selfish tyrant. Lucifer, assuming the guise of godliness, led many Heavenly Beings to come over to his side by misrepresenting God's character, as if God Himself were the Evil One.

Lucifer sowed seeds of murmuring, complaining and strife which germinated into rebellion, and caused divisions among the angels of Heaven. Lucifer tried to weaken the unity of Heaven, thinking this would weaken the power of the Almighty. However, only one third of the Heavenly host chose the side of the god of confusion. *The whole Universe chose only two sides;* there was no middle ground. There was war in Heaven between Christ and Lucifer. *"And the great dragon was cast out, that old serpent, called the Devil, and Satan, which deceiveth the whole world: He was cast out into the earth, and his angels were cast out with him."* Revelation 12:9.

The very plans Lucifer tried to execute in Heaven, he is now conditioning the people of the world to accept. Just as Satan, or Lucifer, concealed his real plans from the angels in Heaven in the beginning to overthow the worship of God, so is Lucifer trying today to overthrow the True worship of God among the inhabitants of this world. Just as Satan did not suddenly expose his real plans that would have demanded the worship of him by Heavenly Beings, so has Satan camouflaged the worship of himself among earthly beings, through a world-wide network of gods and goddesses, and later through false systems of Christianity.

Sun worship was the greatest rival religion of the worship of Jehovah in the Old Testament. It was through Sun worship that the worship of Lucifer was camouflaged throughout this world. Those who obeyed the pagan precepts were actually bowing their knee before the Devil, not gods as they thought. *"Know ye not, that to whom ye yield yourselves servants to obey, his servants ye are to whom ye obey; whether of sin unto death, or of obedience unto righteousness?"* Romans 6:16.

As the angels of Heaven chose sides before Lucifer was cast out of heaven, so will the people of this world join into two distinct groups before the end of this age. The line of distinction, which will be studied in detail in the closing chapter, will be drawn by *the Mark of the Beast* foretold in Revelation 13:11-18 and 14:6-13.

The Luciferian plot to overthrow the worship of Jesus has always worked in secret, using camouflages to remain hidden. It has not come upon the world suddenly, but little by little. Likewise, we must also trace this history of the great Luciferian Conspiracy little by little. We will expose how primitive man was deceived into worshipping Lucifer, then bring the reader down through the centuries and show how Lucifer is being worshipped in these modern 1980's.

To begin this study, let's take a closer look at the name "Lucifer" itself. The name "Lucifer" in Latin means "Light-Bearing" and may also mean the planet Venus, which is the "morning star at dawn."[2] In Greek mythology, Lucifer was personified as a male figure bearing a torch.[3] Hence, we have the origin of the Light-Bearer of the Olympic Games. The Greek transliteration of the name of this incarnation of Lucifer in the myth was Teitan. In middle English his name was Titan, which also meant "Sun-god."[4] A distorted record of the rebellion of Lucifer and that of the rebel giant Nimrod has been preserved in Greek mythology. Titan (Teitan), the personification of Lucifer, was the ancestor of a race of giant humans here on earth who were overthrown by

2. The World Book Encyclopedia, Vol. 12 (1979), p. 847.
3. Encyclopedia Britannica, Vol. 6 (1915), p. 373.
4. The American Heritage Dictionary of the English Language, 1969, p. 1348.

the Olympian gods.[5] Hence, the word *titan* today means "one gigantic in size or power." And, the word *titanism* today in our language means "spirit of rebellion; or a defiance of and revolt against the established order or authority."[6]

As Lucifer was the chief leader that led the angelic host to rebel against God, so did Nimrod cause the early descendants of Noah to rebel against God. Flavius Josephus, the ancient Jewish historian, wrote about Nimrod and how he seduced the people of his day to rebel against God, and was first to teach the arts of masonry, while building the "Tower of Babel." From the book *The Complete Works of Flavius Josephus*, we read the following:

"... *Now it was Nimrod who excited them to such an affront and contempt of God. He was the grandson of Ham, the son of Noah, a bold man, and of great strength of hand. He persuaded them not to ascribe it to God, as if it was through his means they were happy, but to believe that it was their own courage which produced that happiness. He also gradually changed the government into tyranny, seeing no other way of turning men from fear of God, but to bring them into a constant dependence on his own power. He also said he would be revenged on God, if he would have a mind to drown the world again, for that he would build a tower too high for the waters to be able to reach! And that he would avenge himself on God for destroying their forefathers!*

"*Now the multitude were very ready to follow the determination of Nimrod, and to esteem it a piece of cowardice to submit to God; and they built a tower, neither sparing any pains,*

5. Ibid., p. 1348.
6. Ibid., p. 1348.

nor being in any degree negligent about the work.
And by reason of the multitude of hands
employed in it, it grew very high, sooner than any
one could expect; but the thickness of it was so
great, and it was so strongly built, that thereby its
great height seemed, upon the view, to be less
than it really was."
The Complete Works of Flavius Josephus, Whiston, Kregel
Publications, 1960, 1978, p.30.)

Nimrod tried to unite the whole known world
of his day into a One World Government that would
be anti-God or Antichrist. God wanted the sons of
Noah to eventually replenish the earth by traveling
abroad the earth and settling in colonies. This would
have kept in check the wickedness that has always
derived out of the cities. In the beginning, it was not
intended that man be crowded together in large
cities. This tower of Babel, the building of which
Nimrod supervised, was to have two great
significances. The city of Babel would become the
metropolis of the world and unite its inhabitants
under the dictatorial rule of Nimrod. And its tower
was to be a monument to man to stand as a symbol of
the wisdom of its builders. By building the city of
Babel, Nimrod hoped to prevent the people from
scattering abroad into colonies as the Lord intended.
While in the midst of this building, when the tower
reached an height that it could today be called
"skyscraper," our Lord came against it. In Genesis
11:3-9 we read: "And they said one to another, Go to,
let us make brick, and burn them throughly. And they
had brick for stone, and slime had they for mortar.
And they said, Go to, let us build us a city and a tower,
whose top may reach unto heaven; and let us make us
a name, lest we be scattered abroad upon the face of
the whole earth. And the Lord came down to

see the city and the tower, which the children of men builded. And the Lord said, Behold, the people is one, and they have one language; and this they began to do: and now nothing will be restrained from them which they have imagined to do. Go to, let us go down, and there confound their language, that they may not understand one another's speech. So the Lord scattered them abroad from thence upon the face of all the earth: and they left off to build the city. Therefore is the name of it Babel (confusion); because the Lord did there confound the language of all the earth: and from thence did the Lord scatter them abroad upon the face of all the earth.''

Nimrod, who built Nineveh, was worshipped by its early inhabitants under his deified name "Ninus." He was first to incite people to war with their neighbors after the confusion of tongues had scattered the early descendants of Noah over the earth. Trogus Pompeius, who wrote of Ninus, states that the first King of Nineveh caused the people to war against themselves. Alexander Hislop compiled this statement written by Trogus Pompeius, the ancient historian, in his book *The Two Babylons*, p. 23:

" 'Ninus, king of Assyrians,' says Trogus Pompeius epitomised by Justin, 'first of all changed the contented moderation of the ancient manners, incited by a new passion, the desire of conquest. He was the first who carried on war against his neighbours and he conquered all nations from Assyria to Lybia, as they were yet unacquainted with the arts of war.' "

Hislop goes on to quote another ancient historian named Diodorus Siculus and shows how Trogus Pompeius and Siculus both agree with each other.

" 'Ninus, the most ancient of the Assyrian kings mentioned in history, performed great ac-

tions. Being naturally of a warlike disposition, and ambitious of glory that results from valour, he armed a considerable number of young men that were brave and vigorous like himself, trained them up a long time in laborious exercises and hardships, and by that means accustomed them to bear the fatigues of war, and to face dangers with intrepidity.' "
Loizeaux Brothers, Neptune, NJ, 1916.

Hence, Nimrod (Ninus) was celebrated at Nineveh, which he built, as a War-god, and his epics as a hunter, a warrior, and his death were later imitated in the Assyrian, Babylonian, Egyptian, Greek, Roman and American Indian Mysteries. His Egyptian name was Osiris.[7] To the Romans, he was also worshipped as Mars (which means "The Rebel"), from which our name March was derived. He was Zernebogus to the Anglo-Saxon, which means: "The Seed of the Prophet Cush."[8] But, Nimrod's ancient Babel name was Merodach, which means "To Be Bold, or Rebel."[9] So here we find the real meaning of these two gods found in Scripture: "Bel (The Confounder) is confounded, Merodach (The Rebel) is broken in pieces (Jeremiah 50:2)." We will study more of the origin of the name "Bel" later.

In the Babylonian myth of Tammuz, or Thammuz (the equivalent to the Egyptian god Osiris, who actually was Nimrod, the ringleader in the great apostasy against our Lord, was ordered to be killed by a certain king. The reason given for his death was that Tammuz, the incarnation of the Sun-god, tried to promote the worship of Astrology to this certain king. However, this king ordered him to be put to death. Maimonides, another ancient historian, had

7. The Two Babylons, Hislop, pp. 20-22.
8. Ibid., pp. 33, 34.
9. Young's Analytical Concordance to the Bible, Young, p. 656.

read deeply into the learning of the Chaldeans. He describes this myth, quoted by Hislop in *The Two Babylons*, p. 62:

"When the false prophet named Thammuz preached to a certain king that he should worship the seven stars and the twelve signs of the Zodiac, that king ordered him to be put to a terrible death. On the night of his death all the images assembled from the ends of the earth into the temple of Babylon, to the great golden image of the Sun, which was suspended between heaven and earth. That image prostrated itself in the midst of the temple, and so did all the images around it, while it related to them all that had happened to Thammuz. The images wept and lamented all the night long, and then in the morning they flew away, each to his own temple again, to the ends of the earth. And hence arose the custom every year on the first day of the month of Thammuz to mourn and to weep for Thammuz."

Now, in the worship of the Sun-god among the Mexicans, they believed that for the Sun-god to bestow life on the world, he needed also to receive life from it.[10] To show the reader the murderous character of Satan displayed in people, and what human beings can be led to do by his false religious spirit, we will explore some of the reasons behind the rites of human sacrifices.

To the ancient Mexicans, the heart was the seat and symbol of life, and bleeding hearts of men and animals were presented to the Sun-god to maintain him in vigor and enable him to run his course across the sky.[11]

Now, when the Israelites turned their backs

10. The Golden Bough, Frazer, pp. 90 and 91.
11. Ibid., p. 91.

from worshipping the Lord, they adopted the worship of the pagan gods from their neighbors. And
they too were led by pagan high priests to sacrifice
human beings. *"They joined themselves also unto
Baalpeor and ate the sacrifices of the dead. Thus they
provoked him to anger with their inventions: and the
plague brake in upon them. ... And they served their
idols which were a snare unto them. Yea, they sacrificed their sons and their daughters unto DEVILS, and
shed innocent blood, even the blood of their sons and
their daughters, whom they sacrificed unto the idols of
Canaan: and the land was polluted with blood."*
Psalms 106:28, 29, 36-38.

The ignorant Israelites were not sacrificing
their children to gods, as they thought, but unto
devils. Paul, over 1000 years later, said the sacrifices
of the Gentiles which the Israelites adopted were actually "Sacrifices to Devils." *"But I say, that the
things which the Gentiles sacrifice, they sacrifice to
devils, and not to God: and I would not that ye should
have fellowship with devils."* I Corinthians 10:20.

As history has documented, that greatest object in pagan worship was the sun, who was symbolized all over the world as a heavenly bull.[12] The
pagans displayed the cosmic god in their arts as a
bull standing on its hind legs with a tail, hoofs and
horns, with a man's head and arms, with a three-
prong pitchfork in his hand. So the ancient cosmic
symbol of the Sun-god, with hoofs, a tail, horns and a
pitchfork, is where we today get our symbol for
Satan as having hoofs, a tail, and horns, with a pitchfork in his hand.

In pagan philosophy, lightning was the
manifestation of their god's wrath and an agent of
his punishment. The thunder was the voice of his

12. Beware It's Coming — The Antichrist 666, W.F.G. Inc., pp. 19-24.

warnings.[13] In ancient Greece, thunder and lightning were believed by the worshippers of Zeus to be manifestations of his presence. Any spot struck by lightning became sacred. The very name "Zeus" (skt. *dyaus*, "The Bright Sky") identifies him as the god of the sky and its phenomena.[14] In Rome he was worshipped as Jupiter, in Scandinavia, Thor, and in Canaan, Baal, the Storm god.

Lightning from the sky separates into branches; hence, the lightning bolt found in the hand of the supreme god of the sky was stylized into a pitchfork. This was a symbol for his power, as he who controls the lightning bolt.

Besides Satan's personation of Christ just before Jesus' Second Coming, what other power of God is the second beast of Revelation 13:11-17 going to counterfeit through lying wonders? *"And he doeth great wonders, so that he maketh fire come down from heaven on the earth in the sight of men."* And this is still future.

The prince of the power of the air is also the prince of darkness. Just as the pagan was deceived by Satan in ancient times, so has the Christian in modern times. And, if man can learn how to bring electricity down from the sky and harness its energy, how much more could Satan, a supernatural being, who is even called in the Bible "The Prince of the Power of the Air" (Ephesians 2:2), able to cause destructive storms! And not only this, but also give his followers secret knowledge how to do the same to their enemies.

Because the Sun-god was believed to have this

13. Funk and Wagnall's Standard Dictionary of Folklore, Mythology and Legend, p. 621.

14. Harper's Dictionary of Classical Literature and Antiquities, edited by Harry T. Peck, Cooper Square Pub., 1965, p. 1682.

power and would also give it to his followers, if they were obedient, or would zap his enemies with his bolt, the pagans worshipped their gods through fear. In Bible Truth, it is the goodness of God that turns an evil person to worship Him (Romans 2:4). But in pagan belief, it was the anger of the Storm god, his hatred for man, his unmerciful attributes, that made the pagans bow before him. Not through love, but through fear. Their whole worship revolved around winning the evil one's favor by pacifying him through sacrifice and appeasement.

The main features behind the pure demon worship of ancient Babylon can be seen today by the open worship of the Yezidis of Kurdistan, Armenia, and the Caucasus. In their pagan worship they believe it is "Melek Taus," who is the Devil, that was the co-creator of the world.[15] Their religion today is the worship of both Good and Evil, or Christ and Satan. They have adopted some heretical elements of Christianity, and some precepts of Islam. They regard Jesus as an angel in human form and recognize Muhammad as a Prophet with Abraham. They practice circumcision and baptism. Instead of Christ as the creative agent of the Godhead (Ephesians 3:10), they regard the Devil as the creative agent of the Supreme God, and seek even today to (appease) him as the author of evil. They also avoid mentioning the name of the Devil in fear of offending him.[16] We will study another religious movement that has the dualism of good and evil to be worshipped from today's Rock Era a little later. This study should be particularly interesting for people who called themselves Christians during the epidemic of the Beatle hysteria.

15. Encyclopedia Britannica, 14th edition, Vol. 23, p. 891.
16. Ibid., p. 891.

The Yezedis, like most pagans, believe their destinies are not determined by a good, loving, kind and gentle God, but by the Evil One, who has no mercy, who delights in destroying mankind. They believe that the good God will forgive no matter how they regard him. But, it is the Evil One whose favor they must secure. He, as the destructive deity, must be pacified by offering him sacrifice, penance, and worship.

Is this not similar to how multitudes who call themselves Christians are led to worship the Lord of the Scriptures? Is it not pictured by erring priests and pastors that God is a vengeful God, who is ever waiting to cast the unrepentant into a burning place of torment, or sent the repentant to purgatory, so they may be tortured by fire until they suffer enough to be purified for Heaven? Is it not screamed, dramatized and shouted to congregations about how gruesome are the tortures of them who are now, so they say, in Hell, the burning place of torment?

There is hardly a Christian denomination that doesn't teach the doctrine of Life After Death or Immortality of the Soul. But the Bible clearly states that no one lives on after death. "For the living know that they shall die: But THE DEAD KNOW NOT ANYTHING, neither have they any more a reward: for the memory of them is forgotten. Also their love, and their hatred, and their envy, is now perished: neither have they any more a portion for ever in any thing that is done under the sun." Ecclesiastes 9:5,6.

If the wicked are tormented in Hell Fire as taught by most Christian priests and pastors, when the wicked die, would they not have some knowledge of the torment they are supposed to be experiencing? "Whatsoever thy hand findeth to do, do it with thy might: For there is no work, nor device, nor knowledge, nor wisdom, in the grave, whither thou goest." Ecclesiastes 9:10.

If the righteous go to Heaven after death as taught in most Christian churches, would they not be praising the Lord? The Bible says: "The Dead Praise Not The Lord, Neither Any That Go Down In Silence." Psalms 115:17.

If man goes to Heaven at death like most Christian churches tell their members, wouldn't these righteous people have some thoughts or ideas where they are? The Bible says: "His breath goeth forth, he returneth to his earth; in that VERY DAY HIS THOUGHTS PERISH." Psalm 146:4.

Some go to the gravesites to talk to their dead friends or relatives, but the Bible says: "His sons come to honour, and he knoweth it not; and they are brought low but he perceiveth it not of them." Job 14:21. "For in death there is NO REMEMBRANCE OF THEE, IN THE GRAVE WHO SHALL GIVE THEE THANKS?" Psalms 6:5.

Jesus plainly stated that the dead are still in the graves at His Second Coming, not in Heaven: "Verily, Verily, I say unto you, The hour is coming, and now is, WHEN THE DEAD SHALL HEAR THE VOICE OF THE SON OF GOD: AND THEY THAT HEAR SHALL LIVE." ... "MARVEL NOT AT THIS: FOR THE HOUR IS COMING, IN WHICH ALL THAT ARE IN THE GRAVES SHALL HEAR HIS VOICE, AND SHALL COME FORTH; they that have done good, unto the resurrection of life and they that have done evil, unto the resurrection of damnation." John 5:25,28,29.

Both the wicked and the righteous are still in their graves. However, there is a Hell Fire where the wicked will surely be destroyed. But this is still future. This hell fire comes from Heaven, not from some secret place where the dead are now receiving their punishment. The Devil is not in charge of some secret place called Hell that is under the earth where all the wicked have been thrown. Nor does the Devil run around with his pitchfork, sticking and burning the wicked both day and night. The fire is from Heaven and will destroy the wicked and also the Devil himself. Revelation 20.

Peter foretold Christ's Second Coming would be in fire: *"The Lord is not slack concerning his promise, as some men count slackness: but is longsuffering to us-ward, not willing that any should perish, but that all should come to repentance. But the day of the Lord will come as a thief in the night; in the which the heavens shall pass away with a great noise, and the elements shall MELT WITH FERVENT HEAT, THE EARTH ALSO AND THE WORKS THAT ARE THEREIN SHALL BE BURNED UP."* II Peter 3:9, 10.

David foretold Christ's Second Coming 1,000 years before Jesus was born. In Psalm 50:3-5, we read: *"Our God shall come, and shall not keep silence: a fire shall devour before Him, and it shall be tempestuous round about Him. He shall call to the heavens from above, and to the earth, that He may Judge His people. Gather my saints together unto me; those that have made a covenant with me by sacrifice."*

Paul also foretold that Jesus would be a consuming fire to those who have rejected the Gospel. II Thessalonians 1:7-9, *"And to you who are troubled rest with us, when the Lord Jesus shall be revealed from heaven with his mighty angels, In flaming fire taking vengeance on them that know not God, and that obey not the Gospel of our Lord Jesus Christ: Who shall be punished with everlasting destruction from the presence of the Lord, and from the glory of His power."* In Isaiah 29:6 we read: *"Thou shalt be visited of the Lord of hosts with THUNDER, AND WITH*

EARTHQUAKE, AND GREAT NOISE, WITH STORM AND TEMPEST, AND THE FLAME OF DEVOURING FIRE."

The doctrine of the wicked being thrown into ever burning fire cannot be found in either the Old or New Testaments, but it is found on the pages of Sun worship. The Hell Fire Jesus plainly described in Scripture has *two time periods.* There are *two* different times fire and brimstone shall rain from Heaven. The first shall be at Christ's Second Coming. But the consuming fire that finally destroys the Devil, his angels, and the wicked will not be until after the 1,000 years described in Revelation 20:1-6, 9, 10. This is when the wicked will be raised from the dead, and Satan will make a last effort to destroy the New Jerusalem: *"And they went up on the breadth of the earth, and compassed the camp of the saints about, and the beloved city; and fire CAME DOWN FROM GOD OUT OF HEAVEN, AND DEVOURED THEM. AND THE DEVIL THAT DECEIVED THEM WAS CAST INTO THE LAKE OF FIRE AND BRIMSTONE, WHERE THE BEAST AND THE FALSE PROPHET ARE, AND SHALL BE TORMENTED DAY AND NIGHT FOR EVER AND EVER."* Revelation 20:9, 10.

This whole earth is going to be covered with fire. Fire is a purifying agent. And it will be fire that our Lord will use to purify the earth of its pollutions caused by Satan and man for 6,000 years.

In the book of Malachi we read the following: *"For behold, the day cometh, that shall burn as an oven: and all the proud, yea, and all that do wickedly, shall be stubble: and the day that cometh shall burn them up, saith the Lord of hosts, that it shall leave them neither root nor branch."* Malachi 4:1.

The Lord destroyed everything in Noah's day

by water; that was just a shadow of the earth when it shall be covered by fire. Peter saw this was to come and said in II Peter 3:5,6, *"For this they willingly are ignorant of, that by the word of God the heavens were of old, and the earth standing out of the water and in the water: Whereby the world that then was, being overflowed with water, perished: But the heavens and the earth, which are now, by the same word are kept in store, reserved unto FIRE against the day of judgment and perdition of ungodly men."*

As stated before, there are two periods of this Hell Fire predicted by both the Old Testament Prophets and by the New Testament Apostles. And, there are also to be *two* resurrections. In Revelation 20:1-9, it plainly states the resurrection of the wicked and their destruction will not happen until the 1,000-year millenium is over. *"And I saw an angel come down from heaven, having the key of the bottomless pit and a great chain in his hand. And he laid hold on the dragon, that old serpent, which is the Devil, and Satan, and bound him a thousand years, And cast him into the bottomless pit, and shut him up, and set a seal upon him, that he should deceive the nations no more, till the thousand years should be fulfilled: and after that he must be loosed a little season. And I saw thrones, and they sat upon them, and judgment was given unto them: and I saw the souls of them that were beheaded for the witness of Jesus, and for the word of God, and which had not worshipped the beast, neither his image, neither had received his mark upon their foreheads, or in their hands; and they lived and reigned with Christ a thousand years."* We will study more of this very important doctrine later.

Now, among the first inhabitants of the earth, Lucifer's first lie was "YE SHALL NOT SURELY DIE (Genesis 3:4)." And, this same LIE of the Devil has been used from Adam and Eve's day to our present time today. Here lies the origin of the foundation of the falsehood of immortal soul, reincarnation, all forms of Spiritualism, Astrology, Black Magic, Necromancy, Purgatory and Hell, the burning place of torment. The whole system of the Mystery of Iniquity is based on this lie of the Devil, "Life After Death." But the Bible is very clear: *"THOU SHALT SURELY DIE."* Genesis 2:16, 17.

Man does not continue to live after death as most have been deceived into believing. *"For the living know that they shall die: but the dead know not any thing."* Ecclesiastes 9:5.

As stated before, the myths about "Life After Death" can be traced in the legends of Nimrod who became the great god of the Assyrians and Babylonians.[17] At Nineveh, Austen H. Layard, from the British Museum, uncovered the ancient city and discovered over 25,000 tablets describing the ancient history of the Assyrian Empire.[18] Layard found inscriptions at Nineveh that said it was Ninus who built the city.[19] The word "Nineveh" itself means "The Habitation of Ninus."[20] But it has been discovered that the name Ninus was just a deified name the early Assyrians called Nimrod, because the Bible itself says it was Nimrod who built Nineveh (Genesis 10:11). Nimrod (Ninus) was said to have been killed, according to the inscriptions, but his "spirit" became immortal and flew up to the Sun and he became "Beelsamon," "Lord of Heaven."[21]

17. The Two Babylons, Hislop, Loizeaux Brothers, Inc., pp. 21-44.
18. Beware It's Coming — The Antichrist 666, W.F.G. Inc., 1980, p. 15.
19. Ibid., p. 15.
20. Encyclopedia Americana, Vol. 20, Americana Corporation, 1980, p. 373.
21. The Two Babylons, Hislop, pp. 165, 264.

In all forms of witchcraft, as in all modern forms today, the doctrine of "Immortality of the Soul" was the center of their whole pagan belief and worship. Pagans believed that when they died they took possession of one of the stars in Heaven. The ignorant pagans, like multitudes of Christians today, believe that the spirits of the dead are "ministering spirits, sent forth to minister for them who shall be heirs of salvation." Hebrews 1:14.

If the reader has ever read into the history of any nation, the history of the people shows that their whole culture was surrounded by the belief in "Life After Death," "Reincarnation," and communicating with the dead. Multitudes of pagan traditions, worldwide, have their origin in the Legends of Nimrod.

The Babylonians taught that the fate of everything was dependent on the sky. The Babylonians, as most ancient people, believed that each mortal, like the gods, had his own star in the sky.[22] Here we can begin to see why primitive men believed their chief gods inhabited the planets and named the planets as the homes of their gods. Saturn (the Roman god of crops) is believed to be the star-god Stephen said the ancient Israelites worshipped in their apostasy under the name of Remphan.[23] *"Yea, ye took up the tabernacle of Moloch, and the Star of your god Remphan, figures which ye made to worship them: and I will carry you away beyond Babylon."* Acts 7:43, see also Amos 5:26.

This will also help us to understand the cosmic religion of Astrology, and how Astrology ties in with Sun worship. Astrology was actually the origin of the pagan sciences and pagan symbols. John, in the book

22. The Mythology of All Races, Holumberg, Vol. 2, Cooper Square Pub. Inc., 1964, p. 365.

23. Young's Analytical Concordance to the Bible, Young, 1970, p. 806.

of Revelation, was given this sacred number 666 of Astrology to identify who this beast is (see Revelation 13:1-11, and 18) that Jesus warns not to be identified with (Revelation 14:9,10).

In the ancient Babylonian astrological system, it is the Sun-god who is the ruler and main god of the zodiac. And all the gods of heaven (the stars) were considered offspring of the sun. According to pagan philosophy, all the star gods you have heard about in school were actually manifestations of the heat, fire and light which flowed from the sun. It was believed that it was the Sun-god who was the source of all things, and all the other gods were but emanations of the sun, "flesh of his flesh." Therefore, all the manifestations of the gods of nature were just manifestations of the one god, the Sun, whose worship by primitive man was in reality to Satan. Even Lucifer's name means "Day Star," the "Illuminated One," or "Shining One."[24]

The Egyptians, Persians, Greeks, Romans, Hindus and American Indians, like the Babylonians, all believed that their gods were just representations of the one god. The ancient people, shortly after the flood, had a knowledge of the True God of Noah, Shem, and Abraham. But the worship of the True God of Noah, Shem, and Abraham soon became perverted into idolatry by the larger population when Nimrod tried to unite the whole world into a One World Government. And this anti-God movement shall be attempted by some modern Nimrods in our time!

Both history and the Bible reveal that the greatest mystery to mankind has always been the Universe. And Satan, the Prince of the Power of the Air, used man's curiosity about the heavenly host

24. Young's Analytical Concordance to the Bible, Young, 1970, p. 806.

to cause man to worship them instead of their Creator. *"And the children of Israel did evil in the sight of the Lord and served Baalim (the Sun-god)."* Judges 2:11.

The word *Baalim* is a term to describe the whole system of Sun worship. Augustine said in his book, *The City of God,* that all the learned pagan doctors declared that all the chief gods of the Greek-Roman world were 'one and the same Jove,' and that all the stars were part of Jove and had rational souls.[25]

All the chief gods of Greece and Rome were the same gods worshipped in Babylonia, Assyria, Egypt, Persia, and North and South America.[26] Only the names were different, like their languages and cultures were. It was from Babylon (Babel) that Sun worship started. And, it is also where all ancient and modern nations today receive their system of Astrology.[27]

In pagan philosophy, the stars controlled the affairs of the human race. Hence, the science of Astrology claims to interpret the will of the star gods. The chief star gods of the pagans were the gods of Astrology, which were believed to be just emanations of the one god, the Sun-god,[28] the ruler of the Zodiac. Astrology is the foundation of all the pagan sciences of the occult, whose author is Lucifer, and his spirit guides are his angels. Spiritualism, which is just another name for Witchcraft, is today, among the young, the biggest rival of Jesus Christ. It will be through Spiritualism that men and women will come with all manner of lying wonders that will gather the whole world under Satan's banner. *"Then if any man*

25. City of God, Book 4, chapter 11, Everyman's Library. 1973, pp. 122, 123.
26. Beware It's Coming - The Antichrist 666, W.F.G. Inc. 1980, p. 42.
27. The Religions of Ancient Egypt and Babylonia, Sayce, T&T Clark, pp. 236, 237.
28. Ibid., pp. 90, 249, 250.

shall say unto you, Lo, here is Christ, or there, believe it not. For there shall arise false Christs and false prophets, and shall show great signs and wonders; insomuch that, if it were possible, they shall deceive the very elect." Matthew 24:23,24.

Spiritualism (Witchcraft) will deceive the whole world into accepting a strong delusion that will bring Satan to finally use his crowning deception that will cause most to lose their salvation. Lucifer, this Old Serpent, called the Devil, will personate Jesus Christ just before the real Christ comes the Second Time. This will be Satan's last effort to destroy mankind. However, students of the Bible, who have made Scripture their only standard to judge between truth and error, will not be fooled into worshipping Satan as Christ. For the satanic movement to unite the world under one banner and Christ walking upon this earth again is a complete contradiction of Scripture. But to actually understand any of this, the reader must not be ignorant of Satan's devices; so we need to examine what the Bible says Spiritualism or, what Witchcraft is. This we will study in Part II of this Chapter.

CHAPTER I

Part 2

1. The modern term for witchcraft taught in Colleges today.

2. The origin of the "Great Rite" among modern day witches.

3. What is Phallicism?

4. The Jewish Star of David is not originally from Judaism, but Babylonian Witchcraft.

5. The Pentagram and Pentagon.

6. Sacred Numbers and Letters in Witchcraft That Deceive Today.

7. The Origin of the Number 666.

8. Names for the Devil and Sun-gods That Add to 666.

9. The Origin of the Name Phoenix (Fenex), an Ancient Name for Lucifer.

Part 2

Little do young Rock and Rollers know they are deceived by an unseen host of agents of the Devil. The Bible warns it will be *demons, using people as their instruments,* that will lead others into rejecting the True Christ. *"For they are the spirits of DEVILS, working miracles, which go forth unto the kings of the earth and of the whole world, to gather them to the battle of that great day of God Almighty."* Revelation 16:14.

There is absolutely nothing romantic about Satan. He will give some power to work miracles, but this is his way of deceiving. Just as God uses man to lead others to Him, so does Satan. However, unlike God, once Satan has used a person for his own purposes, Satan will cast away all whom he has used to deceive others, like a man casts away his trash into the trash can. So to help a Bible student avoid falling into any of Satan's traps, one can learn from the Scriptures and from those whom Satan has already used, how not to become another one of his victims.

To start, we need to study again the first deception at the Garden of Eden. As we stated before, the Devil uses camouflages to keep his worship hidden. The Sun and Nimrod were only a front used by Lucifer to get multitudes to bow before him. However, the first camouflage he used to deceive Adam and Eve was the serpent. The very thing Satan used to deceive Adam and Eve became eventually one of the most sacred symbols of Sun worship! Instead of the serpent as being a symbol of Satan and deception, as the Bible instructs, the serpent became a symbol of the "Great Benefactor and Healer" of mankind. The serpent was worshipped as the "God of Healing" and "Life-Restorer." *"YE SHALL NOT SURELY DIE,"* Genesis 3:3, was Lucifer's first lie to our first parents. The serpent, the god of healing, was generally represented in the pagan arts entwined on a stick, staff or a stock of a tree.[1] Here we find the origin of the strange symbol that the American Medical Association (AMA) uses today. This medical insignia was originally the symbol of the Egyptian god *Hermes,* who we will see in a moment was Nimrod's father, Cush. And it's here we find the origin of the word *hermetic.* This ancient word found in classical literature actually derived from the ancient Egyptian god of medicine. This name is actually Chaldean and the Greeks and Egyptians adopted this god from the Babylonians. The very word *hermetic* means the hidden knowledge of magic, occult sciences, etc.[2] Not only was the serpent worshipped by the ignorant pagans as "The Great Benefactor" for mankind, the serpent ironically enough was worshipped also as "The Great Enlightener." What did Satan say to Adam and Eve besides, "Ye shall not surely die."? In Genesis 3:5 we read: *"FOR GOD DOTH KNOW THAT IN THE DAY YE EAT THEREOF, THEN YOUR EYES SHALL BE OPENED, AND YE SHALL BE AS GODS, KNOWING GOOD AND EVIL."*

In *The Two Babylons,* by Hislop, p. 227, we read the following:

"Along with the sun, as the great fire-god, and, in due time, identified with him, was the serpent worshipped. In the mythology of the primitive

1. New College Edition, The American Heritage Dictionary, Houghton Mifflin Company, Boston, p. 186.
2. Beware Its Coming - The Antichrist 666, W.F.G. Inc., p. 35

world, says Owen, 'the serpent is universally the symbol of the sun. In Egypt, one of the commonest symbols of the sun, or sun god, is a disc with a serpent around it. The original reason of that identification seems just to have been that, as the sun was the great enlightener of the physical world, so the serpent was held to have been the great enlightener of the spiritual, by giving mankind the 'Knowledge of Good and Evil.' ' "

The ancient Mayans of the Yucatan in Mexico worshipped the serpent god under the name of Can. Can means "serpent" in the Mayan language, as Can or A-Can was the ancient Sumerian and ancient Scottish word for serpent. Here we find the origin of our word canny, shrewd or serpent-like. The Babylonians worshipped Can the serpent and Vul, the god of fire. The Romans simply combined the two words into 'Vulcan," the Roman god of fire from when also comes our word "volcano."[3] This seems to be how the Mayans and Mexicans named their gods. They too combined two words to describe their serpent god. "Kulkul" means "beautiful bird," and "Can," serpent. Hence, "Kulkulcan," which means "Bird Serpent" in the Mayan language. This is the exact same meaning for Quetzalcoatl, the Mexican pagan messiah in central Mexico.[4]

Interestingly enough, the cosmic symbol for Quetzalcoatl was a feathered serpent! Here is another interesting observation. The origin of the word "Vatican" also derived from two words. The Latin word "vatic" or "vatis" means "prophet or soothsayer."[5] The combined word, "Vatican," appears to mean "divination by the serpent"! The sym-

3. The American Heritage Dictionary of the English Language, Morris, p. 617.
4. Mexican and Central American Mythology, Nicholson, p. 82.
5. Webster's New Twentieth Century Dictionary Unabridged, 2nd ed., p. 2023.

bol for Astrology is often shown in pagan arts as a serpent in a circular position with his tail in his mouth. This represented eternal life.

There is the strong evidence from Scripture that the serpent originally had wings and flew, instead of having legs as the evolutionists say. The Scriptures reveal it was a curse for the serpent to travel on his belly as he does now. *"And the Lord God said unto the serpent, because thou hast done this, thou art cursed above all cattle, and above every beast of the field: upon thy belly shalt thou go, and dust shalt thou eat all the days of thy life."* Genesis 3:14.

Hence, that feathered serpent that has been displayed in pagan arts and worshipped as the god of healing, is none other but "that Old Serpent, called the Devil, and Satan, which *deceiveth the whole world.*" Revelation 12:9.

While Satan changed the image of the serpent into something to be adored and worshipped, the goat, from antiquity, symbolized the Devil. The goat, known for its agility, stubborn character and having its own way, is what Astrologers say people are who are born under the sign of Capricorn, the He-Goat. Witches in the Middle Ages were widely reputed to worship the Devil in the form of a goat.[6]

During the Middle Ages there was a widespread witch panic that produced witch hunts and witch trials. Witches were often charged with poisonings and other injuries as well as murder. The charge of murder might have been derived from making a wax image of a hated person and consuming it over a slow fire or sticking it with pins. African witchdoctors, Haitian experts in VooDoo, and American Indian medicine men indulged in this Satanic Black Art. The Middle Ages witch trials

6. Man, Myth and Magic, Vol. 8, Cavendish, pp. 1118-1121.

record how multitudes of witches confessed, under torture, that they held local meetings called *covens* to adore their master, make plans to execute the diabolic will, and partake in bestial rites. In southern Europe the site where the witches met was called a *synagogue*; in Germany it was called a *blocksberg*.[7] These meetings usually took place at midnight. It was brought out during the trials that witches claimed they came to their meetings by being carried by the Devil: others were able to fly by anointing themselves with oils from the bodies of murdered infants; still others rode broomsticks, or a cow or a goat. At the rendezvous Satan appeared as a black animal, often a goat, or as a man with cloven feet.[8]

There are many different sects in modern witchcraft today; however, modern day witches do not believe that the Devil exists. They are not Satanist old women with long black hair and a wart on their nose. A Christian will be shocked to know that ancient Witchcraft has been revived and modernized among the young people today. And, it is the religion of some of those who control the wealth of the world! Their covens (churches) are today Federally recognized tax exempt churches, and enjoy the same rights under the protection of the law as do the Christians. And, believe it or not, there are millions of both male and female witches here in the United States alone. Witchcraft is the biggest rival religion of Christianity in England and America.[9]

It is interesting enough, however, that these modern witches exalt the horn gods and the pagan goddesses such as the Egyptian pagan trinity Osiris, Isis, Horus, which originated in the worship of

7. Colliers Encyclopedia, Vol. 23, 1980, pp. 549-552.

8. Ibid., p. 550.

9. Man, Myth and Magic, Vol. 14, Cavendish, p. 1866.

Nimrod (the Sun), his wife Semiramis (the moon), and Tammuz (the Morning Star).

Like their pagan brethren, modern day witches are ignorant to the fact that these gods do not exist. Even though they claim the Devil does not exist, they too are in reality bowing their knee before him. They exalt the gods Satan hid behind to deceive the ancient nations. Pan or Bacchus is another god the witches exalt and worship. It depends on what coven they belong to. Anyway, how was this ancient pagan god displayed in pagan art? He had a man's head with horns and cloven feet!

Now witchcraft, as stated before, has been modernized. Modern day witches who worship the gods of cosmic forces claim now to work magic and cast spells for the general good of the community. This kind of witchcraft is called *white magic*. Those who practice casting spells that injure people practice what is known as *Black Magic*.

However, most of these modern day witches claim to be good witches as in *The Wizard of Oz*, and unlike medieval witchcraft that made an image out of wax to stick pins in it so the person the wax image looked like would die, these modern day witches claim now that this wax image is used to heal people. This revised and modern form of witchcraft is called today *Wicca*, which is the feminine form of an Old English word, "Wicce," meaning — "Witch."[10]

The main feature of Wicca is, however, nature worship. Just as the ancient Baal worshippers in Babylonia believed it was the cosmic Star gods that were responsible for pouring out the rain from Heaven and caused fertility among the plants and mankind, so do these ignorant people in these modern witch covens teach their little ones these things.

10. Ibid., p. 1866.

The god Pan, symbol of the Universe and the Sun.
He was Bacchus to the Phoenicians.

The word *Baal*, so often seen throughout the Old Testament, was used to describe a god. The word means "Lord" or "Master"[11] and in the Bible it was the name for the Sun-god.

Now, kings of pagan nations often were considered the incarnation of the Sun-god, and to identify with the Sun-god the kings would adopt the name of his god as Jezebel's father did in I Kings 16:31. His name was "Ethbaal" which means "with Baal" or "Baal's man."[12]

Just as ancient Sun-kings pretended to be the ancient incarnation of the Sun-god, so does modern witchcraft teach that the High Priest is the personification of the horned god Pan, or Osiris. And, the High Priestess of these covens, like ancient Sun worship, is the personification of Isis, Diana, or one of the other names this pagan goddess has throughout the world. Baal worship was basically a fertility cult that taught its followers that the Sun-god and Moon-goddess controlled the seasons, brought fertility, etc. Here we find the origin of the beliefs of Wicca.

Witches, ancient and modern, take off their clothes during their meetings as a symbol of freedom, and so the power they say they receive from their gods can freely flow from their bodies. A circle is drawn to contain and concentrate the power the witches claim to receive through lewd dancing and chanting. On nights of the full moon and other festivals, the High Priest of witchcraft performs a ritual known as "Drawing Down the Moon." This is taught to new members to explain how the High Priestess becomes the incarnation of the Moon-goddess.[13].

11. Young's Analytical Concordance to the bible, Young, p. 65.
12. Beware Its Coming — The Antichrist 666, W.F.G. Inc., p. 25.
13. Man, Myth and Magic, Vol. 14, Cavendish, p. 1866.

Witches believe that the build-up of power is achieved much more readily when the participants are naked, and when a certain sexual tension is present. When these witches reach the power they want charged in their atmosphere, they begin to cast their spells. They claim the spells should always be for the good; an evil spell, they say, rebounds threefold upon the head of its creator. After their spells are cast, the witches settle down to a ceremony that is similar to the holy communion held for the Egyptian god Osiris. However, instead of a round disk wafer that was an Egyptian symbol of the sun, some modern day witches make cakes in the shape of a five pointed star called the Pentagram. This to the occultist is one of the most powerful weapons in magic. The Pentagram symbolism is based on that of the number five which, according to Astrology, stands for the living world of nature, such as Air, Fire, Water, Earth, and the Spirit of their god and pagan goddess who used the elements, according to witchcraft, to create the Universe.

The number five in Astrology also represents the four directions and the center, for the five senses (smell, taste, sight, touch and hearing).

Witchcraft, like all forms of Spiritualism, teaches man is a microcosm (miniature universe); man is the ruler of nature, and as the miniature image, the potential master of all things.[14] So, the Pentagram (five pointed star) with one of its point projecting upwards is imagined in Witchcraft as a man's body with arms and legs extended, and is a symbol of the dominance of the divine spirit. It is used as a magical weapon for invoking good influences and keeps the evil spirits at bay, say those who practice white magic.

14. Man, Myth and Magic, Vol. 16, Cavendish, p. 2159.

Many of our youth reject the religion of the Bible, and now worship the created things instead of the Creator through this new modern form of Witchcraft because Witchcraft today is attractive and has taken on a brighter look. Instead of the satanic evil looking people of the Middle Ages, the witches of today have been, for the past century, portrayed as good people, who fight against the evil forces of this world, such as "Wonder Woman," with her sign of white magic (the Pentagram) displayed on her forehead. But to distinguish the bad witches from the good witches, say the occultists, a reversed Pentagram with *two points upward* is a symbol of Black Magic, and of those who do worship the Devil. The two points of the star pointed upwards suggests the horns of the Devil symbolized as a goat attacking the Heavens with his horns.[15] This five pointed star which has two points upward was, and is today, worn as an amulet by open Devil worshippers, and by many modern day magicians and wizards. Originally this evil sign was worn to show Satan that they had chosen him as their leader.[16]

Is this not chilling and frightening to know that multitudes of women of high fashion may not be aware that when they wear that little gold chain around their neck, with this five pointed star with two points upward, they are showing they have chosen the Devil's side, and seek his protection? Is it not chilling to know that they who call themselves Freemasons, and the ladies who call themselves "The Order of the Eastern Star" display this evil sign in their lodges? We will study even more shocking truths about the origin and purpose of these Secret Societies in the next chapter.

15. Man, Myth and Magic, Vol. 16, Cavendish, p. 2159.
16. Ibid., p. 2159.

The Pentagram in Witchcraft symbolizes today Black and White Magic. The Pentagram with one point up symbolizes White Magic. The Pentagram with two points up represents Black Magic or Satanism. There are occultists who believe in Satan and there are occultists that do not.

As stated earlier, there are many sects of modern witchcraft today, and many variations found in their rituals. In some covens the cakes they use in their communion are made into the shape of a crescent, which is the symbol of the Moon-goddess. These cakes, by the way, are made of salt, honey, wine, meal, oil and, in some covens, blood. They are eaten in honour of the Egyptian god Horus[17] or whatever god the coven exalts.

In ancient witchcraft the cakes were round with a cross drawn on them that represented the first letter of the name of the ancient dead and risen pagan messiah "Tammuz," who was the incarnation of the Sun-god, and the son of the Moon-goddess (the Queen of Heaven). Even the Israelites, when they turned from the worship of our Creator, made these same cakes that honoured the pagan Queen of Heaven and her god-child Tammuz. In Jeremiah 7:18 our Lord condemned this ancient ritual in the worship of these cosmis gods. *"The children gather wood, and the fathers kindle the fire, and the women knead their dough, to make cakes to the queen of heaven, and to pour out drink offerings unto other gods, that they may provoke me to anger."*

Today, the Roman Catholic Church dedicates these same cakes to the Virgin Mary whom they ironically call the Queen of Heaven.[18] These cakes are called by Roman Catholics "Hot Cross Buns."[19] The name of this pagan goddess the Israelites worshipped and dedicated these cakes to is found in Judges 2:13. Her name to the Israelites was Ashtaroth. To the early Romans her name was Venus, the goddess of love.

17. Encyclopedia of the Unexplained: Magic, Occultism and
   Parapsychology, Cavendish, Rainbird Reference Books, Ltd., 1974, p. 277.
18. The Catholic Encyclopedia, Broderick, Thomas Nelson, Inc., 1975,
   p. 518.
19. Beware Its Coming — The Antichrist 666, W.F.G. Inc., pp. 29, 48.

Witchcraft is just another word for Spiritualism, but the modern word used to cover-up the evil name of Witchcraft so it may be taught in Colleges is "Parapsychology." Now, to understand this other abomination found in both ancient and modern Witchcraft, the reader must understand that it was the Sun-god and Moon-goddess who created the whole Universe, according to these witches. To honour this pagan belief, a ritual called "The Great Rite" is strictly observed among these so-called "good" witches. Since the High Priest in a coven is believed to be the incarnation of Pan, the Sun-god, and the High Priestess is the incarnation of the Queen of Heaven, the Moon-goddess, these two mimic the myth in the creation of the Universe by the Sun-god and the Moon-goddess when they perform "The Great Rite" ritual, which is engaging in sacred prostitution.

This is justified by the witches on the grounds of fertility, because after all, they say, Wicca is a fertility cult.[20]

To try to understand any of this perversion so you can teach others how to avoid it, the reader simply needs to realize that this abominable practice of sacred prostitution found today in modern witchcraft is nothing new. All ancient heathen worship of the Sun-gods had within its philosophies Phallicism. What is Phallicism? It is the veneration and worship of male and female sex organs. The union of male and female organs is symbolized in witchcraft as a point within a circle, and also as two triangles uniting to make a "Hexagram,"[21] better known today as the "Star of David." The truth is, King David of Israel never carried this emblem that is now the symbol of Israel. This emblem was

20. Man, Myth and Magic, Vol. 14, Cavendish, p. 1867.

21. Ibid., p. 1300.

adopted from witchcraft by some Jewish priests who had explored deep into the Babylonian religion during their captivity in Babylon. From here sprang witchcraft in another garb called *the Cabala*.

The Mexican Indian, centuries before seeing a white man, had the Hexagram as the symbol of their phallic worship of the cosmic gods. Often the Hexagram is displayed as a symbol of the 7 planets that serpentine their way through the Zodiac. The Sun in the center is displayed in a circle with a point in its center.

Usually before these modern day witches partake of the cake and wine to honour Horus or Pan, as we examined in part one of this chapter, a ceremony for any new initiates into their coven is performed. This involved blinding, binding, and whipping new members for the purpose of purification. However, this ceremony is not as brutal as in medieval covens; they are good witches, so the whip they use now is said to be of embroidered silk. However, those present with sadomashochistic tendencies might be satisfied. The following five-fold kiss bestowed by the High Priest or Priestess on the feet, knees, genitals, breasts and lips of a new member speaks for itself.[22]

In *Man, Myth and Magic, An Illustrated Encyclopedia of the Supernatural*, Vol. 14, p. 1867, Cavendish, we read the following:

"*Only three pieces of magic can be performed at each meeting, they claim, and the spells should always be for the good; an evil spell rebounds threefold upon the head of its creator. Sometimes the spell is cast telepathically: for instance, in the case of a spell cast to cure a person of a bad leg the witches would stand silently and 'will' the leg*

22. Man, Myth and Magic, Vol. 14, Cavendish, p. 1867.

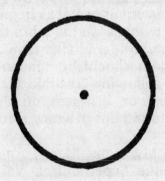

The Hexagram is one of the most evil signs in Witchcraft. It is commonly worn today by both deceived Jews and some Christians. The circle with point in center is another phallic symbol representing the Universe and the Sun-god.

to heal. On other occasions they might use a doll, or 'fith-fath,' to represent the sick person - bathe the doll's leg with a healing potion, or the high priestess might 'bind' the spell, wrapping her girdle around the blade of her athame in a special way."

How popular has this modern witchcraft become? In the September 12th, 1982 *Arkansas Democrat* "Family Weekly," Georgia Frontiere appeared on the front page. Georgia inherited the Los Angeles Rams when her late (sixth) husband drowned in the riptides off the Florida coast in April 1979. He was 72. But what we really are interested in bringing to your attention is her openness about being able, says she, to talk to her dead husband's spirit, and how she dabbles in the occult. On page 11 of the Sept. 12 issue we read the following:

"Georgia gives Nolan Cromwell an unasked for raise ... and Georgia, who dabbles in the occult (she says she's talked to Carroll's spirit), mysteriously waves a hand at half-time over Haden's injured leg, which is believed to be broken.

'I thought for sure she was nuts,' Haden says. 'Then, incredibly, after the doctors told me they were sure it was broken, the X-rays were negative.' "

Why are more and more people coming out publicly and admitting to be connected with Spiritualism? About 25 years ago they would be afraid to make such statements for fear of public ridicule and harm. However, most Christians never heard of the Fraudulent Mediums Act of 1951 which only applies to those who obtain money from the public under the pretext of possessing supernatural power. This allows those who really can perform these lying wonders to practice their arts legally in the open for the first time in hundreds of years.[23]

Most witches, because they believe in the immortality of the soul, teach that every human being has a spirit guide that they can contact for advice. This is also where the Psychics claim their advice and information comes from. These departed souls, they say, are the spirits of loved ones, ancient Indian Chiefs, or Egyptian, Hindu, or Chinese Sages, or Wise Men from past ages. These spirits, they say, have much wisdom because the spirit guides have experienced many reincarnations and have mastered the lessons they were meant to learn while on earth, and now have the power to benefit the living.[24]

As we already read from Scriptures, the doctrine of "Life After Death," or the belief in an immortal soul is a *lie from the Devil*. But the miracles and spells that some witches have are very real. They may not know it, but they receive their power from Devils who, after they use them to deceive other humans, will destroy the very ones they have used.

However, a person who has chosen the teachings of Jesus Christ, and made His Spirit a guide through a knowledge of the Scriptures, knows that these spirit guides are not spirits of past Sages, but spirits of devils impersonating them. And, the believer who has chosen the God of the Bible is promised protection from those who practice Voodooism and spell casting. In Numbers 23:23 we read: "Surely there is no ENCHANTMENT (Witchery) *against Jacob, neither is there any DIVINATION against Israel.*"

23. Man, Myth and Magic, Vol. 14, Cavendish, p. 1867.

24. Ibid., p. 1867.

As established earlier, the ancient pagans believed that when they died their souls flew up to the Heavens and took possession of one of the stars. The chief gods of the Zodiac, which were but emanations of the Sun-god, all HAD A SACRED NUMBER. Space does not allow us to examine all of these numbers in Astrology. However, to help us understand why this mysterious number 666 was given to John the Apostle in Revelation 13:18, warning us not to be identified with it, it is necessary now to examine some ancient pagan numerology.

Ancient Astrology teaches that one of the sacred numbers of the Chief god of the Zodiac (the sun) was the number one. The Sun symbol, we saw earlier, was a Heavenly Bull and a serpent. Since Babylon was the birth place of Astrology and the rest of Idolatry, we will see how this Babylonian system of gods and goddesses spread throughout the ancient world and has penetrated into modern culture today.

Originally, the letters of the various alphabets had, and still have to some extent, a numerical significance. The English language has lost track of this, for there are no numbers that identify with each letter of our alphabet. But, the first letter of the alphabet in many languages still carries with it a reference to the Sun-god (one) whose main symbol was either a serpent or a bull. Take, for instance, the first letter in the Hebrew and Chaldee alphabet. It was a symbol of a bull.[25]

The Greek word *aleph* (*alpha*) is the name of the first letter in their alphabet, and it means bull or ox. It is interesting to note that the ever-revered bull-god of the Orient (the elephant) has the same root (eleph) in his name, and almost every Hindu temple has its phallic idol to commemorate the life-giving

25. The American Peoples Encyclopedia, Spencer Press, Inc., 1953, p. 647.

qualities of their god (one). So to honour the Sun, the god (one), the Heavenly Bull-god, the first day of the week[26] (Sunday) and the first of everything was dedicated to the bull-god as sacred. The first day of the month, the first day of the year, the first born son and the first fruits of the harvest and of the flocks, were kept sacred and dedicated to him.

Indeed, most Christians cast away the original day of the worship described in Genesis 2:1-3 (before Jews were ever heard of) for the observance of Sunday, the first day of the week! We will investigate this mystery later.

The number 2 in ancient Astrology is considered a female number and a symbol for the Mother goddess who, according to pagan belief, is the second member of the godhead. However, pagan philosophy teaches that the number 2 was thought upon as an evil number. In ancient paganism, women were considered as evil and the cause of death. Some scholars claim that our very word, evil, is eve-il.

The name of the second letter of the Hebrew-Chaldean alphabet is *Beth*, a feminine proper name which means house. The moon, which is the symbol of the Mother goddess, is ever considered as the monthly house of the Sun in Astrology.

The number 3 is a sacred number identified with the pagan godhead of Baal, Ishtar, and Tammuz. Sometimes the number 3 represented a triple aspect of the Sun-god as the ruler of Heaven. While the sun appeared in the sky it was symbolized as a Heavenly Bull. The Serpent was the symbol of the sun in the spiritual realm of things.[27] However, when the sun sinks into the Western ocean at the end of

26. The Encyclopedia of Religious Knowledge, Vol. 4, p. 2259.
27. The Two Babylons, Hislop, pp. 226, 227.

the day and spends the night in the realm of darkness and the dead, he then becomes the fish god, Lord of the Underworld. The Fish-god to the Babylonians, Assyrians, and Philistines was Dagon. This name Dagon, like Kulkulcan of the Mayans, is derived by combining two words. *Dag* means Fish, and *On* means Sun. Hence, the part man and part fish gods worshipped in the Old World. To the Romans he was Neptune, who was ever displayed in ancient Roman arts as part man, part fish, with a pitchfork in his hand. It was during a festival to celebrate the capture of Samson, and to give thanks to Dagon for delivering Samson into the Philistines' hands, that Samson pulled down the house in which the Philistines were celebrating, on himself and three thousand Philistines. Judges 16:23-31.

It is an interesting observation that the High Priest of Dagon wore a robe and a mitre that resembled a fish. This mitre the pagan priests wore is the origin of the mitre the Popes and Cardinals wear today. This mitre that resembles a fish head was worn centuries before the birth of Christ by pagan High Priests of Dagon.[28]

In India, their trinity is based on the 3 phases of the Sun-god. When the sun rises in the East, he is Brahama, when he gains his meridian, he is Siva, and when he sets in the West, he becomes Vishnu. This explains why the gods of the orient sometimes were displayed with three heads and three pairs of arms on one body. Many pagans believed in the three aspects of the Sun-god, who has 3 phases in which he travels across the sky. Hence, the number 3 in Astrology represents the trinity in Witchcraft.

The number 4 is the sacred number in Astrology for the Sun as Ruler of the four quarters of the

28. The Two Babylons, Hislop, pp. 216, 217.

Universe, or the four divisions of the Zodiac, the four seasons, and the four directions, It is interesting to note the name of Tammuz, where the cross originally came from. It was originally the initial T in Tammuz, which was known as the sacred *Tau*. The cross was a symbol of the sun worshippers centuries before Jesus was born. The number 4 itself is little more than a cross. Take away the angular bar and we have a cross. As the reader probably has observed, no Catholic will pray a prayer or worship God until he makes the four directions across his head and body to resemble it. That which is now called the Christian cross was originally the mystic Tau that the Chaldeans used to sacrifice a first born child to the Sun-god.[29] And, it was this very thing that was used to crucify Jesus on. No greater insult could Satan give the Christ than to sacrifice Him on his own symbol of heathen worship.

We have already explored some of the reasoning behind the number 5 in Astrology such as the 5 pointed star (Pentagram), but it is the number 6 that should capture our close attention. The hidden meaning and symbols represented by the number 6 are so involved that an entire book could be written about this number and its origin. Here, again, we explore the worship of the serpent, because the number SIX has ever been connected with the serpent.

It is interesting to note that man and the serpent, along with the other land animals, were created on the sixth day (Genesis 1:24-31). The words used to say SIX, *sex* in Latin, *seis* in Spanish, *seks* in Norwegian, *shest* in Portuguese, *sechs* in German and *sas* in Chaldean-Hebrew, as in most languages, start with the letter S. The letter S derived, believe it or not, from a pictograph of a cobra, erected in its

29. Beware It's Coming — The Antichrist 666, W.F.G. Inc., pp. 44, 45.

Α α	1	א	1
Β β	2	ב	2
Γ γ	3	ג	3
Δ δ	4	ד	4
Ε ε	5	ה	5
Ζ ζ	7	ו	6
Η η	8	ז	7
Θ ϑ	9	ח	8
Ι ι	10	ט	9
Κ κ	20	י	10
Λ λ	30	כ * ך *	20
Μ μ	40	ל	30
Ν ν	50	מ * ם *	40
Ξ ξ	60	נ * ן *	50
Ο ο	70	ס	60
Π π	80	ע	70
Ρ ϱ	100	פ * ף *	80
Σ σ * ς *	200	צ * ץ *	90
Τ τ	300	ק	100
Υ υ	400	ר	200
Φ φ	500	ש	300
Χ χ	600	ת	400
Ψ ψ	700		
Ω ω	800		

The Greek and Hebrew alphabets, showing the numerical values corresponding to each letter.

striking position. The hissing sound of the letter S represented the voice of the serpent. We can note that *snake, serpent* and *Satan* begin with the serpent letter S. On the heads of cobras there are usually distinct markings in the shape of letters. They are V, U and O. Hence, the ancients invented names for different serpents with these letters, such as the U in Uraeus. That was the Egyptian name for their sacred Asp, which ever appears on the forehead, or crown, of the Pharoah, who claimed to be the vicar, or the earthly incarnation, of his god.[30]

The O occurs in the Greek *Ophis*, the name of the serpent whom the Gnostics worshipped. During their celebration of their Lord's Supper, they let a snake, whom they called Ophis, crawl over their bread. They became known in history as the Ophites.[31]

In the Greek numerical system the symbol S is called the *sigma,* and was originally the sixth letter of the Greek alphabet. It was also represented as the number six. However, today the letter S, or Σ in Greek, has a number significance of 200. With the dropping of the sacred sigma from the sixth position in the Greek alphabet, it appears the Ethioptic and some other alphabets did the same thing with their 6th letter. This has been one of the most baffling mysteries to people who have studied into the origin of the alphabets. No one seems to know why the ancients did this. The Z or *Zeta,* used everywhere to stand for 7, fell into the 6th position, and is used in the mysteries of the occult for both 6 and 7. Remember this, because it is important to know to be able to unlock secret symbols that hide, or add to, the number 666. Why should so much importance be

30. Encyclopedia of Religion and Ethics, Vol. 2, p. 402.

31. Ibid., p. 404, 405.

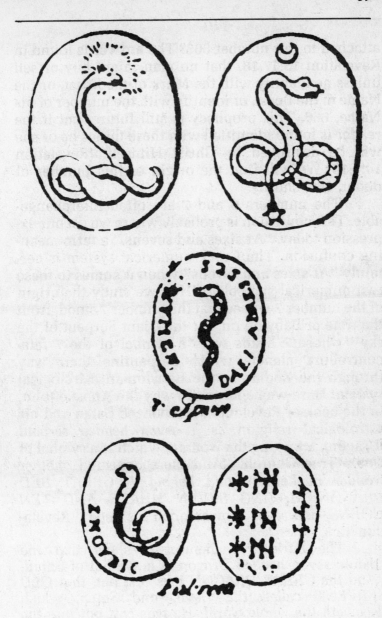

These are Gnostic coins showing serpents in their striking positions forming the letter S and the number 6.

attached to this number 666? The answer is found in Revelation 13:17,18, that no man might buy or sell unless he identify with the Mark of the Beast, or the Name of the Beast, or identify with the number of his Name, 666. This prophecy is still future, but if the reader is found identified with these things he or she will be destroyed by Christ Himself. (Revelation 14:9,10) We will find the origin of this number of doom, 666, shortly.

The numbers 6 and 7 are often interchangeable. This confusion is probably where we get our expression today, "At sixes and sevens," a term meaning confusion. The Greek numerical system is certainly "At sixes and sevens" when it comes to these two numerical symbols. WHen we study the origin of the number 7 we see that the number 7 stood, from the time of Babylon on, for the Giant Serpent of the sky[32] whose 7 heads were a symbol of the 7 fate-controlling planets which serpentine their way through the Zodiac in the Babylonian astrological system. Here we begin to see why the Apostle John, in the book of Revelation, symbolized Satan and his astrological religion as a *seven headed serpent* (Dragon), attacking the woman, which is a symbol of God's True Church. *"And there appeared another wonder in heaven; and behold A GREAT RED DRAGON, HAVING SEVEN HEADS AND TEN HORNS, and seven crowns upon his head."* Revelation 12:3.

The Scriptures themselves show that the cosmic *seven headed Dragon* is a symbol of Satan. *"And the GREAT DRAGON was cast out, that OLD SERPENT called the Devil, and Satan, which deceiveth the whole world: He was cast out into the earth, and his angels were cast out with him."* Revelation 12:9.

32. The Religion of Ancient Egypt and Babylonia, Sayce, p. 240.

Now in Revelation 17:1-5 we observed earlier that *Mystery, Babylon the Great, the Mother of Harlots* is riding a Seven Headed Beast. However, this is not a Dragon (Devil), but a beast which in symbolic language represents a *"Political Power."* See Daniel 7:1-8, 17, 23 and 24. We will study more about how a beast in Bible prophecy is a symbol of "Political Power" further on.

It will also be shown later on that this beast from the bottomless pit with seven heads and ten horns is Satan's last political movement that will try to unite the world under one banner.

As we already established, the serpent was ever displayed in the pagan arts as an emblem of the Sun-god. It is eye opening to learn that even many of the names used for the Sun-gods actually add to 666. For instance, all the avatars (incarnations) of the Sun-god, which were ten, according to the Hindu belief were called *Buddhas* or *Rasees of the Siun,* or Sun. The Greek word to describe the Buddhas, or Rasees, is *Xiuv.* This means Wisdom of the Sun, or Solar Wisdom. In the ancient Greek language, this word to describe avatars of the Sun added to 666.[33]

X I U N

600 10 6 50 = 666

We will see more names of pagan gods that add to 666 as we go on. But first, we need to know more about the origin of the number 6, how some of our letters today derived from this number, and how letters were used in the Babylonian mysteries to hide the number 666.

We have noted that S is the initial of most words used for SIX. In several Greek dialects, the S was replaced by F which the Greeks called *Bau, Vau,*

33. Anacalypsis, Vol. 2, Higgins, p. 210.

etc. If you take away the cross bar on F, it too resembles a snake in striking position. There is a very striking resemblance between S, F, and V. It can never be understood why the occultists used these letters in their mysteries, unless the reader remembers the S, F, and V represent the number SIX. V is the 6th letter in the Hebrew-Chaldean family of alphabets. F replaces it in Western alphabets and it must be noted as stated before, like 6 and 7, F and V are ever interchangeable. Take for instance "knife" and "knives."

Another letter that is a serpent symbol in Greek was the letter M. This letter represents, in the mysteries, the number 12, and is the 12th letter of the Greek alphabet. M is frequently used for the letter S because it is just a sigma on its side Σ.

Now if M is but a sigma on its side and refers to the second 6, or 12th, letter, it would appear significant that the symbol for the letter following the sigma should be nothing more than a Z or *Zeth* on its side. In the mysteries of paganism the second six (M) or the number 12 stands for the Zodiac. As we have seen, the dropping of the sacred sigma as the sixth letter numeral causes the Z to drop back into the sixth place. However, like the letter S, the Z also resembles a hissing sound, so the ancients never lost the significance of the number 6.

Now since history says our letters F, M, S, V, and Z derived from the ancient pictures of a serpent in his striking position, and have the numerical value of SIX in most other alphabets, we now might be able to understand the symbolic language.

Just as a number in our present numerical system has place values, such as 6 written alone equals six, two sixes together equals sixty-six, and three sixes together would equal six hundred sixty-six, so did the ancient learned doctors of witchcraft use the letters S, V, Z or the other serpentine letters to hide the number 666. Just as Freemasons have secret signs and grips to let each other know they are Masons, so did the learned doctors of witchcraft let each other know who they were by camouflaging this sacred number 666. Only the learned pagan knew the significance. The number 666 was written in serpentine letters like SSS, VVV, ZZZ = 666. They also arranged the letters different ways; sometimes they would turn them upside down or sideways. The SSS sometimes could be seen with a line drawn through the middle of all three S's and turned sideways. This is the origin of the popular amulet called the *Oriental cross.*

Another way the number 666 was hidden which can be unmasked, is in learning the origin of the trident sign. Earlier we learned that the Sun-god's weapon was the lightning bolt and it was stylized into a pitchfork. The pitchfork had three prongs to it, hence, we have today the trident sign, which by the way is used to symbolize the number 666 also.

Beware of these schemes to deceive, for it is still not clear how this number of doom, 666, will keep God's people from buying and selling. It is not only the Mark of the Beast, which we will study in the last chapter, that will prevent God's people from buying and selling, but also the *number of his name* (666). Revelation 13:17, 18.

However, we can trace the origin of the number 666. *And this number of doom derived out of Astrology.* The Zodiac is a narrow band about 18° wide making a complete circuit of the sky around the earth. As we noted before, this was symbolized in pagan arts by a serpent with his tail in his mouth

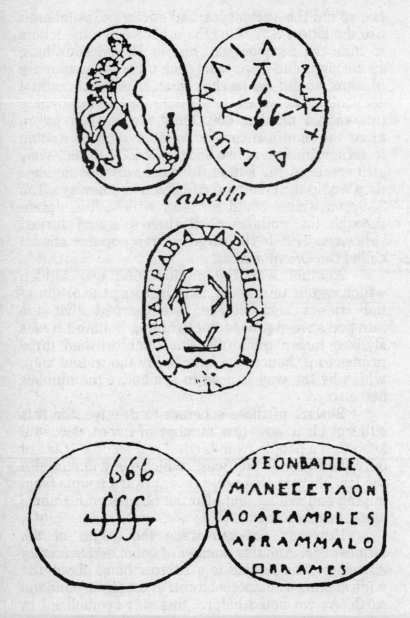

Cavello

The symbols occultists have worn to secretly display the sacred number 666 of Astrology.

forming a circle. This represented to the occultist endless time or eternal life.[34]

As we established earlier, astrology taught that the fate of mankind was ever decided by the position of the stars. Now the chief gods of the Zodiac were the 7 planets who serpentined their way through the 36 rooms of the Zodiac. The 7 planets travel through the narrow band of the Zodiac at varying speeds. The Zodiacal band itself was divided into 12 houses, one for each month of the year, and each house was divided into three rooms, making 36 rooms in all, one for each 10° of the Zodiacal circle.[35] Here we find the origin of our present time-keeping. Believe it or not, the dial of a clock is derived from the 12 houses of the Zodiac. Thus the Zodiac was a Heavenly Clock with which today we measure time. Here's another interesting fact: It was not by chance that our ruler has 12 inches to a foot. Both of these systems of measuring time and length were based upon the 12 houses of the Zodiac. It was not by chance we have 12 units to a dozen. Here we can find the origin of the "Chance of Fate." It is not by chance that the original Roulette wheels have a 360° circle with 36 divisions of 10° each, with a blank or zero division to represent the 5 days beyond the 360 days in a year.

It is not by chance that there are 36 numbered cards in a 52 card deck. One card each represents the 52 weeks with 12 face cards, four Kings, four Queens, and four Jacks, and four suits, that represent the four seasons. Why do you suppose fortunetellers use a deck of cards to predict the future? Because the deck of cards is derived from Astrology! Burn them!

It is not by chance that our present townships

34. Astrology, McCaffery, pp. 28, 29.
35. Ibid., pp. 28, 29.

are composed of 36 square miles, for several writers point out that the ancients divided the earth according to the divisions in the sky. Just as truly as our 12 inch ruler was once a symbol of the 12 house Zodiac, so is our 36 inch yardstick based upon the 36 rooms into which the heavenly houses were divided.

Now, the entire remainder of the sky outside of the Zodiacal band was also divided into 36 constellations, 15 on the south side and 21 on the north side. A god of each constellation was appointed to rule over one of the 36 rooms of the Zodiac. Every star in the sky was considered as a god and the abode of departed spirits and was included in a constellation, over whom was appointed a god who ruled over a Zodiacal room. Each Zodiacal house god rules over a month of the year, and the 7 planetary gods regulated, according to Astrology, the affairs of mankind by their relative positions in the various rooms of the Zodiac. Over them all ruled the Sun-god (The All-Seeing Eye), who was considered the central fire from which each had sprung. As you will recall, the learned doctors of paganism believed that all the other gods were but emanations of the one god, the Sun-god.

Now 1, 6, 12, 36, 111, and 666 were the most sacred numbers in Astrology. Priests of Sun worship used the numbers mathematically by the way the stars travel across the sky to predict future events. They invented magic charts to perform this most popular form of divination. Like the Roulette wheel, the charts were divided into 36 numbered divisions. There were 6 columns in all directions with the numbes 1 to 36 placed inside the entire chart. Any direction you add the columns, they add to 111. There are six squares in each column and $6 \times 111 =$ 666. If you add all the numbers from 1 to 36 they will also add to 666. So you see, the number 36 was a sacred number that identified with the 36 room gods of the Zodiac, and the number 666 was a summary number of the Sun-god, because it was his sacred number as the Ruler of the Zodiac.

Most will agree that this is very interesting, but there is still another, deeper deception the Apostle John, in the book of Revelation, was told to warn the people of the world about. This is the number of the Beast that will cause the world to worship Satan under a false system of Christianity. *"Take heed lest any man deceive you. For many shall come in my name, saying, I am Christ; and shall deceive many."* Mark 13:5,6.

"Here is wisdom. Let him that hath understanding count the number of the beast: for it is the number of a man; and his number is Six hundred three-score and six." Revelation 13:18.

The Hebrew-Chaldean, Latin, Greek and Arab languages have a numerical value for the letters of their alphabets. Take for instance the original Roman Numerals. They were I V X L C D. And if you add these Roman Numerals themselves, along with their numerical values we get:

I V X L C D
1 5 10 50 100 500 = 666

The letter M was not in the original system, it was added later. Now the pagans had a custom of adding their names according to the value of their letters of their own alphabet. As their languages are different, so were the values of each of their letters in their alphabets. The I in Roman Numerals equals 1; in the Greek language, however, the I has a value of 10.

6	32	3	34	35	1
7	11	27	28	8	30
19	14	16	15	23	24
18	20	22	21	17	13
25	29	10	9	26	12
36	5	33	4	2	31

This is an Astrological chart pagan high priests used to predict future events. If you add all the numbers together they will add to 666.

The new Testament was originally written in the Greek language, and an ancient Greek name for Satan in its transliterations as we examined earlier was *Teitan*. And if you add Teitan in its Greek numerical values for the letters we get:

T E I T A N
300 5 10 300 1 50 = 666

Now since the Sun-god, the Heavenly Bull, brought both light and darkness as he rose from east to west, he was worshipped also as both good and evil. He was worshipped not only as a good and evil god, but both male and female. The reasoning behind this heathen philosophy is that the Sun-god was believed to be the source of all things. So since there is good and evil, and male and female, the Sun-god had to be good and evil, and double-sexed, because men and women were created in the image of their god. And since everything derived from the Sun-god, the ancients believed that the soul of man was a divine spark that returned to the central fire (the sun) from which they originally came. And since the pagans believed the stars were but emanations of the sun, all the Star-gods were believed to be once men[36], that had visited this planet.

This could explain why Quetzalcoatl, the Mexican and Aztec messiah, was pictured in their arts as a good man who was a great benefactor of mankind. He visited the earth to teach the arts of civilization, and promised his followers he would return, but he was pictured also as an evil serpent which devoured mankind.

36. Roman Religion As Seen in Pliny's Natural History, Casper, pp. 10-30.

37. The Book of the Dragon, Allen/Griffiths, Orbis Pub. Limited, 1979, p. 60.

The American Indians, both in the North and in the South, considered the bird and the snake as sacred. The bird, because of its power of flight, contained the spirits of the dead, and was associated with lightning. Both lightning and birds of prey can be seen to descend sharply from above and strike with lethal effectiveness.[38]

Hence, the mythological time-cycle bird of fire was called the *Phoenix* not only by many Indian tribes of North America, but also by the Egyptians and the Phoenicians. Sometimes called *Benu* by the Egyptians, the Phoenix was worshipped as the bright and morning star. The morning star to the Egyptians was the nocturnal representation of the hidden Sun-god Osiris, or his soul. The Phoenix was known as *"The One Who Ferries Osiris."*[39]

In the earliest texts, the morning star and Orion, the ruler of the sky, are often compared. For some, gods with a similar name seem to be confused with the morning star, like *Athtar*, who was worshipped as the god of vegetation, as was Tammuz.[40] However, this name *Athtar*, according to *Mythology of All Races*, means *Lucifer*.[41]

Now, it just so happens that one of the old spellings of Phoenix is *Phenex* or *Fenex* in Greek transliterations. Like the name *Lucifer*, Phoenix means "Shining One."[42] And if we add FENEX in its Greek value we get:

$$\text{F} \quad \text{E} \quad \text{N} \quad \text{E} \quad \text{X}$$
$$6 \quad 5 \quad 50 \quad 5 \quad 600 = 666$$

38. Ibid., p. 60.
39. Mythology of All Races, Vol. 12, p. 54.
40. Beware Its Coming — The Antichrist 666, W.F.G., Inc., 1980, p. 29.
41. Mythology of All Races, Vol. 12, p. 54.
42. Ibid., pp. 413, 414.

It depended on what area of the world the pagan lived as to what type of bird was called the Phoenix. To the Egyptian, it was the heron. To the Babylonians, Assyrians, and Hindus it was a peacock. To the North American Indian, it was the Eagle. To the Central and South American, he was the quetzal.

In China, Japan and India, the phoenix is the peacock and the symbol of the sun. In Bali, the peacock is a symbol of the entire sky.[43] The pagan believed that when he died his spirit (soul) would become immortal, and take possession of one of the stars in Heaven from whence he originally came.[44]

It is significant that the Peacock Throne made at Delhi, India, in 1628 is supported by 12 pillars, one for each of the 12 signs of the Zodiac. It is eye opening to discover the Peacock Sun-bird, a symbol of Lucifer, the god behind all false gods, pictured on a Roman Catholic Church window, encircled by the Zodiac. In the church of St. Maurice at Reims, France, we find a woman (probably the Virgin Mary) pictured in a sun-halo, and crowned with seven stars. In one hand she holds a peacock, around which stretches a circular band having on it the 12 signs of the Zodiac. Another shocking observation regarding the Roman Catholic Church is her exaltation of her Pope when in procession, as he is carried on his portable throne. During this procession, two grooms carry large fans of peacock feathers in such a way that the seated Pope seems to have two wings on his shoulders which are constantly in motion and they make him appear as if he is flying.

In ancient Rome and Greece, heaven was considered filled with eyes, the eyes representing the

43. Dance and Drama in Bali, deZoete/Spies, p. 91.
44. The Book of Talismans, Amulets, and Zodiacal Gems, Pavitt, p. 39.

stars, the stars representing the homes of the dead. The god Argus was said to have hundreds of eyes.[45] These eyes of Heaven were represented by the eyes found on the peacock feathers.

Juno, Queen of Heaven to the Romans, had a peacock as her sacred bird.[46] The peacock or Phoenix has long been connected with the Zodiac. The Yezidis, the open Devil worshippers we mentioned earlier, to this day have seven stone images of peacocks which they say represent the 7 planets and which they call *Seitan*, which is merely the Arabic spelling for Teitan or Satan.

In Hinduism, the Ramayana relates that when the god Indra transforms himself into an animal, he becomes a peacock. In India the peacock was believed to have a thousand eyes in its feathers and had power to kill snakes.[47] This sacred bird that symbolized the heavenly host is known to have been kept in Babylon for religious purposes. Aristotle mentions the peacock bird, and a reference in a play by Aristophanes may imply that a Persian ambassador brought a gift of peacocks. Alexander the Great imposed heavy penalties on those who killed Indian peacocks. The birds were depicted on Greek coins. They were sacred to Hera and a myth relates how the goddess set the hundred eyed Argus to guard her husband's mistress, Io, after Zeus sent Hermes to charm and kill Argus. Hera used the giant's eyes to ornament the peacock's tail.[48] In Java, the peacock was associated with the Devil.[49] In Mosul in northern Iraq, there is a sect of Yezidis who hold that the Devil is not evil, and call him the Peacock Angel. The

45. Bulfinch's Mythology, Bulfinch, pp. 28, 30.
46. Man, Myth and Magic, Cavendish, p. 2153.
47. Ibid., p. 2153.
48. Ibid., p. 2153.
49. Ibid., p. 2154.

worshippers of Satan could have chosen no better animal to represent the heavenly host as the proud ruler of the year, and god behind all gods.

It is interesting to note that the very symbol of the proud ruler of the universe, according to heathen belief, is used as a symbol for the NBC Television Network! And CBS Television Network uses the "All-Seeing Eye," which was the symbol of the Sun-god,[50] the Ruler of the eyes (stars) in heaven. Also, ABC Television Network uses the Sun-disk as a symbol of their organization.

It is very important that the reader have some knowledge of the various religions that derived out of Astrology so that he may understand the esoteric mysteries found in the goals and purposes of Secret Societies. However, before we begin to study the Secret Societies which we shall examine in the next chapter, there are a couple of more important facts about astrology and spiritualism the reader should be aware of.

Astrology teaches that this world is to pass through a time period about 26,000 years. This is the length of time it takes, according to astrology, for the Earth to pass through the influence of each of the twelve signs of the Zodiac. Each Great Month or Sign is figured about 2,100 years.[51]

Hence, the entire time period of Twelve Months having about 2,100 years each, is known to astrologers as The Great Year. This Great Year is divided by seven ages: Leo, Cancer, Gemini, Taurus, Aries, Pisces and Aquarius.[52]

During this so-called Great Year, or 26,000 years, astrology claims to have predicted the evolutionary progress of man from century to century.

50. Mythology of All Races, Vol. 12, pp. 28, 29.
51. The Aquarian Gospel of Jesus the Christ, Levi, p. 9.
52. The Compleat Astrologer, Parker, p. 44.

The starting point for the seven continual Ages began 10,000-8,000 BC, which was known as the Age of Leo. From the book *The Compleat Astrologer*, Parker, we read the following:

"*The earliest Month of which we have real knowledge was that of Leo (10000 - 8000 B.C.): The Lascaux cave paintings show the Leonine creative influence but the thought-motivation behind the effort is Aquarian in spirit. The Age of Cancer (8000 - 6000 B.C.), witnessed the earliest development of settled farming and constructed dwellings - both of which are Capricornian in essence. During the Geminian Age (6000 - 4000 B.C.) the founding of the earliest libraries comes under Sagittarius. Perhaps the most striking polarity of all was in the Taurean Age (4000 - 2000 B.C.), for the Egyptians were much preoccupied with death and the afterlife, themes strongly related to Scorpio. The war-like Arian Age expressed its polarity with Libra in the magnificent beauty and balance of Greek Architecture (2000- B.C. - Birth of Christ).*"

(*The Compleat Astrologer*, Parker, McGraw-Hill Book Company, 1971, p. 44.)

Now, according to Astrology, we are living in the Age of Pisces (0 - 2000 A.D.). The Age of Pisces is considered the Christian dispensation. Pisces was symbolized in Astrology in the form of a fish because the Mother goddess Venus and Cupid hurled themselves into the river Euphrates and became fishes after being terrified by the giant Typhon.[53] Hence, we find the real origin of the fish symbol that some erring Christians display to show they are Christians.

Spiritualism teaches that during this evolu-

53. The Compleat Astrologer, Parker, p. 128.

tionary time table of the 26,000 years, Masters of Wisdom, or Christs, were to arise. Some were to be founders of great religions, say occultists, and they would have a variety of titles such as Mahatmas, the Hierarchy, the Great Ones, the Secret Brotherhood, the Inner Government of the World, the Great White Lodge of Masters of the Wisdom. One of these so-called Masters was Koot Hoomi, who is said to have inspired a witch named Alice Bailey.[54] She claimed to be one of these Masters.[55]

She was the author of many occult books, one of which was *Discipleship in the New Age*. In her book she states the following:

"We stand now on the verge of a similar but still more momentous event - the appearance of the fifth kingdom, as a result of the planned activity of the New Group of World Servers, working in collaboration with the Hierarchy of perfected souls, and under the guidance of the Christ Himself. This will usher in the New Age wherein five kingdoms in nature will be recognised as existing side by side upon earth."

Discipleship in the New Age, Bailey, Lucis Publishing Co., 1944, p. 32.

Bailey goes on to say that this New Age we are entering into will call for a universal New World Religion.[56] This philosophy is based on the theory found in Astrology that this world is entering into the Age of Aquarius. Hence, the reader may look at this song found among Rock 'N' Rollers in a different light. For "This is the dawning of the Age of Aquarius" was written by disciples of this New Age Movement to help promote the idea of a One World Government and a One World Religion.

54. Man, Myth and Magic, Vol. 13, Cavendish, p. 1769.
55. Discipleship in the New Age, Bailey, p. 43.
56. Ibid., p. 38.

Now, Aquarius is also known as the great coming New Month. In the book *The Compleat Astrologer*, Parker, p. 44, we read the following:

"In the Age of Aquarius, we may conjecture that man will consider a system of WORLD GOVERNMENT, which will involve the organizational characteristics of Leo."

Alice Bailey told her brethren that Christ Himself would usher in this New Age. Bailey goes on to say how this New Age will call for a New World Religion. In her book *Disciples in the New Age*, p. 38, we read the following:

"The Workers in the Field of Religion form this group. Their work is to formulate the universal platform of the NEW WORLD RELIGION. It is a work of loving synthesis, and it will emphasize the unity and the fellowship of the spirit. This group is, in a pronounced sense, a channel for the second Ray of Love-Wisdom, that of the World Teacher - an office held at present by the Christ. The platform of the NEW WORLD RELIGION will be built by the many groups working under the inspiration of the Christ and the influence of the second ray and these - in their totality - will constitute this sixth group."

Reader, be not deceived! The Christ here that Alice Baily is referring to is NOT JESUS OF NAZARETH! Spiritualism does not deny the existence of Jesus, but they do deny Jesus was God Manifested in the Flesh. And as we continue to follow the history of the Great Luciferian Conspiracy, the reader will see how Spiritualism uses Christianity to destroy Christianity. We may examine this fact by reading the writings of another disciple of this New Age Movement who called himself Levi. In his book *The Aquarian Gospel of Jesus the Christ*,

THE WORLD HAS HAD *enough*...OF HUNGER, INJUSTICE, WAR.

IN ANSWER TO OUR CALL FOR HELP, AS WORLD TEACHER FOR ALL HUMANITY,

THE CHRIST IS NOW HERE.

HOW WILL WE RECOGNIZE HIM?

Look for a modern man concerned with modern problems—political, economic and social. Since July, 1977 the Christ has been emerging as a spokesman for a group or community in a well known modern country. He is not a religious leader, but an educator in the broadest sense of the word—pointing the way out of our present crisis.

We will recognize Him by His extraordinary spiritual potency, the universality of His viewpoint and His love for all humanity. He comes not to judge, but to aid and inspire.

WHO IS THE CHRIST?

Throughout history humanity's evolution has been guided by a group of enlightened men, the Masters of Wisdom. They have remained largely in the remote desert and mountain places of earth, working mainly through their disciples who live openly in the world. This message of the Christ's reappearance has been given primarily by such a disciple trained for his task for over 20 years.

At the center of this "Spiritual Hierarchy" stands the World Teacher, Lord Maitreya, known by Christians as the Christ. And as Christians await the Second Coming, so the Jews await the Messiah, the Buddhists the fifth Buddha, the Moslems the Imam Mahdi, and the Hindus await Krishna. These are all names for one individual.

His presence in the world guarantees there will be no third World War.

WHAT IS HE SAYING?

My task will be to show you how to live together peacefully as brothers. This is simpler than you imagine, My friends, for it requires only the acceptance of sharing.

"How can you be content with the modes within which you now live, when millions starve and die in squalor, when the rich parade their wealth before the poor, when each man is his neighbor's enemy, when no man trusts his brother?"

"Allow me to show you the way forward into a simpler life where no man lacks, where no two days are alike, where the Joy of Brotherhood manifests through all men."

Take your brother's need as the measure for your action and solve the problems of the world.

WHEN WILL WE SEE HIM?

He has not as yet declared His true status and His location is known to only a very few disciples. One of these has announced that soon the Christ will acknowledge His identity and within the next two months will speak to humanity through a worldwide television and radio broadcast. His message will be heard inwardly, telepathically, by all people in their own language.

From that time with His help we will build a new world.

WITHOUT SHARING THERE CAN BE NO JUSTICE;
WITHOUT JUSTICE THERE CAN BE NO PEACE;
WITHOUT PEACE THERE CAN BE NO FUTURE.

This announcement is appearing simultaneously in major cities of the world

This announcement was seen in several leading newspapers throughout the world in 1982.

Astrology teaches that the human race will pass through seven ages. Before each age a Christ, according to Spiritualism, was to appear to usher in each New Age. We live in the Age of Pisces, 0-2000 AD, and according to Spiritualism we are about to enter into the "Age of Aquarius," which will begin in the year 2000 AD. Whether or not this is the long awaited appearance of the Antichrist foretold from Scripture still remains to be seen. For there "are many antichrists." I John 2:18. The Devil himself will appear as Jesus Christ just before the real Jesus of Nazareth appears in the heavens. II Thessalonians 2:3-11. Satan will personate Jesus as He is described in Revelation 1:13-15. This false Christ Maitreya, according to this newspaper article, will appear as an ordinary modern man.

Levi shows how Spiritualism is trying to unite Christianity into its ranks which untold millions have already been deceived:

"The Christ is son, the only son begotten by Almighty God, the GOD OF FORCE and God omniscient, God of thought; and Christ is God, the God of Love."

Levi goes on to say:

"Christ is the Logos of Infinities and through the word alone are thought and Force made manifest."

(The Aquarian Gospel of Jesus the Christ, Levi, DeVorss & Co., Publishers, 1964.)

Spiritualism teaches that Jesus was just one of the Masters that would come into the world. And the word Christ in Spiritualism is a principle (Logos) and does not refer to any particular person.[57] Jesus was just another avatar[58] among modern day occultists.

Again, we quote from The Aquarian Gospel of Jesus the Christ, by Levi, as follows:

"What relationship existed between Jesus of Nazareth and the Christ? Orthodox Christian ecclesiastics tell us that Jesus of Nazareth and the Christ were one; that the true name of this remarkable person was Jesus Christ. They tell us that this man of Galilee was the very eternal God clothed in flesh of man that men might see his glory. Of course this doctrine is wholly at variance with the teachings of Jesus Himself and of His apostles."

(The Aquarian Gospel of Jesus the Christ, Levi, DeVorss & Co., Pub., 1967, pp. 35, 67.)

Contrary to what Levi said in his book, there are numerous Scriptures found in the Bible, both in

57. The Aquarian Gospel of Jesus the Christ, Levi, p. 12.

58. Ibid., p. 13.

the Old and New Testament that supports the doctrine that Jesus was God Himself clothed in a human body. *"And without controversy, great is the mystery of godliness: God was manifest in the flesh, justified in the Spirit, seen of angels, preached unto the Gentiles, believed on in the world, received up into glory."* I Timothy 3:16.

Jesus Himself said in John 14:8,9, *"Philip saith unto him, Lord, shew us the Father, and it sufficeth us. Jesus saith unto him, HAVE I BEEN SO LONG TIME WITH YOU AND YET HAST THOU NOT KNOWN ME, PHILIP? HE THAT HAT SEEN ME HATH SEEN THE FATHER; and how sayest thou then, shew us the Father?"*

Here is another truth the Scriptures call to attention. *"Who is a liar but he that denieth that Jesus is the Christ? He is antichrist, that denieth the Father and the Son."* I John 2:22. *"And every spirit that confesseth NOT that Jesus Christ is come IN THE FLESH IS NOT OF GOD: and this is that SPIRIT OF ANTICHRIST, whereof ye have heard that it should come; and even now already is it in the world."* I John 4:3.

Spiritualism teaches that at the beginning of every Age there has been a Christ to usher them in. Jesus was the Christ who according to Astrology ushered in the Age of Pisces (0 - 2000 A.D.). Today, Spiritualism calls Christ "The God of Force."

Little do these modern Luciferians know that the Christ of the Holy Scriptures, the Lord of the Sabbath, foretold through His Prophets how Spiritualism would try to unite the world into a One World Luciferian Socialistic Government. The Apostle John was given a vision from our Lord, Jesus of Nazareth, that symbolized this New Age Movement as the Beast that ascendeth out of the Bottomless Pit.

Revelation 11:7; 17:3, 7-14. While Daniel, the Prophet, was given a vision of this New Age Movement almost 700 years before the Apostle John of Revelation received his vision. Daniel even used the same language modern Luciferians and occultists use today to describe it. In Daniel 11:36-39 we read the following: "And the king shall do according to his will; and he shall exalt himself, and magnify himself above every god, and shall speak marvellous things against the God of gods, and shall prosper till the indignation be accomplished: for that that is determined shall be done. Neither shall he regard the God of his fathers, nor the desire of women, nor regard any god: for he shall magnify himself above all. But in his estate shall he honour the GOD OF FORCES: and a god whom his fathers knew not shall he honour with gold and silver, and with precious stones, and pleasant things. Thus shall he do in the most strong holds with a strange god, whom he shall acknowledge and increase with glory; and he shall cause them to rule over many, and shall divide the land for gain."

In the following chapters of this book, we will understand more of the meaning of this prophecy, and we will learn what other names this New Age Movement is coming under.

Chapter II

Part 1

Chapter II

Part 1

To trace the origin and purposes of Secret Societies, we need to go back again to the book of the beginnings (Genesis) to Adam and Eve's fall. The book of Genesis showed us how Satan caused a serpent to deceive Eve, then later managed to get the very instrument used to deceive to be worshipped and adored. Now in this chapter we will study the bait Satan used to actually induce the first humans to commit their deadly mistake, and how Lucifer has used this same bait to deceive others.

What did the Father of Lies say unto Eve? "For God doth know that in the day ye eat thereof, then your eyes shall be opened, and ye shall be as gods, knowing good and evil." Genesis 3:5.

Here is the Truth about how multitudes are swept into the high ranks of Witchcraft to be used by Satan to deceive others. It was by creating a desire to obtain forbidden knowledge that Adam and Eve were swept from the protection of God, and lost eternal life, not only for them but also their offspring. Satan implanted in Adam and Eve a desire to be like gods, knowing good and evil. This covetousness produced self-exaltation in the minds of the earth's first couple, and it is this very thing that led to Lucifer's own fall in Heaven.

Man, from the time of Adam and Eve, has ever strived to progress forward into the knowledge of the secret things of the Universe. As with Adam and Eve, Lucifer tries to kindle a desire to explore what God has not made known to us. The Bible reveals to man there are secrets of the Universe the Lord does not want to reveal to man. It is not because God is selfish, as the serpent implied, but because of the evil heart in man - he can't be trusted with them. Look at the condition that man has created for himself in the world today. He is constantly in fear, world wide, because of his evil inventions that could destroy the world. He is plagued day by day with the threat of war, crime, and national ruin within his own country. It was Christ who created the Universe and all that is in them. John 1:1-3, 14; Ephesians 3:9; Hebrews 1:1,2. Jesus is the owner, and it's His right to judge what knowledge man can or cannot be trusted with. Saith the Lord: *"The secret things belong unto the Lord our God: but those things which are revealed belong unto us and to our children for ever, that we may do all the words of this law."* Deuteronomy 29:29.

How were these secrets about the Earth's history revealed? Saith the Lord: *"Surely the Lord God will do nothing but he revealeth his secret unto His servants the prophets."* Amos 3:7. For those things that were to be revealed to us, God chose people that he knew he could trust and would faithfully carry out His prescriptions. These people were called Prophets. They were to write down and record what was revealed to them by Visions and Dreams.

Saith the Lord: *"And he said, hear now my words: If there be a prophet amng you, I the Lord will make myself known unto him in a VISION, and will speak unto him in a dream."* Numbers 12:6.

However, as there is a Mystery of Godliness (I Timothy 3:16) so is there a Mystery of Iniquity (II Thessalonians 2:7). And, as the Lord has His Prophets, so has the Devil. *"For such are false apostles,* deceitful workers, transforming themselves into the apostles of Christ. And no marvel; for Satan himself is transformed into an angel of light. Therefore it is no great thing if his ministers also be transformed as the ministers of righteousness; whose end shall be according to their works." II Corinthians 11:13-15.

Now, one of the clear ways to test a prophet is found in Isaiah 8:20: "To the Law and to the Testimony if they speak not according to this word, it is because there is NO LIGHT IN THEM." If a man or woman claims to receive a vision or a dream from the Lord, but contradict the teaching in the Law (Torah), which means the first five books of the Bible (Genesis, Exodus, Leviticus, Numbers, Deuteronomy), or contradicts the teachings found in the Testimony (the rest of the books of the Bible), it is because the Lord has not sent them. Another way the Lord has given His people to detect a true or false prophet is found in Deuteronomy 13:1-5: "If there arise among you a prophet or a dreamer of dreams and giveth thee a sign or a wonder, And the sign or the wonder come to pass, whereof he spake unto thee, saying, Let us go after other gods, which thou hast not known, and let us serve them; thou shalt not hearken unto the words of that prophet, or that dreamer of dreams: for the Lord your God proveth you, to know whether ye love the Lord your God with all your heart and with all your soul. Ye shall walk after the Lord your God, and fear him, and keep his commandments, and obey his voice, and ye shall serve him, and cleave unto him. And that prophet, or that dreamer of dreams, shall be put to death, because he hath spoken to turn you away from the Lord your God which brought you out of the land of Egypt, and redeemed you out of the house of bondage, to thrust thee out of the way which the Lord thy God commanded thee to to walk in. So shalt thou put the evil away from the midst of thee."

As stated clearly above, the Lord said there are some people who can predict something to happen (give a sign), or can work wonders, but at the same time could be trying to lead us into the worship of one of these religions of Satan's we have been examining. Can we not today, in our time, observe such things?

Here is another way the Lord gives His people knowledge and understanding to see who is being led by the Holy Spirit, or being used by the Devil. "*I have also spoken by the prophets, and I have multiplied visions, and used similitudes, by the ministry of the prophets. And by a prophet the Lord brought Israel out of Egypt, and by a prophet was he preserved.*" Hosea 12:10, 13. A true prophet's ministry will tend to preserve the people.

When a man or woman claims to receive a message from the Lord about something to happen, but it doesn't, the Bible warns: "*But the prophet, which shall presume to speak a word in my name, which I have not commanded him to speak, or that shall speak in the name of other gods, even that prophet shall die. And if thou say in thine heart, How shall we know the word which the Lord hath not spoken? When a prophet speaketh in the name of the Lord, if the thing follow not, nor come to pass, that is the thing which the Lord hath not spoken, but the prophet hath spoken it presumptuously: thou shalt not be afraid of him.*" Deuteronomy 18:20-22.

A genuine prophet of God is distinguished from a false prophet according to Scripture by his life, Doctrines, Predictions, and who he or she worships. If a prophet predicts certain events to happen and only some of the events come to pass, it is because he is not receiving messages from the Lord. A genuine prophet of God, according to Scripture, is never wrong in predicting future events, because the messages he is receiving are from the One who knows the end of things from the beginning. A prophet who foretold something to the Lord's people in ancient times, but that prediction did not come to pass, was to be killed for deceiving the people.

Now here is another important note from the Scriptures to remember in testing prophets: *"There shall not be found among you any one that maketh his son or his daughter to pass through fire or that useth divination, or an observer of times, or an enchanter, or a witch, or a charmer, or a consulter with familiar spirits (spirit guides), or a wizard, or a necromancer. For all that do these things are an abomination unto the Lord: and because of these abominations the Lord thy God doth drive them out from thee."* Deuteronomy 18:10-12.

The God of the Bible says He communicates to His Prophets through VISIONS AND DREAMS. He does not reveal messages through Astrologers, Palm Readers, or through cards, or by crystal ball visions. This is prophecy by divination. He does not reveal messages through a magician, sorcerer, or psychic. The Lord does not reveal messages through a hypnotist, called a charmer in Scripture. The Lord does not relay messages through spirit guides which the psychics, mediums and witches claim to be ancient sages or wise men. *"The dead know not any thing."* Ecclesiastes 9:5. The Lord does not communicate through wizards (male witches), or necromancers, *"For all that do these things are an ABOMINATION UNTO THE LORD."* Deuteronomy 18:12.

As we tried to show you in the last chapter, Astrology is the basic foundation of Witchcraft.

In Isaiah, the Bible foretells what will happen to Astrologers and people who trust in them. Unlike Astrology, the Bible predictions have never failed: *"Thou art wearied in the multitude of thy counsels, Let now the Astrologers, the Stargazers, the monthly Prognosticators, stand up, and save thee from these things that shall come upon thee, Behold, they shall be as stubble: the fire shall burn them: they shall not deliver themselves from the power of the flame: there shall not be a coal to warm at nor fire to sit before it."* Isaiah 47:13,14.

"Remember the former things of old: for I am God, and there is none else, I am God, and there is none like me, declaring the end from the beginning and from ancient times the things that are not yet done, saying, My counsel shall stand, and I will do all my pleasure." Isaiah 46:9.

Our Lord, from ancient times, has revealed the mysteries of the Godhead and what he desires us to know about the Universe, and its future, through His Holy Prophets. However, instead of believing these words: *"Believe in the Lord your God, so shall ye be established; believe his prophets, so shall ye prosper,"* II Chronicles 20:20, Satan has led man away from the Gospel by keeping him interested in the secrets of the Universe. While abandoning the most ancient book we have about the world's history, the Bible, men are led to think there is Truth beyond Bible Truth, and have invented false sciences which totally contradict the Scriptures. The way out speculations and pure guess work used to support their findings leads them to eventually lose hold on what little faith they had in God, to even reject that there is a God.

When the Jews were deceived into worshipping the cosmic gods of nature and were sent into captivity by the Lord to Babylon as a punishment for their idolatry, certain Jewish priests, while in Babylon, studied deep into the ancient Babylonian mysteries (Witchcraft). These priests produced what became a philosophy called the *Cabala, Cabbala,* or *Qabbalah* (some of the English spellings of a Hebrew word whose more correct transliteration is *Kabbalah*), whose meaning is "Receiving," or "that which is received." The Cabala's central doctrine, say the Cabalists, deals with the unfolding of the hidden and unknowable God into the fullness of the manifest God, known by his works.[1] In other words, they try to explain that which is hidden that the Lord has not revealed. The scientific name for this science is Metaphysics. The word Cabala actually derived from the Hebrew verb, *kabel,* which means to receive and implies that the Cabala was received, in the form of special revelations, by a few of the elect, who were especially chosen for the privilege, because of their saintliness.[2]

This Jewish movement didn't catch on among the Jews as a whole until about nine centuries after the resurrection of Christ. It reached its height in Spain when a Cabalist's Bible called the *Zohar* was published.[3] The *Zohar* was compiled by Moses de Leon at the end of the 13th century. He incorporated into the Zohar, which means "book of brightness," the doctrines of the infamous Gnostics and Neoplatonists[4] that the soul is immortal and its attachment to the body is unfortunate, but temporary. Cabalists believe in reincarnation and that God supplies all knowledge. They claim that the Scriptures contain important symbols that, properly analyzed, reveal

1. Man, Myth and Magic, Vol. 3, Cavendish, p. 382.
2. Collier's Encyclopedia, Vol. 5, 1977, p. 85.
3. Ibid., p. 84.
4. Ibid., p. 84

secrets concerning the creation of the Universe. They believed that these secret combinations of words and symbols could be manipulated to achieve magical results.[5]

Unlike ancient Witchcraft, the Cabalists believe that the Godhead consists of 10 emanations of the one God. However, these Jewish Cabalists do not believe that these emanations are gods, as paganism teaches, but a complex organism consisting of ten emanations, potencies, or focal points, called the Sefiroth. These ten aspects, stages, or manifestations of the Living Deity, the World of Emanation, or World of the Sefiroth, is not the Universe (stars), say Cabalists, but the Godhead in its existent aspect.[6]

It is mind boggling to try to understand any of this nonsense; however, we ask the reader to keep patience, for the reader must have a little knowledge what the Cabala is so he can understand the philosophies behind the Secret Societies. It is from the Cabala that modern Witchcraft and the Secret Societies say they draw many of their crafts.

Like Witchcraft, the Cabala teaches that man is a microcosm (miniature universe), and has both male and female elements in the Godhead. The female element of the Godhead is found in one of the ten emanations (Sefiroth). The Shekhinah, they say, is the female element because it is the passive aspect to the Deity, the manifestation of the divine power which vitalizes all creation.[7]

Cabalists say man has spiritual intercourse with God through the Shekhinah. From *Hasidic Prayer*, by Louis Jacobs, page 61, we quote the following:

"But of Moses of the Zohar does say that he had intercourse with the SHEKHINAH! Tishby has,

however, shown that there are, in fact, many passages in the Zohar in which erotic symbolism is used for man's relationship with God and not only with regard to Moses."

Jacobs goes on to say:

"For instance, the Zohar states that when a man cannot be with his wife, for example, when he is way from home, or when he is studying the Torah, or when she has her periods, then the Shekhinah is with him so that he can be male and female."

Another sacrilegious claim of the Cabala is also found in their philosophy about the 10 emanations (Sefiroth). Cabalists claim that the 10 Sefiroth is the Tree of Life from which the Universe emanated or came into existence, and that man can unite himself with, or become, the One 'by rising through the spheres,' spiritually climbing the ladder of the Sefiroth to reach God.[8] In magic, the adept (an expert) must experience and master all ten Sefiroth in order to achieve supreme perfection and power, for the Tree of the Sefiroth is believed to be a cosmic diagram, the basic pattern which shows how the Universe is arranged and how its phenomena are connected. And since man is a miniature replica of the Universe (microcosm) and of God, man is capable of spiritually expanding himself to become God.[9]

Is not this blasphemous language nothing but an echo from Eden? "YE SHALL BE AS GODS," Genesis 3:5. The Cabala teaches that man can reach the magnitude of the Omnipotent God. Who would dare make such a statement? As we saw earlier, his words are recorded in Isaiah 14:12-15.

5. Student's Encyclopedia, Vol. 3, 1971, p. 579.
6. Man, Myth and Magic, Vol 3, p. 384.
7. Ibid., p. 384.
8. Man, Myth and Magic, Vol. 3, Cavendish, p. 387.
9. Ibid., p. 387.

Like Roman Catholic Church doctrines, there are enormous amounts of blasphemous claims against the God of Heaven that can be found in their literature. However, space does not allow us to venture too far into this diabolical scheme to deceive. But to summarise what basically the Cabala is, it can be summed up in one word, MAGIC, and its roots are found in Babylon. Cabalistic magic is mainly arranging numbers and combining Hebrew letters and their numerical values into magical squares and anagrams.[10]

The Cabalists claimed Moses used magic to bring the plagues against the Egyptians. However, it wasn't Moses who caused the plagues to fall upon the Egyptians, it was God Himself. There will be more unveiling of the Cabala and how multitudes have been deceived by it as we study into the doctrines and purposes of the Secret Societies. However, before we study the origin and purposes of the Secret Societies, we need to examine an ancient mystical name given to schools or groups that taught Babylonian mysticism. They were known for centuries as the *Illuminati*. And they called Babylonian mysticism ILLUMINISM.

The *Encyclopedia Americana*, p. 698, says *The Illuminati* is a name taken, or given, to various groups of individuals existing during the past 2,000 years, who believed in and taught a doctrine of illumination or inner light (Illuminism).[11] However, this mystical name derived from its original source at a much earlier time. The Western equivalent to this Eastern mysticism is Hermeticism and Gnosticism, which we will also examine as we go on.

10. Man, Myth and Magic, Vol. 3, Cavendish, p. 387.

11. The Encyclopedia Americana, Americana Corporation, 1947, p. 698.

12. Ibid., p. 698.

The Illuminati taught living a life of purity and service would open their so-called inner senses so that they would obtain spiritual sight or Clairvoyance, known as the Third Eye, become Seers, and be able to converse with angels and with dead saints.[12] The individual who became spiritually or intellectually enlightened in the ancient Babylonian Mysteries was initiated into the mysteries when qualified, and called an Illuminated.[13]

In France, under the name of *Illumines*, another Witchcraft school appeared in Picardy in 1623, but only continued a short time because of the repressive measures taken by the Papacy. However, another sect of Illumines appeared in the south of France about 1722 AD and continued until 1794. They traced their origin to the Gnostics.[16]

Here is an interesting note. It is from a sect of the Illuminati who existed in the 15th century that the Rosicrucians, an international Secret Society, claim their modern fraternal order originated. They also continue to claim that it actually derived out of the Egyptian mysteries before that time. Rosicrucism is a mixture of both Christianity and Witchcraft.

The number 13 in Witchcraft plays a very important part in the practice of Witchcraft as we saw earlier. And so it does in this fraternal Order of the Rosicrucians. Here from one of their own publications, *"The Rosicrucian Cosmo - Conception,"* by Max Heindel, we read the following:

"The Order is not merely a secret society; it is one of THE MYSTERY SCHOOLS, and the Brothers are Hierophants of the lesser Mysteries, Custodians of the Sacred Teachings and spiritual power

12. Ibid., p. 698.
13. The Encyclopedia Britannica, Vol. 14, 1910, p. 320.
16. The Encyclopedia Britannica, Vol. 14, 1910, p. 320.

more potent in the life of the Western World than any of the visible Governments, though they may not interfere with humanity so as to deprive them of their free will."

Heindel goes on to say,

"Like all other Mystery Orders, the Order of Rosicrucians IS FORMED ON COSMIC LINES: If we take balls of even size and try how many it will take to cover one and hide it from view, we shall find it will require 12 to conceal a thirteenth ball. The ultimate division of physical matter, the true atom, found in interplanetary space, is thus grouped in twelve around one. The twelve signs of the Zodiac enveloping our Solar System, the twelve semitones of the musical scale comprising the octave, the twelve Apostles who clustered around Christ, etc., are other examples of this grouping of 12 and 1. The Rosicrucian Order is therefore also composed of 12 Brothers and a 13th."

We will come back to the Rosicrucians in a moment, but let's go on and take another look at some other Mystic Schools who adopted this name "Illuminati." There were other little sects of Illuminism recorded in history like the Illuminati of Avignon and the Illuminati of Stockholm; but none of them became a threat to freedom, liberty of conscience, and Christianity like the Illuminati of Bavaria. This Secret Order was founded May 1, 1776, by one Adam Weishaupt, a professor of Canon Law at Ingolstadt, Germany, and an ex-Jesuit Priest.[17] Weishaupt, and his Order of Illuminati, we shall study in the next chapter.

Now, the Rosicrucians, who claim also to be Illuminated or Enlightened, say that Thutmose III of

17. Encyclopedia of Occultism and Parapsychology, Vol. 1, 1978, p. 460.

Egypt was the founder of their Secret Order. He erected two obelisks bearing a record of his achievements. One of these obelisks is now located in Central Park in New York.[18]

According to the Rosicrucians, after Thutmose III died, his son Amenhotep took up his father's work in their Brotherhood about the end of September 1448 BC. He was succeeded by his son Thutmose IV, who ruled from 1420 to 1411 BC. Then came Amenhotep IV, with whose history all the Rosicrucians are greatly concerned. He was the Great Master in the family of the founders, and the one to whom they owe their philosophies and writings used so universally in all their Lodge work throughout the world. He was born in the Royal Palace at Thebes, according to the Rosicrucians, in 1378 BC.[19]

To qualify to be initiated into the mysteries, the new initiate had to want to become an expert (adept) in Astrology, Magic, Sorcery, Fortune-telling, Necromancy, etc., which, by the way, is an abomination unto our Lord (Deuteronomy 18:10-12).

On this side of the resurrection of Jesus Christ, there were various other schools of these mystics besides the ones we already stated, who were given, or assumed, this name Illuminati, on the grounds of having superior knowledge of God, and of divine things which they claimed to be able to perform. The Rosicrucians and the Illuminati's first cousins were the infamous Gnostics, from whom Simon Magus borrowed his mysteries and mixed them with Christianity. Another group of Gnostics found in the book of Revelation were called the Nicolaitanes (Revelation 2:15), who were followers of one Nicolas, a

18. Rosicrucian Questions and Answers with Complete History, Lewis, p. 28.
19. Ibid., pp. 28, 29.

deacon in the time of Paul, who fell into licentious doctrines and practices.[20]

Another such school for higher learning of Witchcraft was found in Spain around 1520 AD, and was called in the native language *Los Alumbrados*. It continued for about a century, then disappeared as victim of the Spanish Inquisition. Ignatius Loyola, the founder of the Society of Jesus (the Jesuits), almost became a victim of the Spanish Inquisition himself when the Roman Catholic Church got wind of his connection with the Alumbrados. But he was acquitted before the Inquisition Court with an admonition.[21]

However, there are some who hold today that the Illuminati is a front for the Roman Catholic Church to unite the world under her banner again. And, it was this same Ignatius Loyola who founded the Illuminati.[22] But, we will learn from history that it was not Ignatius Loyola who founded the Order of the Illuminati in Germany which has continued since 1776 AD. It was Adam Weishaupt, an ex-Jesuit.

Now, coming back to the Rosicrucians who also used the name Illuminati for their Order: The reason the Rosicrucians look back to the reign of Amenhotep IV was because he was the last of the Great Pharaohs of Egypt, and Hermes Trimegistus, the Prophet, was born during his reign. There is much confusion in ancient and modern learned circles about who Hermes actually was. Scholars of mythology said he was just a myth, as was Mercury, his equivalent to the Romans. His Egyptian equivalent, say some scholars, was the Egyptian god "Thoth." The god Thoth or Hermes, was the moon

20. Encyclopedia Britannica, Vol. 9, p. 702.

21. The Encyclopedia Britannica, Vol. 14, 1910, p. 320.

22. The Godfathers, Chick Publications, 1982, pp. 9-11.

god, who was the god of time and of its divisions. He was the measurer and the god of measurements. He was also the conducter of the dead, and god of human Intelligence, to whom are attributed all the productions of human Art. To the pagan Egyptians, all the literature of Egypt is attributed to Hermes. All the writings that relate to the different sciences, mathematics, astronomy, medicine, and music of the Egyptians were called by the Greeks "The Hermetic Books."

In Greek mythology, Hermes was known as the son of Zeus and Maia. He was the god who invented dice, music, geometry, the interpretation of dreams, measures and weights, the arts, letters, etc. He was also regarded as the patron of public treaties, as the guardian of roads and writing. Thoth to the Egyptians was considered a great king, a teacher of mankind, who had left books of magic and mystery behind him. Numerous books of such a sort once existed in Egypt. Clement of Alexander claimed he knew of 42 so-called Hermetic fragments which could be found in the works of Stobaeus, Cyrillus, Suides and Lactantus.

The Hermetic Books fall into two groups. The first deals with Astrology, Alchemy, etc.; while the others are dialogues describing the soul's regeneration in terms like the Cabala. This is the blasphemous doctrine that man can reach perfection through his own efforts by journeying through the higher spheres of knowledge, then after death, become God. Tradition says the Egyptian mysteries were a key to a complete knowledge of the Universe and man. And this so-called knowledge was preserved in these Hermetic Books which were believed for centuries to be written by Hermes Trismegistus. These books were universally accepted among the doctors of occultism as authentic books of Hermes until the early 17th century, when they were proven to be a fraud. They had actually been written as late as the second and third centuries AD, by a succession of anonymous Greeks living in Egypt.

However, even though these Hermetic Books were not directly from Hermes, as the occultists said, there are still some interesting facts to learn about who Hermes was, this legendary god of wisdom. To start, we need to take a deeper look at the other gods of the Orient who were the Eastern equivalent to the Western god Hermes. They were known in history as *Nebo (Nabu)* and *Bel.* Alexander Hislop, who spent years tracing down ancient gods to Babylonian origin, has some very interesting facts compiled from the ancient past in his book *The Two Babylons.* In this book Hislop states the following:

"If Ninus was Nimrod, who was the historical Bel? He must have been Cush; for Cush begot Nimrod, Gen. 10:8, and Cush is generally represented as having been a ringleader in the great apostacy. But again, Cush, as the son of Ham was Hermes or Mercury; for Hermes is just an Egyptian synonym for the "son of Ham." Now, Hermes was the great original prophet of idolatry; for he was recognized by the pagans as the author of their religious rites, and the interpreter of the gods."

(*The Two Babylons,* Hislop, pp. 25, 26.)

To the occultist, tradition says the Egyptian Mysteries were a key to a complete knowledge of the Universe and of man. But the truth is, Egypt received its knowledge of the ancient Mysteries from Babylonia. In the traditions of the ancient writers, Ninus is said to be the son of Bel who Gesenius the ancient scribe identifies as Nebo, the Babylonian prophetic god. And Hyginus, another ancient scribe, shows that Nebo was Mercury. And, Hyginus tells how a similar legend was written about the confusion of tongues as stated in the Bible. Hyginus is quoted by Hislop:

"For many ages men lived under the government of Jove (evidently not the Roman Jupiter, but Jehovah of the Hebrews), without cities and without laws, and all speaking one language. But, after that Mercury interpreted the speeches of men (whence an interpreter is called Hermeneutes), the same individual distributed the nations, then discord began."

(The Two Babylons, Hislop, p. 26.)

Now the pagans often named places, cities, and towns after their chief gods. A mount called Nebo east of Jordan over against Jericho, in Moab, part of the Abarim range, with a top called Pisgah, is where our Lord told Moses to view the land which he couldn't enter because of his transgression, Deuteronomy 32:49. The word "Nebo" means height.[23]

The word "Baal" means Lord, but the name "Bel" means "The Confounder."[24] The ancients often got the two names Baal and Bel mixed up as do modern scholars today. The Scriptures themselves show that Baal and Bel were two distinct gods with TWO distinct names. In Jeremiah 50:2; 51:44 we read: "Declare ye among the nations, and publish, and set up a standard; publish, and conceal not; say, Babylon is taken, Bel is confounded, Merodach is broken in pieces, her idols are confounded, her images are broken in pieces." "And I will punish Bel in Babylon, and I will bring forth out of his mouth that which

23. Young's Analytical Concordance to the Bible, p. 689.
24. The Two Babylons, Hislop, p. 26.

he hath swallowed up: and the nations shall not flow together any more unto him: yea, the wall of Babylon shall fall.''

Now, Bel the Confounder or, in other words, the god of confusion, was himself to be confounded by the destruction of Babylon, the origin of all pagan religions. The name Babylon itself means "Confusion."[25] Today, the city of Babylon is just as it was predicted to be, and now is a symbol of religious confusion throughout the world which will, in these last closing days, unite under one banner.

To the Romans the god Bel, who actually was Nimrod's father Cush, was worshipped as Janus, the two faced god, the god of gods. Hislop quotes Ovid, another ancient scribe who wrote of a hymn dedicated to Janus.

"From whom all the other gods had their origin is made to say of himself: 'the ancients . . . called me Chaos.' "

This god Chaos' name is used in our language today to mean confusion. The symbol of this god of confusion was a club, and Hislop goes on to say the following:

" . . . that symbol is a club; and the name of a 'club' in Chaldee comes from the very word which signifies 'to break in pieces, or scatter abroad.' He who caused the confusion of tongues was he who 'broke' the previously united earth, Genesis 11:1, in pieces and scattered the fragments abroad. How significant, then, as a symbol, is the club, as commemorating the work of Cush, as Bel, the Confounder? That significance will be all the more apparent when the reader turns to the Hebrew of Genesis 11:9, and finds that the very word from which a club derives its name is that

25. Ibid., pp. 25, 26.

which is employed when it is said, that in consequence of the confusion of tongues, the children of men were scattered abroad on the face of all the earth. The name of Cush is also 'Khus,' for sh frequently passes in Chaldee into s; and Khus, in pronunciation, legitimately becomes Khawos, or, without the digamma, Khaos."

(The Two Babylons, Hislop, p. 27.)

In Isaiah 46:1, it appears that Nebo and Bel are synonymous. "Bel boweth down, Nebo stoopeth." And the symbol of this god (the club) is called the hammer in Scripture. "How is the HAMMER of the whole earth cut asunder and broken! How is Babylon become a desolation among the nations." Jeremiah 50:23. Hence, it was Bel and Baal, or Cush and Nimrod, who caused the inhabitants of the earth to be scattered all over the earth by introducing Astrology, Magic, Necromancy, etc., building an antichrist society that would change "the glory of the uncorruptible God into an image made like to corruptible man, and to birds, and fourfooted beasts, and creeping things. Wherefore God also gave them up to uncleanness through the lusts of their own hearts, to dishonour their own bodies between themselves, Who changed the truth of God into a lie, and worshipped and served the creature more than the Creator, who is blessed forever. Amen." Romans 1:23, 24.

Now look at the name "Hermes," from whom these Secret Societies and occult fraternities say they draw their philosophies. The word Her, says Hislop, in Chaldee is synonymous with Ham, or Khem,[26] the burnt one. This name formed a foundation for covertly identifying Ham with the Sun, and so deifying the Patriarch after whose name the land of Egypt was called.[27] The Scriptures themselves state that

26. Ibid., p. 25.
27. Ibid., p. 25.

Egypt was founded by Ham. "*Israel also came into Egypt; and Jacob sojourned in the Land of Ham.*" Psalms 105:23, 27, Hislop goes on to say:

> "*Her is the name of Horus, who is identified with the Sun (Bunsen, Vol. I, p. 507), which shows the real etymology of the name to be from the verb to which I have traced it. Then, secondly, 'Mes' is from Mesheh (or, without the last radical, which is omissible [see Parkhurst, Sub Voce, p. 416], Mesh, 'to draw forth.'*"
> The Two Babylons, Hislop, Loizeaux Brothers, p. 25.

What all this means is "Mes" was used by the ancient Egyptians to show the genealogy of the name applied. This will explain the Egyptian names of Kings of Egypt such as Rameses, which means "Rameses" - "The Son of Ra," who was the Egyptian Sun-god, whose incarnation was "Osiris." Hence, "Hermes" or "Her-Mes" means "The Son of Her," or Ham, who was Cush.[28] "*And the sons of Ham: Cush, Mizraim, and Phut, and Canaan.*" Genesis 10:6.

Now it was really Cush who was worshipped as Hermes, Bel, Nebo, Mercury, etc., that was generally represented by the ancients as their god who was the author of Astrology, Magic, Spiritualism, etc., on this side of the flood. Here are some more astonishing facts about modern Secret Societies that even most of their own members are not aware of.

Like the Rosicrucians, the Freemasons trace their origins to the Hermetic writings. And, ironically enough, the Freemasons admit that it was Nimrod along with Hermes (Cush), who founded their order. The following will be taken from an authorized publication of Freemasonry called *An Encyclopedia of Free-*

28. Ibid., p. 26.

masonry and Its Kindred Sciences, by Albert G.
Mackey 33°, p. 322:

"HERMES" * IN ALL THE OLD MANU-
SCRIPTS, RECORDS WHICH CONTAIN THE
LEGEND OF THE CRAFT, MENTION IS MADE
OF HERMES AS ONE OF THE FOUNDERS OF
MASONRY."

Mackey goes on to say:

"He found one of the two pillars of stone, and
found the science written therein, and he taught it
to other men. There are two persons of the name
of Hermes mentioned in sacred history. The first
is the divine Hermes, called by the Romans Mercury. Among the Egyptians he was known as
Thoth. Diodorus Siculus describes him as the
secretary of Osiris; he is commonly supposed to
have been the son of Mizaim, and Cumberland
says that he was the same as Osiris. There is,
however, much confusion among the
mythologists concerning his attributes.

"The second was Hermes Trismegistus or
Thrice Great, who was a celebrated Egyptian
legislater, priest, and philosopher, who lived in the
reign of Ninus, about the year 2670 (BC). He is
said to have written thirty six books on theology
and philosophy, and six upon medicine, all of
which are lost. There are many traditions of him;
one of which, related by Eusebius, is that he introduced hieroglyphics into Egypt. This Hermes
Trimegistur, although the reality of his existence
is doubtful, was claimed by the alchemists as the
founder of their art, whence it is called the
Hermetic science, AND WHENCE WE GET IN
MASONRY, HERMETIC RITES AND HER-
METIC DEGREES."

Now in the same volumes of An Encyclopedia

of Freemasonry *and its Kindred Sciences,* by Albert G. Mackey, Vol. 2, p. 518 we read who this other founder of Freemasonry was:

"NIMROD." THE LEGEND OF THE CRAFT IN THE OLD CONSTITUTIONS REFER TO NIMROD AS ONE OF THE FOUNDERS OF MASONRY."

It was indeed NIMROD who was first to teach the arts of masonry! Now here lies a key to understanding the mysterious rituals of Freemasonry. Just as the women who worshipped Thammuz were led to weep for the god because in the myth all the images wept for him, so does the Freemason mimic the myths of the Sun-gods during their Hermetic Rituals. Just as the Roman Catholic is taught to mimic the death of Jesus Christ during Holy Week, so does Freemasonry imitate most of the myths of Baal worship. Here from their own publications we will learn the real purposes and goals of the leaders of Freemasonry.

In the Booklet, "The Masonic Report," published by C.F. McQuaig, a former 32nd Degree Mason, with an Introduction from James D. Shaw, a former 33rd Degree Mason and past Master of all Scottish Rite Bodies, we have now one of the complete studies into the Secret behind Freemasonry. These former high ranking Freemasons now EXPOSE Freemasonry for what it actually is, in hope that deceived Masons will see who is really the hidden teacher of their mysteries, and choose Jesus Christ as their Lord and Saviour, and will openly withdraw from it. Space won't allow us to examine the entire booklet; however, we will examine Masonic books the booklet quotes, and also other Masonic books that we have ourselves. After the reader has examined these things from their own literature, the reader will learn that Freemasonry is nothing less than WITCHCRAFT! All this will be completely exposed in the part 2 of this chapter.

CHAPTER II

Part 2

1. A Comprehensive Study into the Secret Doctrines of Freemasonry.

2. Documentive Proof that Albert Pike was an open worshipper of Lucifer.

3. The Promotion of Modern Witchcraft by Apostles of Lucifer.

4. Charles Manson, *aka* Jesus Christ God.

5. Shocking facts about the Beatles Rock Group's *White Album*, and other Rock Groups.

6. Shocking facts about Witchcraft signs being the origin of Symbols of the United States Government.

CHAPTER II

Part 2

Freemasonry, says Albert Pike 33°, is a continued effort to seek light. Albert Pike was a Confederate general during the Civil War who was honoured among Masons in the South as a great Confederate hero. He was honoured also among Masons as "The Prince Adept, Mystic, Poet, and Scholar of Freemasonry." In the South he was almost considered a god-man, a genius, a hero among multitudes. Pike, also a well known American poet, was born in Boston and studied at Harvard. From 1833 to 1836, Pike was the associate editor, and then proprietor, of The Arkansas Advocate. His best known poems were "To the Mocking Bird," "The Widowed Heart" and "Dixie." Little did the people of Arkansas understand who they were naming their parks, streets, and a county after, when they used the name Albert Pike. And ironically enough, in Tennessee and Arkansas, a tourist will find lakes and towns named after Nimrod. Albert Pike made his mark before the war in Arkansas as a lawyer and writer, but as a Confederate Brigadier General, he was, according to the Arkansas Democrat of July 31, 1978, a complete "WASH-OUT," not a hero. Yet, Gen. Albert Pike is the only Confederate general with a statue on federal property in Washington, DC. He was honoured, not as a commander or even as a lawyer, but as Southern regional leader of the Scottish Rite of Freemasonry. The statue stands on a pedestal near the foot of

Capitol Hill. Albert Pike states in his book *Morals and Dogma*, which is a Bible of Freemasonry, that *"Masonry is a search after Light. That search leads us directly back, as you see, to the Kabalah*. In that ancient and little understood medley of absurdity and philosophy, the Initiate will find the SOURCE OF DOCTRINES; AND MAY IN TIME COME TO UNDERSTAND THE HERMETIC PHILOSOPHERS, the Alchemist, all the Anti-Papal Thinkers of the Middle Ages and Emanuel Swedenborg."*   Morals and Dogma, Pike, p. 741

All a reader needs to do is glance at the pages of Masonic books and he will see this same philosophy taught from the Cabala we examined earlier. Here from Martin Wagner's book *Interpretation of Freemasonry*, p. 27, we read the following:

"The Temple is a glyph for the universe, the MACROCOSM, and for the MICROCOSM (THE INDIVIDUAL HUMAN TEMPLE), sometimes referring to the one and sometimes to the other. The details given in the ritual concerning Solomon's Temple, its artizens, apprentices, fellowcrafts, masters, pilasters, etc., are related to conceal the real Masonic meaning, or give an apparently rational explanation to the ceremony. These things are the rubbish of the temple under which the REAL MASONRY IS CONCEALED."
    Quoted in *Masonic Report*, McQuaig, p. 14

Masonry uses symbols of the Bible to hide the real Masonic meaning behind their Hermetic Rites. They just use the name Solomon for their Temples. The truth is, Solomon, the King of Israel, was not a Mason, nor did he ever have any connection with Freemasonry. The real reason Freemasonry uses the name Solomon is to hide the real NAMES OF THE SUN-GODS FROM THREE DIFFERENT NATIONS.

* (Cabala) the Jewish Book of Magic

Again, from *An Interpretation of Freemasonry*, by Martin Wagner, p. 97, we read the following:

"*This name Solomon is not the Israelitish king. IT IS NAME IN FORM, BUT DIFFERENT IN ITS MEANING. IT IS A SUBSTITUTE WHICH IS EXTERNALLY LIKE THE ROYAL NAME. THIS NAME IS A COMPOSITE. SOL-OM-ON, THE NAMES OF THE SUN IN LATIN, INDIAN, AND EGYPTIAN, AND IS DESIGNED TO SHOW THE UNITY OF SEVERAL GOD-IDEAS IN THE ANCIENT RELIGIONS, AS WELL AS WITH THOSE OF FREEMASONRY.*"
Quoted from the *Masonic Report*, McQuaig, p. 13.

Freemasonry Lodge meetings at this present day are usually held in the upper chambers of their lodges. The worshippers of Baal (the Sun-god) erected their idols and altars on top of hills, among sacred groves, or on the roofs of houses. Now in another authorized Masonic publication we read the following:

"*Lodge meetings at present day are usually held in upper chambers, and the reason for this custom is that 'Before the erection of temples the celestial bodies were worshipped on hills and the Terrestrial ones in valley's.'* "
General Ahiman Relon, by Daniel Sickles, p. 75.
Quoted in *Masonic Report*, McQuaig, p. 15.

Here again from an authorized Masonic publication, more shocking information about these Masonic Lodges, and the secret meaning of G.A.O.T.U., from *The Master's Carpet*, by Edmond Ronayne, past Grand Master of Lodge 639 in Chicago, on pages 301-302 we read the following:

"*The Lodge room then is brought before us as a symbol of the Universe, GOVERNED BY THE SUN-GOD, and its cubical form expressed in the language of the ritual is made to represent the united power of light and darkness, and the constant conflict which is supposed to be always going on between them. In other words THE LODGE ROOM IS THE REAL HEAVEN (IN MINIATURE), WHERE THE GOD OF NATURE THE G.A.O.T.U. - ALWAYS PRESIDES, WHERE HIS SYMBOL IS ALWAYS DISPLAYED, WHERE HIS WORSHIP IS ALWAYS PRACTICED, and when the good Mason dies he is simply transferred from this lower heaven of this Lodge below, to the mount Olympus of the craft, called the Grand Lodge above."*

Quoted from *Masonic Report*, McQuaig, p. 15.

Now here we see who this god of nature, the G.A.O.T.U., really is. It is the Sun-God! And just as the Witches hold their meetings at night, so does the Freemason meet at night. Here from *Symbolism of Freemasonry*, by Albert G. Mackey 33⁰, p. 157:

"Darkness, like death, is the symbol of initiation. It was for this reason that all the ancient initiations were performed at night. The celebration of the mysteries was always nocturnal. The same custom prevails in Freemasonry and the explanation is the same."

Quoted from *Masonic Report*, McQuaid, p. 16.

In the Hindu religion, the Sun-god, as in many others, was worshipped as we saw earlier as a Trinity. The Trinity was formed because of the three phases of the sun's course. At sunrise the Hindu worshipped his Sun-god as Brahma, at noon he was Siva, and at sunset, he became Vishnu. Now, the high priests of Sun worship pretended to be the incarnation of the Sun-gods, and so do the Worshipful Master, the Senior Warden and the Junior Warden of these Masonic Lodges. Here from *Freemasons Guide*, by Daniel Sickles, on page 66 we read the following:

"The Worshipful Master represents the sun at

its rising, *the Senior Warden represents the Sun at its setting, and the Junior Warden represents the Sun at Meridian."*

Quoted from the *Masonic Report*, McQuaig, p. 18.

In Baal worship, which is Witchcraft, it is taught that the god of nature, the Ruler of the Zodiac, the Sun, was both male and female. Now the three gods of the Trinity, or three great lights (sun, moon and stars) were symbolized as the geometric symbol which the Greeks called the *Delta*, or the Triangle.[1]

The Egyptian pyramids to the Sun are solid figures on a triangular square with sloping sides meeting at an apex. The male and female elements of the Sun-god were symbolized, as we saw earlier, by two pyramids or triangles: The male symbolized as a triangle pointing upward, the female pointing downward. As we saw earlier, the pagans combined the two to form what is called the Hexagram. This is one of the most evil signs of Witchcraft. It is used in magic to control spirits (demons). It is used by witches to cast a spell, to charm, or injure a person or his property.[2] One of the most common uses for this symbol is the Star of David in the Jewish faith. This six pointed star commonly used by the deceived Jews is called the Seal of Solomon among Masons.[3] And the five pointed star called the Pentagram, that witches get in the center of to cast their spells, is also a Masonic symbol. They call the Pentagram the Blazing Star.[4]

Now keeping in mind that Freemasonry is astrological in all areas as this will help us see other deceptions as we go on. All Star worship, as originally taught by the Babylonians, says man's soul is immortal, and at death he had a place in Heaven among

1. Webster's Dictionary, Allee, p. 89.
2. Man, Myth and Magic, Vol. 8, Cavendish, p. 1300.
3. Morals and Dogma, Pike, p. 799.
4. Ibid., pp. 14,15.

the stars. However, the chief gods of the Zodiac were the Seven Stars:

1. Sun
2. Moon
3. Venus
4. Mars
5. Jupiter
6. Mercury
7. Saturn

The Morning Star, which is the East Star (the Phoenix, or Venus to the Romans), was the nocturnal representation of the hidden Sun-god Osiris, or his soul according to Egyptian mythology. He was called "Athtar," the East Star, among the Arabs, which actually meant "Lucifer," the Illuminated One. The Masons have adopted the name "The Blazing Star" to describe this symbol which the evil sign of Witchcraft (the Pentagram) derived with its two horns (points) attacking Heaven.

Albert Pike says in his book *Morals and Dogma*, on pages 15 and 16:

"Our French Brethren place this letter Yod, in the centre of the Blazing Star. And in the old Lectures, our ancient English Brethren said, 'The Blazing Star or glory in the centre refers us to that grand luminary, THE SUN, which enlightens the earth, and by its genial influence dispenses blessing to mankind."

Pike goes on to say,

"They call it also in the same lectures, an EMBLEM OF PRUDENCE. The word Prudentia means, in its original and fullest signification, Foresight; and accordingly, the Blazing Star has been regarded as an EMBLEM OF OMNIS-

In Freemasonry and the Order of the Eastern Star, the Blazing Star with its five points represents, as in Witchcraft, the male and female principle. The white star represents the male, the black star the female. It also is a symbol for Osiris and Isis (see *Masonic Report*, McQuaig, p. 51).

This Eastern Star that has been an ancient symbol for pagan messiahs in Sun Worship has also been, throughout history, a symbol of Lucifer. Lucifer's name itself means *Day Star* in Isaiah 14:12. See margin (KJV).

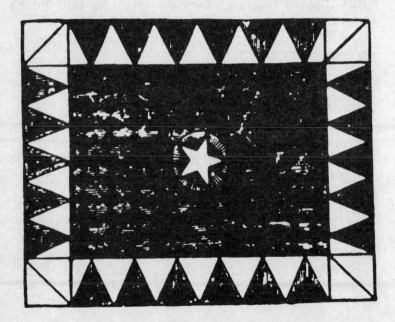

CIENCE, OR THE ALL-SEEING EYE, which to
the Egyptian Initiates was the EMBLEM OF OSI-
RIS THE CREATOR. With the Yod in the centre,
it has the kabalistic meaning of the Divine
Energy, manifested as Light, creating the
Universe."

The pyramid with the ALL-SEEING EYE as the
cap stone, which is a symbol of the EYE OF LUCIFER,
can be found on the back of an American Federal
Reserve Note for One Dollar. We will study how this
satanic occult sign became an emblem of the United
States monetary system in the next chapter. Very few
Americans know that more than 50 of the signatories
of the Declaration of Independence were either
Masons or Rosicrucians, and were much into the
esoteric (secret) sciences such as Astrology,
Numerology, Tarot, Cabala, etc. Our own Benjamin
Franklin and Thomas Jefferson were both expert
astrologers (occultists).[5]

As we saw earlier, the ancients often used
animals and birds to represent their chief deities in
their myths. The "Phoenix" to the Egyptian was a
species of the Heron family with long crest feathers.
The name Phoenix to the Egyptians, as to other
pagan nations, was a name that symbolized the Sun-
god under the names Ra and Osiris, and in later
times was also their embodiment in the planet
Venus, which is the Morning Star, or East Star. The
name Phoenix, as we pointed out earlier, means
"Shining One"[6] and so does the name "Lucifer."[7]

However, it was the Eagle (Sumerian symbol)
which took flight daily across the vault of Heaven
and traversed the celestial dominion of the stars and

5. Occult Illustrated Dictionary, Day, 1976, p. 56.

6. Mythology of All Races, Vol. 12, p. 165.

7. Young's Analytical Concordance to the Bible, Young, p. 624.

constellations, descending toward the Rising Sun from the storm clouds of Adad. The Eagle was a symbol of the Sun-god as the Spring and Morning Sun, victorious over the powers of Darkness and the Underworld through which he passed nightly.[8]

As several times throughout this book, we have tried to show that it is Satan (Lucifer) who is being worshipped through a camouflage of pagan gods symbolized as humans, animals or birds. It was Lucifer who was the original "Light Bearer" (Isaiah 14:12).

Now this sacred bird of light, the Phoenix, who was also symbolized as a peacock and heron, is also worshipped today among the American Indians as the Eagle. Very few Masons, like the Roman Catholics, understand the religion they blindly serve. They're told to do things they don't understand and they do them without questioning why. And so is it among the Protestant circles. They never think to check the words their Pastors have told them with the Holy Scriptures themselves, as the Bible clearly states: *"Prove all things: hold fast that which is good."* I Thessalonians 5:21.

Very few Masons know that Albert Pike, this highest authority of Freemasonry, The Prince Adept, Mystic, Poet, and Scholar of Freemasonry, was himself also the head of the Palladist, another Secret Society which openly worshipped Lucifer and was bent on destroying Christianity, replacing it with the worship of Lucifer himself. Albert Pike, the head of the Freemasons, was also an Apostle of Lucifer! Here from the *Encyclopedia of Religion and Ethics*, Vol. 12, p. 204, we read the following:

"The latter group, with which we are mainly concerned, was known under the alternative names of LUCIFERIANS and PALLADISTS.

8. Man, Myth and Magic, Vol. 5, Cavendish, p. 115.

They were said to adore LUCIFER, the equal and foe of ADONAI, Jahweh. He was in their view the God of Light, the good principle, while Adonai was THE GOD OF DARKNESS, THE EVIL PRINCIPLE. In sort, he was Satan himself. This worship was founded on a dualistic philosophy and was a sort of topsy-turvy Christianity. The name of Palladists is derived from a palladium which they were said to revere, namely the BAPHOMET, or grotesque idol, the worship of which was one of the articles of accusations against the "Knights Templars" in the 14th century. It was alleged that the Baphomet was preserved in secret through nearly five centuries after the suppression of the order and ultimately carried by one Isaac Long in 1801, together with the skull of the last Grand Master, the unhappy Jacques du Molay, from Paris to Charleston in the United States of America. These relics were averred to have there become the sacred objects of a society which was a development of Freemasonry.

"The head of the society, we are told, was one ALBERT PIKE, under whose influence it spread all over the civilized world."

After Albert Pike's death, Adriand Lemmi transferred this Luciferian Secret Society from Charleston to Rome. And it was reported that the most foul, cruel and obscene rites, along with the adjuration of Christ and his religion, accompanied by the appearance of Satan himself, were all part of the ceremonies that took place during their meetings. See *Encyclopedia of Religion and Ethics*, Vol. 12, p. 204.

From the beginning of this book, we have

to show the reader that there is a spiritual conflict between God and Lucifer, and Christians and Lucifer'ans. We have tried to show through history how Satan has indeed been working little by little to condition the world into worshipping him through various camouflages. Just like Lucifer tried to overthrow the worship of Adonai (Jehovah) in Heaven, so does Lucifer have him a Worldwide Conspiracy working today, behind the public eye, that is bent on destroying the Christian religion, and establishing a Luciferian Government on this earth. Just as Christ commissions His people to go and preach the Gospel to every kindred, tongue and nation, so does Lucifer have his apostles who are as determined to promote their god through *"spiritual wickedness in high places."* Ephesians 6:12. Just as our Lord gives His people the *"Spirit of Prophecy"* (Revelation 19:10), so does Lucifer give his people the *"Spirit of Divination"* (Acts 16:16). This gospel of Lucifer is *Illuminism*, and is the foundation of the various Secret Societies.

If the reader has any doubts about Albert Pike's involvement in the Luciferian Conspiracy, let his own words in his own book, *Morals and Dogma*, help convince you. Here from page 787 is how Pike slowly instructs unsuspecting Masons about the importance of the Eagle, which is another emblem of Freemasonry, and from ancient times a symbol of Lucifer.

"A great Black Eagle, King of Birds. He alone it is that can fire the Sun, material in its nature, that has no form, and yet by its form develops color. The black is a complete harbinger of the work: it changes color and assumes a natural form, out whereof will emerge a brilliant Sun."

On page 102 of *Morals and Dogma*, Pike said the following:

"The true name of Satan, the Kabalists say,

is that of Yahveh (God) reversed; for Satan is not a black god, but the negation of God. The Devil is the personification of Atheism or Idolatry. For the Initiates, this is not a PERSON, BUT A FORCE, CREATED FOR GOOD, BUT WHICH MAY SERVE FOR EVIL, IT IS THE INSTRUMENT OF LIBERTY OR FREE WILL. They represent this Force, which presides over the physical generation, under the MYTHOLOGIC AND HORNED FORM OF THE GOD PAN; THENCE CAME THE HE-GOAT OF THE SABBAT, BROTHER OF THE ANCIENT SERPENT, AND THE LIGHT-BEARER OR PHOSPHOR, OF WHICH THE POETS HAVE MADE THE FALSE LUCIFER OF THE LEGEND."

Now, on page 321 of *Morals and Dogma*, Pike says the following:

"Lucifer, THE LIGHT-BEARER! STRANGE AND MYSTERIOUS NAME TO GIVE TO THE SPIRIT OF DARKNESS! LUCIFER, THE SON OF THE MORNING! IT IS HE WHO BEARS THE LIGHT, AND WITH IT SPLENDORS IN-TOLERABLE BLINDS FEEBLE, SENSUAL, OR SELFISH SOULS? DOUBT IT NOT!"

Just as the Word of God is a Light that shines through the darkness (ignorance) of this world, so is there a counterfeit Light called Illuminism that actually derived from the name Lucifer. For "Lucifer," as we have already seen, means "The Illuminated One," or "Shining One." Speaking about this counterfeit Light (Illuminism), Gerald B. Winrod, D.D. states in his booklet, *Communism In Prophecy History America*, p. 37:

"As divine illumination is experience in the soul of the believer through contact with the Holy Spirit, so also there is a counterfeit light that poisons human thought and produces decay.

There are 'seducing spirits' that impregnate human minds with 'doctrines of devils.'

"There is a white light of spiritual illumination. But there is also a black light of demonic illumination. Satan himself is transformed into an angel of light. ... Illuminism is black magic. Jannes and Jambres manipulated these powers in the days of Moses. The attack is as old as sin on the planet."

Luciferians teach it is Christ who is the imposter and the Evil One, while it's Lucifer who is the Good God. Like modern Witchcraft, Luciferians do not believe that Satan exists. They do not believe Satan and Lucifer are the same god.

Another Apostle of Lucifer, like Albert Pike, who was equal in the knowledge of the Hermetic Sciences (Witchcraft) was one Aleister Crowley. We will examine more shocking facts about Albert Pike later on. Aleister Crowley (1875-1947) wrote many books on magic. He was violently against God and Christianity, and saw himself as a Messiah of a new religion. He was a member of the Hermetic Order of the Golden Dawn headed at that time by a Samuel Liddell Mathers, who later expelled Crowley from their Secret Society. This Secret Society, which exists today, taught the use of magical weapons and practiced ceremonial magic mixed with drugs and sex.

As a child, Crowley was brought up in a Christian environment where he learned of the warning about the Beast of Revelation, and its number of doom, 666. However, this warning took just an opposite effect on him. Because of his terrible behaviour as a child, his mother said to Crowley that he reminded her of the Beast of the book of Revelation that came out of the depths of the sea, with horns on his head, blaspheming God. Later as Crowley developed a deep seated hatred for Jesus Christ, he became ever more zealous in trying to destroy Christianity. To show his rejection of God and the Bible, not understanding what the beast symbolized in the Bible, his ignorance led him to proclaim that he was the Beast 666, and finally found a name that he could use that would add to that number, 666. The name he used was "THE WILD BEAST," which in Greek, "TO MEΓA OHPION," adds to 666.[9]

Like Ahab and Jezebel in the Bible, he made an all out effort to promote the Mysteries of Sun worship. He held, according to Crowley, meetings with what he called a Secret Chief (familiar spirit) called AIWAZ. This Aiwaz helped in writing one of his books called The Book of the Law,[10] where Crowley summed up his magical philosophy with his motto: "DO WHAT THOU WILL SHALL BE THE WHOLE LAW."[11]

In Crowley's book, Magick in Theory and Practice, he states the following:

"The Devil is, historically, the God of any people that one personally dislikes. This has led to so much confusion of thought that The Beast 666 has preferred to let names stand as they are, and to proclaim simply that Aiwaz -- the solar-phallic-hermetic "LUCIFER" is His own Holy GUARDIAN ANGEL, AND "THE DEVIL" SATAN OR HADIT OR OUR PARTICULAR UNIT OF THE STARRY UNIVERSE. THIS SERPENT, SATAN, IS NOT THE ENEMY OF MAN, BUT WHO MADE THE GODS OF OUR RACE, KNOWING GOOD AND EVIL; HE BADE "KNOW THYSELF!" and taught Initiation. He is "THE DEVIL" OF THE BOOK OF THOTH, AND HIS EMBLEM IS "BAPHOMET," the Androgyne who is the hieroglyph of arcane perfection."

9. Man, Myth and Magic, Vol. 4, Cavendish, p. 559.
10. Ibid., p. 559.

Crowley goes on to say,

"... But moreover his letter is Ayin, THE EYE; he is Light, and his ZODIACAL IMAGE IS CAPRICORNUS, THAT LEAPING GOAT WHOSE ATTRIBUTE IS LIBERTY."

Now, it was this same Aleister Crowley who helped establish an Order of Rosicrucians in San Jose, California. And Crowley is numbered among other magicians and sorcerers such as Emanuel Swedenborg, Sir Richard Kelly, Eliphas Levi, Alice Bailey, and that pot-smoking medium named Madame Blavatsky (founder of the Theosophical Society which we will study in a moment) as one of the leaders of modern Spiritualism today.

Because the books Aleister Crowley wrote were exposing the secrets of the occult, in 1912 Crowley received an unexpected visit at his flat in Victoria Street, London, from one Theodar Reuss, a high ranking German Freemason, and also an agent of the German Secret Police. Reuss had come over from Germany for the express purpose of meeting Crowley and accusing him of giving away magical secrets.[12] Among the occultists, giving away secrets is a crime punishable by death, as it is in Freemasonry. And since there is very little difference between any of these Secret Societies, this vow of secrecy applies to all occultists.

Now this Theodar Reuss was not only a high ranking German Freemason, but belonged to another Secret Society called *ORDO TEMPLI ORIENTIS*, or *Order of the Templars of the East*, that the infamous pot-smoking Madame Blavatsky and Karl Keller, an associate of Blavatsky, founded in 1902.[13]

Now, special attention should be given to this "Ordo Templi Orientis," for it centers around much

11. Ibid., p. 559.
12. Ibid., p. 561.
13. Ibid., p. 561

of the Antichrist movement among our young people today! The Ordo Templi Orientis claimed that it could communicate in nine Degrees the secrets not only of Freemasonry, but of the Rosicrucians, The Illuminati, the Order of the Holy Grail, the Knights of the Holy Ghost, and the Holy Sepulchre.[14] Blavatsky and her associates claimed they were the key which opens up all Masonic and Hermetic secrets, namely, the teaching of sexual magic (Phallicism), and this doctrine of sexual magic would explain, without exception, all the secrets of Nature, all the symbolism of Freemasonry, and all systems of religion.[15]

So, since Crowley was very learned in these areas and was revealing these things to the ordinary reader in his books, Reuss was sent to tell Crowley: "Since you know our hidden sex teachings, you'd better come into our Order." Crowley agreed, and after a journey to Berlin, he was transformed with due ceremony into the Supreme and Holy King of Ireland, Iona, and all the Britons that are in the Sanctuary of the Gnosis. And he gave himself the magical name of BAPHOMET,[16] which we saw is just another name for Lucifer.

Now, this Order of the Templars of the East, or Ordo Templi Orientis, in the 1960's had a Lodge operating under the name of "The Process Church of the Final Judgment" in Los Angeles.[17] This same "Process Church of the Final Judgment" attracted a male Witch that had studied deep into magic, warlockery, hypnotism, astral projection, Masonic lore, scientology, ego games, subliminal motivation, music, and whose religion was like the Yezidis, Gnostics, and the Palladists, of whom Albert Pike

14. Ibid., p. 561.
15. Ibid., p. 561.
16. Ibid., pl. 561
17. Life Forces: A Contemporary Guide To The Cult and Occult, Stewart, p. 287.

was once a leader, as we studied earlier, and which was a mixture of both Satanism and some elements of the Bible. This religious leader and revolutionary claimed he was both Satan and Christ.[18] His name is Charles Manson. Ironically enough, Manson studied Witchcraft while he was in prison at McNeil Island Penitentiary in Washington.[19]

On March 21, 1967, Manson left prison. He was thirty-two years old. At first he went to the Bay area and hung around the Berkeley and the Haight-Ashbury district, where he met his first disciples (Mary Brunner and Lynn "Squeaky" Fromme). He was introduced to LSD, experienced an hallucination, and thought he was Christ. When the leader of the "Family" was arrested, he was booked as "Manson, Charles M. aka Jesus Christ, God."[20]

Before the slayings that were to become known as the Tate-LaBianca murders, Manson and his Family moved to Santa Barbara and Topanga Canyon, where they supported themselves by theft (especially of credit cards) and drug dealing.[21]

Vincent Bugliosi, the prosecutor during the Tate-LaBianca trials, in his search for a motive for the barbaric slayings, found that the motive was centered around a bizarre religious belief and rock music. Also centered around the infamous Charles Manson Family were found very well-known names in Hollywood and rock music circles.

In his book, Helter Skelter, Bugliosi said Manson had an obsession for the Beatles' music, according to former inmates. While he was in prison, the Beatles song, "I Want To Hold Your Hand" became the No. 1 song on the record charts in January 1964. Manson's

18. Helter Skelter, Bugliosi/Gentry, p. 129.
19. Life Forces: A Contemporary Guide to the Cult and Occult, Stewart, p. 287.
20. Helter Skelter, Bugliosi/Gentry, p. 173.
21. Life Forces: A Contemporary Guide to the Cult and Occult, Stewart, p. 287.

fanatical interests while in prison were scientology, his guitar, and his interest in the Beatles songs. But he told numerous people that, given the chance, he could be much bigger than the Beatles.[22]

Manson believed that the Beatles were modern day prophets that were giving their messages through their music. Manson would quote, verbatim, lyrics from the Beatles songs, finding in them a multitude of hidden meanings. He would also use his interpretation of Revelation chapter 9 to support his own views.[23] Now here lies the bizarre reasoning behind the mass murders he and his Family committed. We are not interested in studying the bloody history of the actual killings, but how these young human beings could be led to do such things.

First of all, the reader must remember that the basic foundation to all Witchcraft is the belief that man will continue to live after death (immortality of the soul). That man is, as it were, stuck in a body, but it is only temporary, because he has a soul that will live in Paradise at death. This first lie, *"Ye shall not surely die,"* as we studied earlier, is not a new doctrine, but is as old as this first lie. To help a Bible believer understand why the chapter 9 in the book of Revelation was more viewed than the 13th, 14th, 16th, 17th or 18th chapters by the Manson Family, we have to know the significance behind the occultist doctrine of the number 9.

In ancient pagan numerology, the number 9 is the number of the circle, which was a symbol of infinity or immortality. Take the zodiac, for instance. As we saw earlier, it was a 360° circle. Now the numbers 36 and 360, both important to astrologers, would add to 9 if their components were separated and added: $3+6=9$ $3+6+0=9$

22. **Helter Skelter, Bugliosi/Gentry, Bantam Books, 1974, p. 300.**
23. **Ibid., pp. 321-330.**

Much medieval magic revolves around the number 9. It was considered one of the most potent of numbers because it was composed of the all powerful 3 that represented the Trinity: $3 + 3 + 3 = 9$. The number nine was sacred to the pagan goddess[24] of death, the underworld and Hell, the burning place of torment. Witches believed that they could be reincarnated nine times.[25]

Charles Manson believed and taught that death was only a change. *"The soul or spirit can't die,"* he said. Death was *"a fear that was born in man's head and can be taken out of man's head, and then it would no longer exist."*[26]

Ancient pagans believed that death was a blessing, for at death they would shed this mortal body and become a ghost. It was recorded that the Aztec Indians in Central Mexico sacrificed 20 thousand human beings a year without the slightest guilt of conscience. Even the victims themselves would line up with little resistance to be sacrificed to the Sungod. Some believed it was a high calling to die for the Sun-god because in their myth, the Sun and the Stars killed each other at night. Huitzilopochtli (the Aztec Sun-god) was reborn every morning. The bloody sacrifices of the Aztecs were believed necessary because the Sun-god was nourished by human blood. Most of the wars carried out against their neighboring tribes were to get unwilling victims to sacrifice.

Charles Manson taught his disciples that they were living in the Age of the Armageddon and the word he used for this Great Battle was "Helter Skelter." He taught his followers that the battle of Armageddon would be fought by a race war between

24. Dictionary of Symbols and Imagery, Vries, p. 342.
25. Dictionary of Symbols and Imagery, Vries, p. 342.
26. Helter Skelter, Bugliosi/Gentry, p. 301.
27. Beware It's Coming - The Antichrist 666.

the blacks and whites. There are two keys to understanding this ignorant man's murderous propaganda, and his false interpretation of the book of Revelation. One, the number 9 in Witchcraft, as we have seen, identified with death, Hell (fire and brimstone), and also the immortal soul. Hence, Manson's whole religion was based on his interpretation of Revelation chapter 9. The second key to understanding the Manson madness was the revolutionary propaganda from the Beatles songs. John Lennon of the Beatles can be quoted as saying, *"Christianity will go. It will vanish and shrink. I needn't argue about that: I'm right, and I will be proved right. We're (the Beatles) more popular than Jesus now..."* St. Louis Globe Democrat, Aug. 5, 1966, quoted from *The Death of a Nation,* Stormer, Liberty Bell Press, 1968, p. 67.

What came to pass about the Beatles and John Lennon's tragic death is public record, but Christianity is still here, and will continue until Christ's Second Coming. Saith the Lord: *"These shall make war with the Lamb, and the Lamb shall overcome them: for he is Lord of lords, and King of kings: and they that are with him are called, and chosen, and faithful."* Revelation 17:14.

A decade after the Tate-LaBianca murders, it was reported that evil propaganda messages were found in some Beatles songs. This article appeared in the *San Antonio Light,* Monday, February 1, 1982. The headline read: *"Backward masked Satan promos found on some Rock'n Roll Records."* Evil messages were not only found in the Beatles' music, but also in other rock groups, such as Led Zeppelin, Queen, Black Oak Arkansas, and the Electric Light Orchestra. This subliminal technique of hiding satanic messages is known as "Backward Masking." Messages that cannot be heard when played forward are implanted in the songs. This backward masking of messages can only be understood when the record is played backwards. This is done by placing the speed of the turntable in neutral position, then spinning it by finger backwards at a speed where the voice of the group is distinguishable. The Led Zeppelin song, "Stairway to Heaven," played backwards can be heard to say: "MY SWEET SATAN. ... THE ONE WILL BE SAD WHO MAKES ME SAD, WHOSE POWER IS SATAN." Forward the lyrics say, "YES, THERE ARE TWO PATHS YOU CAN GO BY, BUT IN THE LONG RUN THERE'S STILL TIME TO CHANGE THE ROAD YOU'RE ON."

The Black Oak Arkansas song, "The Day Electricity Came to Arkansas," contains the backward message, "SATAN, SATAN, SATAN, HE IS GOD." Although the Beatles songs do not mention the name Satan in their White Album, still it is the Beatles song, "Revolution No. 9," with which Manson was obsessed. Charles Manson, a satanist himself, believed that the Beatles, as modern day prophets, were telling Manson through their songs what he was to do and what was going to cause the Battle of Armageddon.[28] Manson's disciples also believed that the Beatles songs were speaking to Charles Manson, especially the songs in their so-called White Album. For instance, in the song "I Will," can be heard: "And when at last I find you/Your song will fill the air/Sing it loud so I can hear you/Make it easy to be near you." Manson interpreted this to mean the Beatles wanted him to make an album too. He firmly believed that he was Christ and the Beatles were looking for him. Manson told his followers that the Beatles knew that Christ had returned to earth again and that he was living somewhere in Los Angeles.[29] Here is confusion. John Lennon, as we saw, was antiChrist.

28. Helter Skelter, Bugliosi/Gentry, p. 328.
29. Ibid., p. 324.

In the Beatles' *White Album* is a song called "Honey Pie," which can be heard: *"Oh honey pie, my position is tragic/Come and show me the magic/Of your Hollywood song."* The song goes on to say: *"Oh Honey Pie you are driving me frantic/Sail across the Atlantic/To be where you belong."* In January and February of 1969 just after the *White Album* was released, Manson and his disciples tried to contact the Beatles through several telegrams, letters, and through telephone calls to England, to invite the Beatles to cross over the Atlantic and join him in Death Valley. However, they were without success.[30]

Manson told his followers that in the Beatles *White Album* were found the messages that would "set up things for the revolution" he believed was the Battle of Armageddon. There were actually five songs that Manson and his disciples took, more than the others found on the album, that they believed were messages directed to him. They were: "Blackbird," "Piggies," "Revolution 1," "Revolution 9" and "Helter Skelter."[31] In the song, *"Blackbird singing in the dead of night/Take these broken wings and learn to fly/All your life/You were only waiting for this moment to arise."* Manson interpreted this to mean that the black man was going to arise, overthrow the white man, and take his turn. And the Beatles, according to Manson, were trying to cause them to start a race war. We will come back to this revolutionary propaganda in a moment.

To understand this satanic delusion, we need to see how Manson butchered the Holy Scriptures to support his prophecy of Helter Skelter (Armageddon). In Revelation 9:1, we read: *"And the fifth angel sounded and I saw a star fall from heaven unto the earth: and to him was given the key of the bottomless*

30. Ibid., p. 324.
31. Ibid., p. 326.
32. Ibid., p. 313.

pit." Now Manson's interpretation of the *bottomless pit* is a cave underneath Death Valley, where his chosen people (the Family) would go during the Negro Revolt (Helter Skelter), that he said the Hopi Indians knew about.[32] Manson said his Family were the original Christians reincarnated, and that the Romans had returned as the Establishment. Hence, Manson and his chosen people would remain in this secret paradise underneath Death Valley until his chosen people grew to the number 144,000. Manson told his disciples that the bottomless pit has a golden city with a river of milk and honey that runs through it, and a tree that bears twelve kinds of fruit, a different fruit each month. You don't need to bring candles, nor any flashlights, down there because the walls will glow, and it wouldn't be cold or be too hot. And there would be warm springs and fresh water, and people would already be down there waiting for him.[33]

The first four angels of Revelation, chapters 8 and 9, Manson interpreted to be the four Beatles and the Locusts (insects) were describing the Beatles also because *"They had hair as the hair of women."* Revelation 9:8. Out of the mouths of the Four Angels (Beatles) *"issued fire and brimstone."* In Revelation 9:17, the fire and brimstone CAME OUT OF THE MOUTHS OF THE HORSES, NOT THE FOUR ANGELS as Manson mis-interpreted. This fire and brimstone represented the lyrics, according to Manson, the power of the songs of the Beatles.[34] Their "breastplates of fire" were the electric guitars. Their shapes "like unto horses prepared unto battle" were their dune buggies. The Horsemen, who numbered two hundred thousand thousand and who would roam the earth spreading destruction, were the

32. Ibid., p. 313.
33. Ibid., p. 313.
34. Ibid., p. 322.

motorcycle gangs. And the Fifth Angel, according to Manson, was himself.[35]

Now in Revelation 9:4, it talks about *"the SEAL OF GOD in their foreheads."* Manson was asked what this meant and he said that this meant there would be a MARK on people that only he would be able to see, and the MARK would designate whether they were with him or against him.[36]

And in Revelation 9:11 we read: *"And they had a king over them, which is the angel of the bottomless pit, whose name in the Hebrew tongue is Abaddon, but in the Greek tongue hath his name APOLLYON."* Abaddon means "destroyer." Manson, who believed he was both Christ and Satan incarnated, believed that this applied to him, for according to Manson, he was "the king, which is the angel of the bottomless pit."

The Beatles song "Revolution 9" contains a segment that, played backward, has another message. The repetition of "number nine, number nine" in reverse says, "Turn me on dead man." "Revolution 1," as given on the jacket insert, reads: *"You say you want a revolution/Well you know/We all want to change the world ... /But when you talk about destruction/Don't you know that you can count me out."* However, when you listen to the record itself, immediately after "OUT" you hear the word "IN," and Manson took this to mean the Beatles, once undecided, now favored the Revolution. Now later on in the song, the lyrics say, *"You say you got a real solution/Well you know/We'd all love to see the plan."* To Manson, the meaning of this lyric was obvious: Manson was to sing out and tell the TUNE-IN people how to escape the Armageddon (Helter Skelter).[37]

35. Ibid., p. 323.
36. Ibid., p. 322.
37. Ibid., p. 328.

In "Revolution 9," the listener hears whispers, shouts, snatches of dialogue from the BBC, bits of classical music, mortars exploding, babies crying, church hymns, car horns and football yells –which, together with a chant of "Number 9, Number 9, Number 9," build to a climax of machine-gun fire and screams, followed by the soft and obviously symbolic lullaby of "Good Night."[38]

Manson said this was the Beatles' way of prophesying the battle of Armageddon, which Manson believes is a race war. In the background of all this noise on Revolution 9, Manson heard the oinking of pigs and a man's voice saying, "Rise." This to Manson was the Beatles' way of telling the black man that now was the time to RISE and start the Armageddon. Manson told his followers that the race war would start by Blacks going to the rich piggy districts and murdering them, cutting bodies up, smearing blood, and writing things on the wall in blood. These super-atrocious crimes would cause the white man to start the war. The statement Manson made signed his own guilt decree. On the walls of the places where the murder victims were found, written in blood were the words, DEATH TO THE PIGS, RISE and HELTER SKELTER.[39]

The whole plan of this revolution and terrorism was to incite the white man into starting another civil war. The question is, was all this an isolated plan of one crazed lunatic, or was Manson himself just a pawn in a much larger circle of hidden instigators that want to provoke revolution, riots, race wars, and anarchy?

John A. Stormer, author of the seven-million-copy best seller, None Dare Call It Treason, has written another book called The Death of a Nation, where

38. Ibid., p. 328.
39. Ibid., pp. 330-331.

he has documentive proof that the riots of the late 1960's were Communist inspired:

"The Riots, Looting, sniper attacks on police and massive civil disturbances which have racked American cities since 1964 are part of the Communist program for destroying America's ability to resist.

"In February 1967, FBI Chief J. Edgar Hoover told a committee of the U.S. Congress: 'Communists and other subversives and extremists strive and labor ceaselessly to precipitate racial trouble and take advantage of racial discord in this country. Such elements were active in exploiting and aggravating the riots, for example, the Harlem, Watts, Cleveland, and Chicago.' "

Quoted from The Death of a Nation, Stormer, Liberty Bell Press, 1968, p. 24.

Now, another question should be asked. Who are the Communists? Where did they actually come from? Did they just appear out of thin air? Or are they too just another pawn for a much larger circle of hidden instigators that want to provoke revolution, riots, race wars, and anarchy? As we continue to study the Great Luciferian Conspiracy, the reader will learn that Luciferian fronts designed to destroy all controlling governments and religions are the real hidden instigators of all the Communist Parties of the world, and Communism actually derived out of Spiritualism (Witchcraft)! And the diabolical scheme of the Manson Family and the riots of the sixties are only a shadow of what Lucifer's plans are for the future. The whole world is to be thrown into riot and Revolution by these conspirators, as a way to frighten the inhabitants into a one world government. Just to show what people can be led to do by a false religious spirit, Susan Atkins, one of the murderers of Sharon Tate and a member of the Manson Family

Conspiracy, with her puppy-dog eyes and childish manner, told a jail inmate that she helped kill Sharon Tate, and said: *"YOU HAVE TO HAVE A REAL LOVE IN YOUR HEART TO DO THIS FOR PEOPLE."*[40]

What could lead these people we just read about to train their consciences to accept these murders and social upheavals they tried to cause? The real source and blame can be placed on those whom Satan used during the 18th, 19th and 20th centuries who were responsible for reviving the sciences of Witchcraft. Manson, and the Communist Party, are products of the writings of Emanuel Swedenburg, Adam Weishaupt, Sir Richard Kelly, Eliphas Levi, Karl Marx, Madame Blavatsky, Aleister Crowley, Margaret Murry, Gerald B. Gardner, just to name a few. We will examine this more as we continue.

To show the reader how Witchcraft is gaining control, on October 31, 1971, Leo Martello, long an activist for civil and gay rights, organized a "Witch-In" in New York's Central Park. He finally obtained a permit from the Parks Department to stage his demonstration with *the determined efforts of the New York Civil Liberties Union.* Martello shortly after formed what was to become the *Witches Anti-Defamation League,* devoted to securing religious rights for Witches.[40] Then later, Isaac Bonewits, a self-proclaimed male Witch, and a number of other occultists formed the AADL, the Aquarian Anti-Defamation League, we often hear about. This organization is dedicated to fighting legal battles on behalf of pagans and occultists.[41]

As stated earlier, Witchcraft is the biggest rival of modern Christianity. The average gullible Christian has no knowledge of what is happening all around

40. Drawing Down the Moon, Adler, p. 47.
41. Ibid., p. 47.

him, even within his own church, about how Spiritualism is a very serious threat. However, we are determined to bring these things out in the light for all to see. But to do this, the reader must have a complete understanding of what these Secret Societies actually are.

Like Witchcraft, Freemasons are bound by oaths and obligations under the pain of death if they should prove willfully guilty of violating any part of their solemn oaths or obligations. One of their obligations is toward their brother Mason. In the *Masonic Hand Book*, on page 183 we read:

"Whenever you see any of our signs made by a brother Mason, and especially the grand hailing sign of distress, you must always be sure to obey them, even at the risk of your life. If you're on a jury, and the defendant is a Mason, and makes the Grand Hailing sign, you must obey it; you must DISAGREE WITH YOUR BROTHER JURORS, IF NECESSARY, BUT YOU MUST BE SURE NOT TO BRING THE MASON GUILTY, FOR THAT WOULD BRING DISGRACE UPON THE ORDER. IT MAY BE PERJURY, TO BE SURE, TO DO THIS, BUT THEN YOU'RE FULFILLING YOUR OBLIGATION, AND YOU KNOW IF YOU LIVE UP TO YOUR OBLIGATIONS YOU'LL BE FREE FROM SIN."

Quoted in *The Masonic Report*, McQuaig, p. 9.

During the Tate-LaBianca trials -- with Susan Atkins testifying to how good it felt when the knife went into Sharon Tate -- Manson was flashing Masonic hand signals to the judge.[42] We made a statement a little while back that Freemasonry is nothing less than BAAL WORSHIP. So that there will be no more confusion about this, we will now let the Masons say so themselves. Here from *The Master's*

42. Life Forces: A Contemporary Guide to the Cult and Occult, Stewart, p.287.

Carpet, by Edmond Ronayne, on page 247 we read
the following:

"So then, Because OUR ANCIENT BRETH-
REN — 'THE OLD SUN-WORSHIPERS' — MET
ON THE HIGHEST HILLS TO WORSHIP
BAAL, OR THE SUN-GOD, AND FREEMASON-
RY BEING THAT SAME WORSHIP REVIVED,
IT MUST NECESSARILY FOLLOW, THAT
MASONIC LODGES MUST BE HELD IN THE
HIGHEST ROOMS OF BUILDINGS, TO CARRY
OUT THE COINCIDENCE."

Quoted from The Masonic Report, McQuaig, p. 15.

Many of the lower Degrees of Freemasonry in
America and England will urge that the things we
have exposed about Freemasonry thus far are false,
because they have been led to believe that Freemasonry is a Christian organization. But the higher
Degrees of Freemasonry should know that nothing
could be further from the truth. Now it is true that in
Christian lands the Bible is placed with a Square and
a Compass on the altar of their Lodges. However, like
the name Solomon, the Bible is just a symbol in Freemasonry, not a standard of measuring truth. Here
again from Albert Pike's Morals and Dogma, page 11,
we read the following:

"The Holy Bible, Square, and Compasses, are
not only styled the Great Lights in Masonry, but
they are technically called the Furniture of the
Lodge; and, as you have seen, it is held that there
is no Lodge without them. This has sometimes
been made a pretext for excluding Jews from our
Lodges, Because they cannot regard the New
Testament as a Holy Book. The Bible is an IN-
DISPENSABLE PART OF THE FURNITURE OF
A CHRISTIAN LODGE, ONLY BECAUSE IT IS
THE SACRED BOOK OF THE CHRISTIAN RE-
LIGION. The Hebrew Pentateuch in a Hebrew

Lodge, and the Koran in a Mohammedan one, belong on the Altar; and one of these, and the Square and Compass, properly understood, are the LIGHTS BY WHICH A MASON MUST WALK AND WORK."

Reader, the truth is, Freemasonry has nothing whatsoever to do with the Bible. It is just used as an ornament to attract Christian men into the lodge in Christian lands. In a book, *Digest of Masonic Law*, on pages 207 through 209 we find a statement that says this:

"MASONRY HAS NOTHING WHATSO-EVER TO DO WITH THE BIBLE, THAT IT IS NOT FOUNDED ON THE BIBLE, FOR IF IT WERE IT WOULD NOT BE MASONRY, IT WOULD BE SOMETHING ELSE."

Quoted from *The Masonic Report*, McQuaig, p. 2.

Now that the Masonic Books have established that Masonry is the pagan religions of the world under one banner, what about the God of the Bible, the Lord Jesus Christ? Is he worshipped in any of these Masonic Lodges? From *The Masonic Hand Book*, page 184, we read:

"Whether you swear or take God's name in vain don't MATTER SO MUCH. OF COURSE THE NAME LORD JESUS CHRIST, AS YOU KNOW, DON'T AMOUNT TO ANYTHING, BUT MAH-HAH-BONE — O, HORROR! YOU MUST NEVER, ON ANY ACCOUNT, SPEAK THAT AWFUL NAME ALOUD. THAT WOULD BE A MOST HEINOUS CRIME...UNMASONIC — UN-PARDONABLE."

Quoted from *The Masonic Report*, McQuaig, p. 2.

Now here we start to see the real colors of Freemasonry. Again, from the *Masonic Hand Book*, page 74, we read the following:

"When a Brother reveals ANY OF OUR

136

GREAT SECRETS; WHENEVER, FOR IN-
STANCE, HE TELLS ANYTHING ABOUT BOAZ,
OR TUBALCAIN, OR JACHIN OR THAT AWFUL
MAH-HAH-BONE, OR EVEN WHENEVER A
MINISTER PRAYS IN THE NAME OF CHRIST
IN ANY OF OUR ASSEMBLIES, YOU MUST
ALWAYS HOLD YOURSELF IN READINESS, IF
CALLED UPON, TO CUT HIS THROAT FROM
EAR TO EAR, PULL OUT HIS TONGUE BY THE
ROOTS AND BURY HIS BODY AT THE BOT-
TOM OF SOME LAKE OR POND."
Quoted from The Masonic Report, McQuaig, p. 3.

Does the reader need to go on and on through the
doctrines of Freemasonry to see for himself that
Freemasonry is antiChrist, and it speaks as a dragon?
However, we want to make clear to the reader that
most Masons do not know these things that have been
shown to you, until they reach the highest degrees of
Freemasonry. The pattern of deception in Freemasonry is the very same pattern of deceptions found in
Witchcraft. There are lower and higher Degrees of
knowledge in Witchcraft too. The lower class worship at first a system of a godhead with a mother goddess and a pagan saviour of the world. In Egypt, the
godhead of Sun worship was Osiris (the Sun), Isis
(the Moon), and Horus (the Star). In Babylon, they
were Baal, Ishtar, and Tammuz. In Mexico, they
were Teotl, Coatlicue, and Quetzalcoatl. All these
gods derived from the first King in the world, the
first builder of cities (mason), and his wife known in
history as Semiramis. Nimrod and his wife
Semiramis are where all the Sun-gods and Moon
goddesses can be traced and so is it with the religion
of Freemasonry.

We have already seen that even Freemasons admit that the founders of their Order were Nimrod
and Hermes (Cush). But even some chief adepts of

these systems of idolatry are ignorant of this fact. However, when the initiate finally reaches the highest level of pagandom and of Masonry, he discovers from the learned Doctors that these gods that he was taught to worship do not exist. Initiates are taught to worship these gods at first because within the worship of these gods are knowledge of secret sciences of the Universe, and the worship of these gods will teach to the student of Freemasonry the discipline of a close knit civilized society which is beneficial to mankind.

Masons are purposely deceived at first, then as they progress through the higher Degrees of Masonry (which is nothing less than learning more about the satanic power of Witchcraft), they are gradually conditioned to accept the Luciferian doctrine that it is Lucifer who is really the god behind all gods. To see this is true, we will go back and quote again a statement by Albert Pike.

Pike, writing about the pagan Trinity of the Anglo-Saxons, states the following:

"Our northern ancestors worshipped this Triune Deity; Odin, the Almighty Father; Frea, his wife, emblem of the universal matter; and Thor his son, the Mediator. But ABOVE THESE WAS THE SUPREME GOD, 'THE AUTHOR OF EVERYTHING THAT EXISTETH, THE ETERNAL, THE ANCIENT, THE LIVING AND AWFUL BEING, THE SEARCHER INTO CONCEALED THINGS, THE BEING THAT NEVER CHANGETH.'" Morals and Dogma, Pike, p. 13.

Above all the gods, Pike says there is another. Now since we have already seen statements found in authorized books on Freemasonry that this other god is not Jesus Christ, it should not be hard for the reader to believe the shocking truth we are now about to show. Pike knows that these cosmic gods of astrology do not exist, and he plainly states how ignorant they are that worship them. From *Morals and Dogma*, Pike, page 375, we read the following:

"In all the histories of the gods and heroes lay couched and hidden astronomical details and the history of the perations of visible nature; and those in turn were also symbols of higher and profounder truths. None but the RUDE UNCULTIVATED INTELLECTS COULD LONG CONSIDER THE SUN AND STARS AND THE POWERS OF NATURE AS DIVINE, OR AS FIT OBJECTS OF HUMAN WORSHIP: AND THEY WILL CONSIDER THEM SO WHILE THE WORLD LASTS: AND EVER REMAIN IGNORANT OF THE GREAT SPIRITUAL TRUTHS OF WHICH ARE THE HIERO-GLYPHICS."

To show that most Masons do not know the true purpose of Freemasonry and its god, here again from *The Masonic Report*, on page 5, McQuaig says:

"That the figures and schemes for the knowledge and properties of Nature ARE PRESERVED IN MASONRY, but not the pseudo-Masonry of the majority of the craft members."

From a Masonic book called *Black and White*, Hartmen, p. 62, we read:

"FORTUNATE IS THE MASON OR PRIEST WHO UNDERSTANDS WHAT HE TEACHES. BUT OF SUCH DISCIPLES THERE ARE ONLY A FEW."

Quoted from *The Masonic Report*, p. 5.

Now, the Blue Lodge Masonry is a deliberate hoax especially designed to deceive Masonry's ignorant masses into believing that they know something about the secrets of Masonry, when in reality they know nothing whatsoever. Albert Pike expresses this in his book *Morals and Dogma* on page 819:

"The Blue Degrees are but the outer or portico of the Temple. Part of the symbols are displayed there to the Initiate, BUT HE IS INTENTIONALLY MISLED BY FALSE INTERPRETATIONS. IT IS NOT INTENDED THAT HE SHALL UNDERSTAND THEM; BUT IT IS INTENDED THAT HE SHALL IMAGINE HE UNDERSTAND THEM. THEIR TRUE EXPLICATION IS RESERVED FOR THE ADEPTS, THE PRINCES OF MASONRY. THE WHOLE BODY OF THE ROYAL AND SACERDOTAL ART WAS HIDDEN SO CAREFULLY, CENTURIES SINCE, IN THE HIGH DEGREES, AS THAT IT IS EVEN YET POSSIBLE TO SOLVE MANY OF THE ENIGMAS WHICH THEY CONTAIN. IT IS WELL ENOUGH FOR THE MASS OF THOSE CALLED MASONS, TO IMAGINE THAT ALL IS CONTAINED IN THE BLUE DEGREES; AND WHOSO ATTEMPTS TO UNDECEIVE THEM WILL LABOR IN VAIN, AND WITHOUT ANY TRUE REWARD VIOLATE HIS OBLIGATIONS AS AN ADEPT. MASONRY IS THE VERITABLE SPHINX, BURIED TO THE HEAD IN THE SANDS HEAPED ROUND IT BY THE AGES."

From the very first deception in the Garden of Eden unto this present day, Satan has caused man to err from the True God by keeping him busy in seeking things that lead away from God. By kindling a desire in Adam and Eve to go outside the law of God, Satan caused Adam and Eve to lose eternal life. It was self indulgence and self glorification that led Eve to seek this mysterious knowledge of good and evil. Satan told Eve by taking the fruit of the tree of knowledge, her eyes would be open and she would become as gods. In other words, she would reach the great heights of wisdom. Her curiosity was aroused and Satan kindled a desire in her to want to know about this forbidden knowledge. This same voice has been preserved and heard through the mouths of the Adepts of Freemasonry, and all other Secret Societies and religions that teach Babylonian precepts. This same trap that made Eve fall into a snare of the Devil is used the same way today. This same forbidden knowledge Satan used on Eve is today called the Mysteries, to the occultists. In the Bible, it's called *"MYSTERY, BABYLON THE GREAT, THE MOTHER OF HARLOTS AND ABOMINATIONS OF THE EARTH."* Revelation 17:5.

Very few Americans know what part Secret Societies have played and are playing in Lucifer's attempt to establish his total rule on this planet. This is and has been a gradual attempt to overthrow Christianity and Jesus Christ. As we stated before, what Lucifer tried to do in Heaven, this world *now is experiencing.* Instead of a struggle only between Lucifer and his angels, and Christ and His Angels, the conflict is now between Christ and His people who have His Spirit, and Lucifer and his people, who are possessed by him and his devils. Satan is pouring out his power to his human agents to work miracles and lying wonders without measure, to deceive and destroy the very elect of God if possible.

"Woe to the inhabitants of the earth and of the sea! for the Devil is come down unto you, having great wrath, because he knoweth that he hath but a short time." Revelation 12:12.

Satan has been hiding behind these Secret Societies to further his plans in his conspiracy to condition the inhabitants of this world to accept his rule. But this is only one of his fronts. We will lay wide-open, as we did Freemasonry, an even more diabolical scheme to cause in inhabitants of this world to lose their part in what Christ promised in Scripture. As we continue to follow history, we will see how Lucifer will deceive the very elect if possible.

Very few loyal Americans know what part Freemasonry has played in helping Lucifer establish his total power and rule in this world. American Freemasonry has become a mass movement. In many small towns of the South and middle West, almost every white male Protestant gentleman belongs to a Masonic Lodge.[43] And sharp distinctions are drawn between those who belong and those who do not. Masons refer to non-Masons as *"Protanes."*[44] With millions of members, tens of millions of dollars of assets and property and billions of dollars worth of insurance in force, this should give the reader understanding about how much power is behind this Secret Society. The Rosicrucians alone spend $500,000 a year seeking recruits through newspapers and magazines. The advertisement promises to open the door of success, prosperity and popularity. All the mysteries of life and death, reincarnation, extrasensory perception, and the secrets of the ancient mystical schools will be revealed to those who return the advertisement's coupon to the Rosicrucian headquarters in San Jose, California. After the reader sends in the coupon and asks for further information about the Rosicrucian organization, he is sent a booklet entitled, "Mystery of Life," which lists very familiar names in history who were identified as Rosicrucians, such as Benjamin Franklin, Isaac Newton, and Rene Descartes.[45]

Now the reader has seen from authorized publications of these Secret Societies that they do not exalt or worship the Christian God of the Bible, but exalt the pagan gods of astrology and teach the mys-

43. Hand Book To Secret Organizations, Whalen, p. 51.
44. Ibid., p. 4.
45. Ibid., p. 51.

teries of the occult, which is Witchcraft. It should not be too hard now for the reader to understand why we have today these signs of Witchcraft mingled within our own United States governmental symbols. Now that the reader is aware of the paganism in these Secret Societies and how their own members are deceived into believing that they are Christian organizations, it should not be hard to realize how the inventor of the occult, the god of these Secret Societies, used deceived Masons and Rosicrucians to help establish this country. Benjamin Franklin, himself an expert in occultism, joined one of the first American Lodges of Masonry, and published an edition of Anderson's Constitution in 1734. George Washington joined the Fredricksburg Lodge of Masonry in Virginia in 1752. Patrick Henry, Paul Revere, and John Paul Jones wore the apron of Masonry, and so did Benedict Arnold.[46] A plaque on the wall that surrounds the Alamo in San Antonio, Texas lists the names of those who died in the Texas Revolution in February and March of 1836. The plaque was dedicated by the Freemasonry Order in honour of Masons who gave their lives there. Among the names are Col. William Travis, James Bowie and David Crockett.

Since there have been, from the start, Masonic Presidents, Governors, Senators, and Congressmen making our laws and governing the affairs of our Nation, it should not be too hard for the reader to understand how a pagan goddess that Witchcraft exalts, that the Roman Catholic Church worships as the Virgin Mary, is standing on top of the Capitol of the United States of America.

It was not by chance that the Capitol Building itself was designed after the rotunda, or dome, of St. Peter's Basilica in Vatican City. James Hoban, be-

46. Ibid., p. 52.

lieve it or not, was a Catholic Freemason who designed the Capitol of the United States and was the chief founder of the Federal Masonic Number 1, in the District of Columbia.[47]

Now here are some more astonishing facts. Has the reader ever wondered how the strange structure called the Washington Monument came into being? Well, in the myth of the Egyptian god Osiris, which derived out of the legends of Nimrod, Osiris was said to have been killed by a rival god and cut into 14 different pieces. After cutting the body of Osiris into 14 pieces, this rival god threw all of the parts of Osiris along the Nile. Isis, his wife, found all the pieces but one, his genital member. Now remember, Osiris was worshipped as the Creator, the Impregnating Force of the Universe, so the mother goddess Isis moulded with her hands an image of the dead god's phallus, and set up one to be venerated as a monument to Osiris.[48] Hence, the origin of Phallicism. So in the Temple services of the pagans, a coffin with an image of Osiris' phallus in it became part of the worship of the Sun-god. This same phallic image has been passed down through history to us today. Its name is the *obelisk*, which even a small child should have seen many times. Gross darkness are the deceptions of Satan! The obelisk, the sacred phallic symbol of Osiris (Nimrod), is now standing in St. Peter's Square at the Vatican, with a cross erected on top of its pyramid. And it's also standing 555 feet high in Washington, DC. *And this is the origin of the church steeple!*

It was not by chance that the Pentagram (5 pointed star) was chosen to represent states in the American Flag. It was not by chance that the Pentagon is shaped after the center of the Pentagram that

47. Ibid., p. 51.
48. The Golden Bough, Frazer, pp. 420-424.

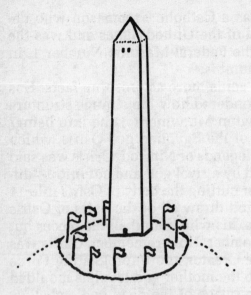

The Washington Monument

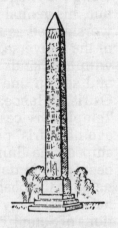

Obelisk (Egyptian)

Church Steeple

Witches and Warlocks get in the center of to cast their spells. It was not by chance that crimson, white and blue, three of the four colors of Witchcraft, were chosen to become the colors of the flag. It was not by chance that the Eagle (the ancient symbol of Lucifer) was chosen to become a symbol of the United States.

Washington, Jackson, Monroe, Polk, Andrew Johnson, Garfield, McKinley, Theodore Roosevelt, Taft, Harding, Franklin D. Roosevelt, Truman and Ford were all Freemasons. President Harding was only a 1st Degree Mason in his hometown Lodge. But when he was elected President, he quickly advanced from 1st to 32nd Dregree. Harry Truman once served as Grand Master of the Grand Lodge of Missouri. Eisenhower and Kennedy were not Masons, but L.B. Johnson took the 1st Degree in a Lodge in Texas, though he did not continue.[49] Gerald Ford is a high ranking Mason today.

Other well known personalities in America who have been members of a Masonic Lodge were John Jacob Astor, Irving Berlin, Luther Burbank, Henry Clay, Thomas E. Dewey, Henry Ford, Barry Goldwater, Samuel Gompers, J. Edgar Hoover, Charles Lindbergh, General Douglas McArthur, Andrew Mellon, General John J. Pershing, Will Rogers, Sigmund Romberg, John Philip Sousa, Mark Twain, and Chief Justice Earl Warren, who by the way investigated the mysterious death of Kennedy which still remains mysterious.

It would not be unusual in any single year for the majority of state Governors, United States Senators, and Representatives to be members of Freemasonry.[50] However, it is quite evident that most of these loyal Americans were not aware of the real satanic character of their fraternities. What our founding fathers designed to protect American citizens

49. Hand Book To Secret Organizations, Whalen, p. 51.
50. Ibid., pp. 51, 52.

from both governmental and religious tyranny was, and is still today, a shield against any religion using legislation to force its beliefs on others, as did the papacy during the Middle Ages.

America, during the brutal Inquisitions, was still a wilderness and became a haven for Bible-believing Christians. This wilderness land that was later to be called the United States hid God's Bible-believing people from the persecuting power of the Dragon, which in Prophecy is a symbol of Satan and Satan's religion. The Roman Catholic Church was a false religious system that caused the Protestants to flee from the Old European countries, to come to America. This was foretold in Revelation 12:14:

"And to the woman were given two wings of a great eagle, that she might fly into the wilderness, into her place, where she is nourished for a time, and times, and half a time, from the face of the serpent."

In the next chapter we will study in detail how the papacy for 1260 years, as foretold, cast the Truth to the ground. And in this next chapter we will see how the Bible foretold Communism and how Communism, like Freemasonry, derived out of Spiritualism.

CHAPTER III

1. Understanding the symbolic term *Harlot* as given in prophecy.

2. A comprehensive study of Revelation, the 17th chapter.

3. A comprehensive study of Daniel, the 7th chapter.

4. Understanding the symbolic Beast from the *Bottomless Pit.*

5. The 1260 year prophecy of the Two Witnesses and the Papal apostasy.

6. Adam Weishaupt, The Human Devil, the 18th century Nimrod.

7. The History of the Secret Society of The Illuminati.

8. The Illuminati becomes a Freemasonry Order.

CHAPTER III

"The Revelation of Jesus Christ, which God gave unto him, to shew unto his servants things which must shortly come to pass; and he sent and signified it by his angel unto his servant John: Who bare record of the word of God, and of the testimony of Jesus Christ, and of all things that he saw.

"Blessed is he that readeth, and they that hear the words of this prophecy, and keep those things which are written therein: for the time is at hand. And, behold, I come quickly; and my reward is with me, to give every man according as his work shall be. I am Alpha and Omega, the beginning and the end, the first and the last. Blessed are they that do his commandments, that they may have right to the tree of life, and may enter in through the gates into the city. For without are dogs, and sorcerers, and whoremongers, and murderers, and idolaters, and whosoever loveth and maketh a lie. I Jesus have sent mine angel to testify unto you these things in the churches. I am the root and the offspring of David, and the bright and morning star. And the Spirit and the bride say, Come. And let him that heareth say, Come. And let him that is athirst come. And whosoever will, let him take the water of life freely. For I testify unto every man that heareth the words of this prophecy of this book, If any man shall add unto these things, God shall add unto him the plagues that are written in this book: And if

*any man shall take away from the words of this book
of this prophecy, God shall take away his part out of
the book of life, and out of the Holy City, and from the
things which are written in this book."* Revelation
1:1-4; 22:12-19.

Of all the books of the Bible, the book of Revelation is the one in which our Lord Jesus promises a
blessing upon those who take the time to read it,
understand it, and obey the truths found in it. This
book is a Testimony from Christ Himself, not from
the Apostle John. The Apostle John was only the
faithful penman who wrote down these things for
Jesus to give us hope, instruction in righteousness,
and to unmask Satan's deceiving schemes in the
human affairs of this world. All through the Bible
you will read, in the beginning of the first chapter of
each book, the name of the faithful writer who wrote
the book under the inspiration of the Holy Spirit,
such as the book of Isaiah, or Jeremiah, or the
Gospels. However, Jesus, speaking about the book of
Revelation, says: *"The Revelation of JESUS CHRIST."*

Most of the prophecies of this ancient book, written about 95 AD, have already come to pass. In this
volume, we will only study the prophecies that concern us today. We will learn about the *three great
powers that Lucifer will use* to cause the whole world
to unite in our day, under one banner. These *three
great powers* we will learn about from the prophecies
are the Roman Catholic Church, The Illuminati, and
American Protestantism. It will be these *three
powers* that will bring Lucifer's great Conspiracy to
its final stage.

To begin this study, we must turn to Revelation
Chapter 17, and study it in detail. Here is the Prophecy:

*"And there came one of the seven angels which
had the seven vials, and talked with me, saying unto*

me, Come hither; I will shew unto thee the judgment of the great whore that sitteth upon many waters: With whom the kings of the earth have committed fornication, and the inhabitants of the earth have been made drunk with the wine of her fornication. So he carried me away in the spirit into the wilderness; and I saw a woman sit upon a scarlet coloured beast, full of names of blasphemy, having seven heads and ten horns. And the woman was arrayed in purple and scarlet colour, and decked with gold and precious stones and pearls, having a golden cup in her hand full of abominations and filthiness of her fornication: And upon her forehead was a name written, MYSTERY, BABYLON THE GREAT, THE MOTHER OF HARLOTS AND ABOMINATIONS OF THE EARTH. AND I SAW THE WOMAN DRUNKEN WITH THE BLOOD OF THE SAINTS, AND WITH THE BLOOD OF THE MARTYRS OF JESUS: and when I saw her, I wondered with great admiration. And the angel said unto me, Wherefore didst thou marvel? I will tell thee the mystery of the woman, AND OF THE BEAST THAT CARRIED HER, WHICH HATH THE SEVEN HEADS AND TEN HORNS. The beast that thou sawest was, and is not, and shall ascend out of the bottomless pit, and go into perdition: and they that dwell on the earth shall wonder, whose names were not written in the book of life from the foundation of the world, when they behold the beast that was, and is not, and yet is. And here is a mind which hath wisdom. The seven heads are seven mountains, on which the woman sitteth. And there are seven kings: five are fallen, and one is, and the other is not yet come; and when he cometh, he must continue a short space. And the beast that was, and is not, even he is the eighth, and is of the seven, and goeth into perdition. And the ten horns which thou sawest are ten kings, which have received no kingdom as yet; but receive power as kings one hour with the beast. These have one mind, and shall give their power unto the beast. These *SHALL MAKE WAR WITH THE LAMB, AND THE LAMB SHALL OVERCOME THEM: FOR HE IS LORD OF LORDS, AND KING OF KINGS: AND THEY THAT ARE WITH HIM ARE CALLED, AND CHOSEN, AND FAITHFUL. AND HE SAITH UNTO ME, THE WATERS WHICH THOU SAWEST, WHERE THE WHORE SITTETH, ARE PEOPLES, AND MULTITUDES, AND TONGUES. AND THE TEN HORNS WHICH THOU SAWEST UPON THE BEAST, THESE SHALL HATE THE WHORE, AND SHALL MAKE HER DESOLATE AND NAKED, AND SHALL EAT HER FLESH, AND BURN HER WITH FIRE. FOR GOD HATH PUT IT IN THEIR HEARTS TO FULFIL HIS WILL, AND TO AGREE, AND GIVE THEIR KINGDOM UNTO THE BEAST, UNTIL THE WORDS OF GOD SHALL BE FULFILLED. AND THE WOMAN WHICH THOU SAWEST IS THAT GREAT CITY, WHICH REIGNETH OVER THE KINGS OF THE EARTH."*

Now, let's back up and read a few verses at a time and search the Scriptures for the interpretation. Verses 1-5 picture a lewd woman with whom the kings of the earth have committed fornication and she also has made the other inhabitants of the earth drunk with the wine of her fornication. This woman was seen in vision as sitting on a scarlet beast, full of names of blasphemy, having seven heads and ten horns. The lewd woman was also arrayed in purple and scarlet colour, decked with gold and precious stones, pearls, having a golden cup in her hand full of abominations and filthiness of her fornication. And on her forehead was a name written *–MYSTERY, BABYLON THE GREAT, THE MOTHER OF HARLOTS AND ABOMINATIONS OF THE EARTH.*

The Scriptures themselves will show that this is not a real woman here described, but a symbol of the astrological religion of Sun worship that we have been studying about. However, there is somewhat of a parallel between this prophecy of this lewd woman and the real life of Semiramis who was the wife of Ninus (Nimrod). It was Semiramis who is history was worshipped in Egypt as Isis, or to the Babylonians as Ishtar, or to the Israelites as Ashtaroth, or in India Isi, or in Rome Cybele, or in Mexico Coatlicue. All the crafts of the occult can be traced back to this evil family of Cush (Hermes), Nimrod (Baal) and Semiramis (Ishtar). As Scripture states, Nimrod was the son of Cush, who was the son of Ham, who was the son of Noah. Genesis 10:6,8.

Now, in the legends of Nimrod, who was Ninus to the Assyrians, it is stated by ancient historians that Ninus, the husband of Semiramis[1], was killed as we have already seen, by a rival god, and cut into several pieces. Both the Babylonian god Tammuz and the Egyptian god Osiris were worshipped as the personification of the Sun-god. And, according to their legends, were killed by a rival god. In the Babylonian version, Tammuz was killed by a "certain king" for trying to introduce the religion of Astrology. Who could this "certain king" be that killed this ringleader of apostasy? Who opposed the worship of the God of Noah and Shem? Hislop says these legends of Tammuz' and Osiris' deaths can be traced through history to Nimrod and Shem. Shem is the Biblical lineage from which Christ was born and Shem in the Egyptian myth was the rival god named Set or Seth or Typhon[2], who was worshipped as the god Shom by the people of India.[3]

So you see, all the legends of the Sun-gods can be traced back to the Babylonian religions. Hence, Bacchus to the Phoenicians, Hercules to the Assyrians, Dionysus to the Grecians, Attis to the Romans, Krish-

1. Encyclopedia Americana, Vol. 20, Americana Corporation, 1980, p. 373.
2. The Golden Bough, Frazer, pp. 422, 423, 550, 551.
3. The Two Babylons, Hislop, pp. 63-65.

na to the Indians (Indians), Quetzalcoatl to the Mexicans, Balder to the Scandinavians, Pan-ku to the Chinese and Pan to both the ancient and modern Witchcraft cults, are just photo-copies of Nimrod as we have already stated many times.

The various goddesses throughout the world also derived out of the legends of the first goddess, Semiramis, who was the wife of Ninus (Nimrod). It was Semiramis (Ishtar to the Babylonians), who was a witch herself, that established the Rite of Sacred Prostitution that witches today call "The Great Rite."

Semiramis was worshipped as the Great Mother Goddess, the Queen of Heaven, the goddess of all impurity, the goddess of Love and Sex, and also of War, and as Athena, the goddess of Wisdom. It appears that it is this version of the Greek goddess who is standing on top of the rotunda of the Capitol of the United States. Another tradition in Greece has this pagan goddess as Aphrodite, the goddess of exciting sexual desires.

During the French Revolution, which we will study later, the revolutionaries banned all Christianity and burned Bibles. The worship of God was forbidden and the Jacobin Clubs had legislated within the laws of their new government that the Christian God of the Bible was a false god. In place of the Bible and the worship of Jesus they exalted this same goddess who was also known as the goddess of Reason and of Liberty. This same goddess is standing in New York Harbor as a gift from France.

Now, in Revelation 17:2, we read the following: *"With whom the kings of the earth have committed fornication, and the inhabitants of the earth have been made drunk with the wine of her fornication."* What is the interpretation according to the Bible, the meaning behind *"wine of her fornication?"* Turn in your Bibles to Ezekiel the sixteenth chapter and we will learn the interpretation thereof. In Ezekiel 16:1-14, the Lord symbolically describes his chosen people as an unwanted baby, on whom the Lord took pity and raised up into a beautiful, prosperous kingdom. However, when the Israelites turned their backs on the Lord and turned to idolatry, the Lord called Israel a *"harlot."* *"But thou didst trust in thine own beauty, and playedst the HARLOT because of thy renown, and pouredst out thy FORNICATIONS on every one that passed by; his it was."* Ezekiel 16:15.

Before the Israelites went into the Promised Land, the Lord told Moses to instruct them: *"I am the Lord your God. After the doings of the land of Egypt, wherein ye dwelt, shall ye not do: and after the doings of the land of Canaan, whither I bring you, shall ye not do: neither shall ye walk in their ordinances."* Leviticus 18:2,3.

However, anyone who has ever read the Old Testament has learned that the Israelites mingled with the people of Canaan and learned their customs. They took the heathen customs and mingled them with the sacred things of God. Even before they entered into the land of Canaan, when Moses went up Mount Sinai to receive the Ten Commandments, the Israelites fell into idolatry.[4] This may also be seen when Joshua died. Judges 2:8-10. After Joshua died, we read in Judges 2:11-14 the following: *"And the children of Israel did evil in the sight of the Lord, and served Baalim. And they forsook the Lord God of their Fathers, which brought them out of the land of Egypt, and followed other gods, of the gods of the people that were round about them, and bowed themselves unto them, and provoked the Lord to anger. And they forsook the Lord, and served Baal and Ashtaroth. And the anger of the Lord was hot against Israel, and he delivered them into the hands of spoilers that spoiled*

4. Exodus 32:1-4.

them, and he sold them into the hands of their enemies round about, so that they could not any longer stand before their enemies."

The problem of the pagan influences penetrating into the ranks of Israel was because the leaders of Israel allowed pagan customs, little by little, to creep in among the sacred things of God. In Ezekiel 22:26 we read: *"Her priests have violated my law, and have profaned mine holy things: they have put no difference between the holy and profaned, neither have they shewed difference between the unclean and the clean, and have hid their eyes from my Sabbaths, and I am profaned among them."*

It was the mingling of pagan philosophies within the sacred ordinances and commandments of our Lord that led Israel to finally abandon the worship of the True God, and bow down and worship images that were symbols of the cosmic gods of Astrology. And so is it today. The whole world has been intoxicated with *"the wine of her fornication"* which means, deceived by the seducing religion and doctrines of the astrological religion of Sun-worship.

You might ask how that could be. Well, in the book *Beware Its Coming - The Antichrist 666*, published by W.F.G. Inc., we read:

"In the legend of the Tauric Goddess Diana, it is said that every stranger who landed on her shore, was sacrificed on her altar. Have you ever wondered what the Christmas Tree has to do with the Birth of Christ? Or the ornaments you place on the tree, or the meaning of the word, 'YULETIDE?' Or where the tradition of the mistletoe came from and how it became a symbol of Christmas? Reader, they have nothing whatsoever to do with the birth of Jesus, but are some of the traditions observed to honor the birth of pagan godchild Tammuz. There is no Scriptural evidence that supports the Birth of Christ as being December 25th;

but history says December 25th was kept thousands of years before the Birth of Christ, in honor of the pagan Messiah. Another name for Tammuz, the pagan god-child, was 'Baal-bereth,' which means: 'Lord of the Fir-Tree.'

"The Sun-god, the Mother goddess, and her son, according to Babylonian mythology were mystically changed into trees. This is the origin of burning the Yule Log. Nimrod deified as the Sun-god was symbolized by a big fir tree stripped of all its branches and cut almost to the ground. But the great serpent which symbolized the life restorer, whose name is Aesculapius, twists itself around the dead stock and lo, at its side a young tree - a tree of an entirely different kind, which is destined never to be cut down by hostile power; even the palm tree, the well known symbol of victory. People of Aryan stock who believed that the oak tree was a symbol of Zeus or Jupiter, believed that this Branch was of Mistletoe which grew on the oak tree, and to be kissed under the mistletoe would insure fertility. The Branch was a name given to the Christ, Isaiah 11:1 – 'AND THERE SHALL COME FORTH A ROD OUT OF THE STEM OF JESSE, AND A BRANCH SHALL GROW OUT OF HIS ROOTS.'

"Now take the word 'Yuletide.' The word yule is as Babylonian as Tammuz. The word yule is the Chaldee word for infant or little child, and the 25th of December was called by the pagan Anglo-Saxons, 'Yule-day,' or Child's Day. The pagan Egyptians, and the Persians both observed the 25th of December as the birthday of their god.

"In Germanic Mythology, they too, had a supreme god to whom they gave sacrifice. These war-like people promised their god, whose name was TIWAZ, that if he would give them victory

over their enemy, they would give to their god all
the spoils of the battle. Like the Babylonians, they
believed their gods could transform themselves
into trees. If the god answered their prayers, they
took their dead victims along with the spoils of
war, and dragged them to their sacred grove, and
there hung them on their sacred trees. Such offerings have been recovered from the bogs in Germany. This begot the origin of hanging ornaments
from the Christmas Tree.

"Little sheep of the Lord's pasture, it is impossible to ignore the pagan Festival of Christmas. The World is commemorating the Birth of
Christ, not Tammuz. There is an advantage during the Christmas season to preach the real Jesus
of the Bible. However, we should keep ourselves
from the vanities of the pagan Festival, not to
mention the cost, and the deaths caused by
lighted Christmas Trees.

"There is, however, an opportunity during the
Christmas Season with its beautiful music, to
make others aware that Christ is no longer a
helpless babe in a manger, but is the Saviour of
the world, the King of kings, Lord of lords. Many
who think the Bible and its message is foolishness
can be reached during the Christmas Season
where it would be almost impossible to talk to
them at another time. Even the Christmas Tree
can be used to teach the children a great lesson.
The children should be taught that it is a historical fact that placing bulbs, tinsel, and lights on a
Christmas Tree is pure pagan heathenism.

"This pagan custom got its start from killing
enemies and hanging their heads and their spoils
from pagan sacred trees. It would not be a sin if
an evergreen tree was set up in the church during
the Christmas Season if it was done to be an ob-

ject lesson. If the parents would take the money
they spend each year on Christmas trees, bulbs,
lights, and expensive presents, and give the
money as an offering to advance the preaching of
the Gospel, would not the Lord be pleased with
such a self-sacrifice?"

There are more shocking facts about pagan
customs that have been adopted into Christianity
that will be revealed as we continue. In the book of
Job, we read: "If I beheld the Sun when it shined, or
the moon walking in brightness; And my heart hath
been secretly enticed, or my mouth hath kissed my
hand: This also were an iniquity to be punished by the
Judge: For I should have denied the God that is
above." Job 31:26-28.

Hence, the symbolic interpretation applied to
this Harlot found in Revelation 17:5 (Mystery,
Babylon the Great, The Mother of Harlots) is Satan's
great religious system with its many various sects,
that taught the world to obey the precepts of the
astrological worship of the Sun, Moon, and the Stars.

The Bible says in I Corinthians 10:11,12: "Now all
these things happened unto them for ensamples: and
they are written for our admonition, upon whom the
ends of the world are come. Wherefore let him that
thinketh he standeth take heed lest he fall."

The records of the history of Israel are types that
will repeat themselves until Christ comes. We are
warned in the Bible to take heed to Israel's fall, lest
we fall. It appears from Scriptures that Israel adopted all the main versions of the Babylonian idolatry in
her apostasy. "Thou has also committed fornication
with the Egyptians thy neighbours, great of the flesh;
and hast increased thy whoredoms, to provoke me to
anger. Behold, therefore I have stretched out my hand
over thee, and have diminished thine ordinary food,
and delivered thee unto the will of them that hate thee,

the daughters of the Philistines, which are a-shamed of thy lewd way. Thou hast played the whore also with the Assyrians, because thou wast unsatiable: Yea, thou hast played the unsatiable: Yea, thou hast played the HARLOT with them, and yet couldest not be satisfied. Thou hast moreover multiplied thy fornication in the land of Canaan unto Chaldea, and yet thou was not satisfied herewith." Ezekiel 16:26, 28.

Now it is time to see from Scripture what the symbol of the *Beast from the Bottomless Pit* means that is carrying this Mother of Harlots. A Beast in prophecy is a symbol of a "political power" or "kingdom" as it clearly shows in Daniel 7:1-8, 17-25. Daniel saw four great beasts and the angel said: *"These great beasts, which are four, ARE FOUR KINGS which shall arise out of the Earth."* Daniel 7:17.

As the Scriptures reveal, the symbolic beasts here represent four pagan nations that would arise in sequence taking dominion, or ruling over the whole known world at that time. These kings were recorded in history as:

1.Babylonian Empire, 605 BC to 539 BC, The Lion
2.Medo-Persian Empire, 538 BC to 331 BC, The Bear
3.Grecian Empire, 331 BC to 168 BC, The Leopard
4.Roman Empire, 168 BC to 476 AD, The Dragon

When Rome fell in 476 AD, it was to have Ten Nations that would arise out of its ruins. *"Thus he said, The fourth beast (Rome) shall be the FOURTH KINGDOM upon earth, which shall be diverse from all kingdoms, and shall devour the whole earth, and shall tread it down, and break it in pieces. And the Ten Horns out of this kingdom are TEN KINGS that shall arise; and another shall rise after them; and he shall be diverse from the first, and he shall subdue three kings."* Daniel 7:23,24.

These *Ten Nations* are also recorded history now as the prophecy of Daniel predicted hundreds of years, earlier. They were the following:

1. Anglo-Saxons
2. Franks
3. Alemanni
4. Lombards
5. Ostrogoths
6. Visigoths
7. Burgundians
8. Vandals
9. Suevi
10. Heruli

After these *Ten Nations* would become history, Daniel the Prophet foretold another *Little Horn* (Nation) was to come up among these Ten Nations and would war with them and would actually destroy three of the Ten Nations. They would be rooted out of that area called Europe today. And, this is precisely what happened. This *Little Horn* (Nation) destroyed the nations of the Heruli in 493 AD, the Vandals in 534 AD, and the last of the three, the Ostrogoths, lost their last battle with this Little Horn (Nation) in 538 AD and were eventually driven out of Italy by 554 AD. However, it was in 538 AD that paved the way for this little Nation to take dominion of that area that would become Europe. In Daniel 7:8 we read about this little horn: *"I considered the horns, and behold, there came up among them another LITTLE HORN, before whom there were THREE OF THE FIRST HORNS PLUCKED UP BY THE ROOTS: and, Behold, in this horn were eyes like the eyes of man, and a mouth speaking great things."*

It is a historical fact that the Roman Catholic Church destroyed the nations of the Heruli, Vandals, and the Ostrogoths. Although it was not the Papacy who actually did the fighting, it was the Papacy who hired mercenaries to destroy them. For more facts about the history of the prophecy of Daniel the 7th Chapter, may we suggest you order a copy of *Beware It's Coming - The Antichrist 666* from our catalogue which is found in the back of this book.

Now in Daniel 7:25 it lists four things that the *Little Horn (Papacy)* was *predicted* in prophecy to do after destroying the Heruli, Vandals and the Ostrogoths. *"And he shall speak great words against the most High, and shall wear out the saints of the most High, and think to change times and laws: and they shall be given into his hand until a time, times and the dividing of time."*

To see how the Papacy has fulfilled the first prediction Daniel described here in 7:25, all one has to do is to pick up a local newspaper and read the words the Papacy speaks when they exalt their present Pope. He is hailed as the *Vicar of God,* Christ in the Flesh. Is this not blasphemy? All one needs to do to see how the Papacy would wear out the saints of the most high, is to pick up an encyclopedia and read about the inquisitions during the Medieval Age. One had merely to be accused of heresy against papal doctrine or authority, and this was enough to burn at the stake. It was the Papacy, not Christ, or His Apostles that changed the original day of worship, the Seventh Day, into the holy day of the Sun-god called today Sunday, the first day of the week. We will study this change in more detail later on.

Now coming back to the last part of Daniel's prophecy of the Papacy as the *Little Horn,* Daniel said the Little Horn would continue *"until a time, times and the dividing of time."* To figure the amount of time the Papacy would commit blasphemy against the Most High, to wear out the saints of the Most High, and would think to change times and laws, we need to read Numbers 14:34 and Ezekiel 4:6: *"After the number of the days in which ye searched the land, even forty days, EACH DAY FOR A YEAR, shall ye bear your iniquities, EVEN FORTY YEARS, and ye shall know my breach of promise."*

In Jewish prophecy a day is counted as a year,

as shown above. Now in Daniel 7:25, the religious dictatorship of the Papacy was to be for a "*time, times and the dividing of time.*" A *time* in Jewish prophecy represents 360 days of the Jewish calendar. So a day in prophecy equals also one year (Ezekiel 4:6). Now a *time* equals 360 days in one Jewish year. *Times* would be two years or 720 days. *Dividing of time* equals half a year, or half of 360 days, which would be 180 days. Now in Jewish prophecy a day is also counted as one year as in Ezekiel 4:6 and Numbers 14:34.

Here is a better way of explaining this:

TIME = 360 days or one year in prochecy
TIMES = 720 days or two years in prophecy
½ TIME = 180 days or ½ year in prophecy

$$
\begin{array}{rcl}
\text{TIME} & = & 360 \\
\text{TIMES} & = & 720 \\
\text{½ TIME} & = & 180 \\
\hline
\text{3½ years} & = & 1260
\end{array}
$$

The starting point for the time, times, and the dividing of time, or the 1260 years of the Papal Religious Dictatorship would be when the last of the *Three Kingdoms* was destroyed. This *Last Kingdom* was the Ostrogoths. The decisive battle between the papal forces and the Ostrogoths was in 538 AD. It was then the Papacy began to claim they were the "Corrector of Heretics"; hence, this began the tyrannical religious dictatorship of the Roman Catholic Church.[5]

It was not until the year 1798 AD, that the Papacy completely lost control to dictate its authority to the world. General Berthier from France, during the Napoleonic Wars, was sent to the Vatican in 1798 to seize Pope Pius VI, and he was dethroned and banished into exile where he later died.[6]

5. Unfolding the Revelation, Anderson, p. 31.
6. Beware Its Coming - The Antichrist 666, W.F.G. Inc., pp. 210-215.

From the year 538 AD to 1798 AD is actually *1260 years*, as the prophecy of Daniel predicted. Here is a diagram of the complete prophecy of Daniel the 7th chapter. The diagram covers a complete picture of the kingdoms of the world that were foretold from Babylon's 605 BC takeover of the known world, down through the centuries to the time when Pope Pius IV was dethroned.

Babylonian Empire	Medo-Persian Empire	Grecian Empire
605-539 BC	539-331 BC	331-168 BC

Roman Empire	Papacy
168 BC-476 AD	538-1798 AD

Now that we have learned what a *beast* is symbolic of in Scripture, let us again examine the 17th chapter of Revelation. As stated before, Babylon the Great represents ALL religions that teach Babylonian doctrines derived from the astrological worship of the Sun-god. This covers all the pagan religions and ALL Christian churches that have mingled heathenism with the sacred things of God. *"Ye cannot drink the cup of the Lord, and the cup of devils; ye cannot be partakers of the Lord's table, and of the table of devils."* I Corinthians 10:21.

Now it's time to look at the *Beast that ascends out of the Bottomless Pit*, that the false religious systems of the World are riding on. In Revelation 17:7-18, we read the following: *"And the angel said unto me, Wherefore didst thou marvel? I will tell thee the mystery of the woman, and of the beast that carrieth her, which hath the seven heads and ten horns. The beast that thou sawest was, and is not; and shall ascend out of the bottomless pit, and go into perdition: and they that dwell on the earth shall wonder, whose names were not written in the book of life from the foundation of the world, when they behold the beast that was, and is not, and yet is. And here is the mind which hath wisdom. The seven heads are seven mountains, on which the woman sitteth. And there are seven kings: five are fallen, and one is, and the other is not yet come; and when he cometh, he must continue a short space. And the beast that was, and is not, even he is the eighth and is of the seven, and goeth into perdition. And the ten horns which thou sawest are ten kings, which have received no kingdom as yet; but receive power as kings one hour with the beast. These have one mind, and shall give their power and strength unto the beast.* THESE SHALL MAKE WAR WITH THE LAMB, *and the* LAMB SHALL OVERCOME THEM: FOR HE IS LORD OF LORDS, AND KING OF KINGS: AND THEY THAT ARE WITH HIM ARE CALLED, AND FAITHFUL. *And he said unto me, The waters which thou sawest, where the whore sitteth, are peoples, and multitudes, and nations, and tongues. And the ten horns which thou sawest upon the beast, these shall hate the whore, and shall make her desolate and naked and shall eat her flesh, and burn her with fire. For God hath put in their hearts to fulfill his will, and to agree, and give their kingdom unto the beast, until the words of God shall be fulfilled. And the woman which thou sawest is that great city, which reigneth over the kings of the earth."*

This prophecy, symbolizing a confederacy of false religious systems and political powers uniting against Jesus (the Lamb), and His people, is for us who live in these closing days of this world's history. The Key that unlocks this prophecy and shows who this beast is that ascends out of the Bottomless Pit, and when it makes its appearance, is in Revelation the 11th chapter. We will compare prophecies of Revelation the 11th chapter with Revelation the 17th chapter. In Revelation the 11th chapter we read the following: *"And there was given me a reed like unto a* rod: and the angel stood, saying, Rise, and measure the temple of God, and the altar and them that worship therein. But the court which is without the temple leave out, and measure it not: for it is given unto the Gentiles: and the holy city shall they tread under foot forty and two months. And I will give power unto my TWO WITNESSES, and they shall prophesy a thousand two hundred and threescore days, clothed in sackcloth. These are the two olive trees, and the two candlesticks standing before the God of earth. And if any man will hurt them, fire proceedeth out of their mouth, and devoureth their enemies: and if any man will hurt them, he must in this manner be killed. These have power to shut heaven, that it rain not in the days of their prophecy: and have power over the waters to turn them to blood, and to smite the earth with all plagues, as often as they will. And when they shall have finished their testimony, the beast that ascendeth out of the Bottomless Pit SHALL MAKE WAR AGAINST THEM, AND SHALL OVERCOME THEM, AND KILL THEM. And their dead bodies shall lie in the street of the great city, which spiritually is called Sodom and Egypt, where also our Lord was crucified. And they of the people and kindreds and tongues and nations shall see their dead bodies THREE DAYS AND AN HALF, and shall not suffer their dead bodies to be put in graves. And they that dwell upon the earth shall rejoice over them, and make merry, and shall send gifts one to another; because these two prophets tormented them that dwelt on the earth. And after THREE DAYS AND AN HALF THE SPIRIT OF LIFE from God entered into them, and they stood upon their feet; and great fear fell upon them which saw them. And they heard a great voice from heaven saying unto them, Come up hither. And they ascended up to heaven in a cloud; and their enemies beheld them. And the same hour was there a great earthquake, and the tenth part of the city fell, and in the earthquake were slain of men seven thousand: and the remnant were affrighted, and gave glory to the God of heaven. The second woe is past; and behold, the third woe cometh quickly. And the seventh angel sounded; and there were great voices in heaven, saying, THE KINGDOMS OF THIS WORLD ARE NOW BECOME THE KING-DOMS OF OUR LORD, AND OF HIS CHRIST; AND HE SHALL REIGN FOR EVER AND EVER. And the four and twenty elders, which sat before God on their seats, fell upon their faces, and worshipped God, Say-ing, We give thee thanks, O Lord God Almighty, which art, and was, and art to come; because thou hast taken to thee thy great power, and hast reigned. And the na-tions were angry, and thy wrath is come, and the time of the dead, that they should be judged, and that thou shouldest give reward unto thy servants the prophets, and to the saints, and them that fear thy name, small and great; and shouldest DESTROY THEM WHICH DESTROY THE EARTH. And the temple of God was opened in heaven, and there was seen in his temple the ark of his testament: and there were lightnings, and voices, and thunderings, and an earthquake, and great hail."

This prophecy will take us from the time the Papacy began to lose its controlling power to dictate to the world until the Second Coming of Jesus. In Revelation 11:1-5, it says: "And there was given me a reed like unto a rod: and the angel stood, saying, Rise, and measure the temple of God, and the altar, and they that worship therein. But the court which is without the temple leave out, and measure it not: for it is given unto the Gentiles and the holy city shall they tread under foot FORTY AND TWO MONTHS. And I will give power unto my TWO WITNESSES, AND THEY SHALL PROPHESY A THOUSAND TWO HUNDRED AND THREESCORE DAYS CLOTHED IN SACK-

CLOTH. *These are the TWO OLIVE TREES, and the TWO CANDLESTICKS standing before God of earth. And if any man will hurt them, fire proceedeth out of their mouth, and devoureth their enemies: And if any man will hurt them, he must in this manner be killed.*"

Again we see this time period of 1260 days, which in prophecy represents 1260 years (Numbers 14:24; Ezekiel 4:6). The periods of 1260 days and 42 months are the same. The ancient Jewish calendar has 360 days in a year and 30 days in a month. Forty two months equals 1260 days (years in Bible prophecy).

$$\begin{array}{r} 42 \text{ months} \\ \times\ 30 \text{ days} \\ \hline 1260 \text{ years} \end{array}$$

This prophecy is the same time period we studied in Daniel 7:25, the *time, times and dividing of time,* that the Papacy was foretold to "*speak great words against the Most High, wear out the saints of the Most High, think to change times and laws.*"

This time period, as we examined, started in the year 538 AD and reached up through the centuries until 1798 AD when the French army seized Pope Pius VI, and sent him into exile where he died. Even though another Pope was reinstated soon afterwards, the Papacy lost its control to run the affairs of the world.

During this time of papal persecution the Holy Scriptures were kept from the ordinary people. The Papacy claimed only priests could interpret the Scriptures, and when the Scriptures were read it was usually given in Latin, which the great masses didn't understand. The suppression of the Holy Scriptures by the Papacy was also foretold in the symbols of the *two witnesses,* who were also symbolized as *two olive trees, or two candlesticks.* "*...and I will give power* unto my TWO WITNESSES, and they shall prophesy a THOUSAND TWO HUNDRED AND THREESCORE DAYS (1260 years) clothed in sackcloth. These are the TWO TREES, AND THE TWO CANDLESTICKS STANDING BEFORE GOD of the earth." Revelation 11:3,4.

The most popular opinion found among the Doctors of Theology is that the *two witnesses* are *two prophets* that shall come during the Great Tribulation Period, while some say that this prophecy of the *two witnesses* has a two-fold meaning. However, the Scriptures and recorded history show that the prophecy about the *two witnesses* has indeed come to pass.

Jesus our Lord said: *"And this Gospel of the kingdom shall be preached in all the world for a WITNESS UNTO ALL NATIONS and then shall the end come."* Matthew 24:14. The Gospel taught from the Scriptures was to be a *witness to all nations* about the loving and saving power of Jesus Christ. It gives its hearers correction in right doing. It gives its believers hope for the future, and the promise of forgiveness for past sins through the sacrifice of Christ's death. *"And that they may recover themselves out of the snare of the Devil, who are taken captive by him at his will."* 2 Timothy 2:26.

However, when the Roman Catholic Church became a religious dictatorship, the Scriptures were hidden from the vast population, and catechism was substituted instead of Bible study. The Gospel of the Bible bacame mingled with the pagan philosophies of Sun worship. The worship of the pagan Mother goddess became the idol of the Roman Catholic Church through the worship of the Virgin Mary.[7]

When the Gospel became perverted through Romanism, God always had a remnant people who

7. The Catholic Encyclopedia, Broderick, pp. 374,375.

were teaching the True Faith during the 1260 years the Papacy cast the Truth to the ground. These faithful followers of Jesus were hunted down by papal authorities as heretics and criminals. They were tortured on the rack, burned at the stake; and it mattered not what age or sex, they were butchered in the name of Heaven.

When those faithful servants who proclaimed the sacred truths from the Old and New Testaments were tortured, murdered, thrown in dungeons and had to flee for their lives from the papal Inquisitors, the True Faith was forced to go underground. The Gospel set forth in the Old and New Testament that had to be preached into all the world for a witness to all nations before Christ would come again, was forced into a state of obscurity. This is what is meant by Revelation 11:3, *"And they shall prophesy a THOUSAND TWO HUNDRED AND THREESCORE DAYS CLOTHED IN SACKCLOTH."*

Sackcloth was worn by the Israelites in times of trouble and grief. (2 Samuel 3:31, 1 Chronicles 21:15, 16; Isaiah 37:1). The sackcloth here mentioned in Revelation 11:3 was to mourn the supression of the Old and New Testament by the papal authorities during the 1260 years. The *two witnesses, the two olive trees, or the two candlesticks represented the light* the Scripture gives its reader.

The Olive Tree was the Israelites' source of oil to anoint their kings and priests. Oil has often, in Biblical language, been a symbol of the Holy Spirit. See Zechariah 4:1-14. The Candlestick represents the illumination a searcher of Truth receives in the heart when he makes the Word of God his standard to measure Truth to live by. *"Thy word is a LAMP unto my feet, and a light unto my path."* Psalms 119:105.

"All scripture is given by inspiration of God, and

is profitable for doctrine, for reproof, for correction, for instruction in righteousness." 2 Timothy 3:16

"And if any man will hurt them, fire proceedeth out of their mouths, and devoureth their enemies: and if any man will hurt them, he must in this manner be killed. These have power to shut heaven, that it rain not in the days of their prophecy. And have power over waters to turn them to blood, and to smite the earth with all plagues, as often as they will." Revelation 11:5,6.

This prophecy is a parallel with that of Jesus in Revelation 22:18, 19. "For I testify unto every man that heareth the words of this prophecy of this book, If any man shall add unto these things, God shall add unto him the plagues that are written in this book: And if any man shall take away from the words of the book of this prophecy, God shall take away his part out of the book of life, and out of the Holy City, and from the things which are written in this book."

This will be fate of ALL those who tamper with sacred Scripture. These warnings were given by God to warn men against changing or adding to anything written in the Holy Scriptures. The Scriptures reveal God's plan for man from the beginning of creation until Christ's Second Coming, and also how he will provide for man after this Age. The Scriptures were given for man as a guide throughout his life to lead him through the gates of the New Jerusalem where he will dwell with God himself. (Revelation 21:1-4).

"And when they shall have finished their testimony, the beast that ascendeth out of the Bottomless Pit shall make war against them, and shall overcome them, and kill them. And their dead bodies shall lie in the streets of the great city, which SPIRITUALLY is called Sodom and Egypt, where also our Lord was crucified."Revelation 11:7.

This beast that ascendeth out of the bottomless

pit is often confused with the Papacy, but this is not a prophecy of the Papacy since this prophecy starts near the end of the 1260 years. For 1260 years the Papacy did exactly what was foretold in Daniel 7:8, 23-25. However, the Papacy never made war on the Scriptures, she just locked them up in an unknown tongue.

This Beast that *ascendeth out of the bottomless pit* is another *political power* that was to take the place of the Papacy in France, that Satan would use to try to destroy the word of God. Ellen G. White in her multimillion seller, *The Great Controversy*, says that this beast that ascendeth out of the bottomless pit is not the Papacy, but ANOTHER NEW manifestation of satanic power:

> "The period when the two witnesses were to prophesy clothed in sackcloth, ended in 1798. As they were approaching the termination of their work in obscurity, war was to be made upon them by the power represented as 'the beast that ascendeth out of the bottomless pit.' In many of the nations of Europe the powers that ruled in church and state had for centuries been controled by Satan through the medium of the papacy. But here is brought to view a new manifestation of satanic power."

Ellen White goes on to say:

> "According to the words of the prophet, then, a little before the year 1798 some power of satanic origin and character would rise to make war upon the Bible. And in the land where the testimony of God's two witnesses should thus be silenced, there would be manifest the atheism of the Pharoah and the licentiousness of Sodom.

> "This prophecy has received a most exact and striking fulfillment in the history of France. During the Revolution, in 1793, 'the world for the

first time heard an assembly of men, born and educated in civilization, and assuming the right to govern one of the finest of the European nations, uplift their united voice to deny the most solemn truth which man's soul receives, and renounce unanimously the belief and worship of a Diety."
The Great Controversy, White, Pacific Press Publishing, 1939, pp. 239, 240.

The beast that ascendeth out of the bottomless pit is the santanic force that caused the French Revolution and the overthrow of papal christianity shortly before the Papacy lost Pope Pius VI as its religious dictator. It is extremely important that the reader have some knowledge of the French Revolution to unmask this same satanic force *working now in our time that will eventually involve the whole world.*

This Secret Revolutionary Force that had its beginnings in the French Revolution is just another tool Lucifer has, and is using to further his plan to establish his eventual total Rule in this world. This Secret Revolutionary Force is predicted by Scripture to unite with the Mother of Harlots, which is a symbol of the Roman Catholic Church, Apostate Protestantism, and all other religious movements that teach Babylonian Illuminism, or Spirtualism. This Confederacy between the false religions and the political powers of this world is just history repeating itself. It is another attempt to unite man under one banner leaving the Lord out, as it was in the days of Nimrod.

We need to look inside the history of the French Revolution and study the subversive groups that actually caused the Revolt. History books tell us that the French Revolution first began in 1787 or 1789,[8] depending on which book you read. However, it was

8. The Peoples Almanac #2, Wallechinsky/Wallace, p. 401.

actually planned by Dr. Adam Weishaupt and the House of Rothschild almost 20 years before the Revolution took place.

Dr. Adam Weishaupt produced the blue print for it, while the House of Rothschild provided the money. This Apostle of Lucifer, Adam Weishaupt was born a Jew, converted to Catholicism, then turned to Witchcraft, where he became an expert, and founded another sect of the Illuminati. This sect of Illuminati was founded May 1st, 1776.[9] Like Freemasonry, the Illuminati is a Luciferian movement to preserve and promote the ancient Black Arts of Babylonian and Druid Witchcraft. Its goals are to destroy Christianity and all world governments, and then unite them under a *one world government* whose ruler is Lucifer.

In the Bible, our Lord chose a priestly Order of Israelites to preserve the sacred things of God. In the Old Testament they were known as the Levites Numbers 1:47, 54. The whole Nation of Israel was to be a nation of priests, but because of her idolatry, our Lord only chose the children of Levi.[10]

The Levites were in charge of the tabernacle of God and all that pertained to it. No one was allowed to set-up, move, or perform any service of the tabernacle, but the Levites. Those who even touched the Ark of the Covenant, other than a Levite, would suffer death.

Like the Levite had his ministry for the chosen people, so had the Prophets of God. If any man claimed to be sent from God and predicted things to come, but they didn't happen, this was to be a sign to the Israelites that this man was not of God, and they were to kill him for deceiving the people. Just as God foretold the future and worked miracles among His

9. Communism In Prophecy History America, Winrod, p. 44.
10. Numbers 1:47-53.

people, so does Lucifer have his system of counterfeiting the power of God. And, just as God chose a people that would preserve and promote His Mystery of Godliness (1 Timothy 3:16), so has Lucifer chosen a people that would preserve and promote his Mystery of Iniquity (2 Thessalonians 2:7).

One such priestly order that preserved the ancient Black Arts of Witchcraft was the Druids. There are modern day Orders of this system of Witchcraft. As the Levites and Prophets were to Israel, so were the Druids to the Celtic peoples. The Celts believed that they were a supernatural people from outer space, and their magical powers were to be preserved through their descendants through the centuries. Much modern English and American Witchcraft is modeled from the pagan religious rites and magic of the Druids, who borrowed their crafts from the Egyptian Sun worship, which came from the Babylonians and Assyrians. Sacrifices were prominent in Celtic ritual; human and animal sacrifices took place at their sacred festivals. The Druids held a dominant position in Celtic society for it was they who invoked the magical powers to ensure prosperity and success. Like the American Indian Witchdoctor, the Druids often fell into trances in order to forecast events.[11]

The modern fraternities of Freemasonry, Rosicrucians, Golden Dawn, Wicca, Church of America, Gardinarian Brotherhood, Church of All Worlds, and Process Church of the Final Judgment (of which Charles Manson was a member), are only a few of the multitudes of Witchcraft groups operating today behind the public eye, preserving and promoting ancient Witchcraft.

However, it was this Witchcraft school called

11. Encyclopedia Americana, Vol. 9, Americana Corporation, 1978, p. 420.

the Illuminati of Bavaria that was predicted to *make open, avowed war on the Bible through the "political world."* This world power, symbolized as the *beast that ascendeth out of the bottomless pit,* was predicted to destroy the Bible (Two Witnesses) in the street of a city that is called (spiritually) Sodom and Egypt, *"where also our Lord was crucified."* Revelation 11:7,8.

This is not Jerusalem, as it has often been interpreted, but Paris, France. During the end of papal supremacy in the 1700's, Adam Weishaupt began to write down his plans to destroy all governments and religions. Atheism was to be used as a tool to destroy the Roman Catholic Church, which then was the controlling power in Europe. Adam Weishaupt's revolutionary force was first launched under the name of the Perfectibilists (Gesellschaft dur Perfectibilisten), which posed as a political movement to destroy tyranny and ignorance, and further the cause of Reason, Freedom and moral virtue.[12]

Adam Weishaupt was a professor of Canon Law at Ingolstadt, and he also was an ex-Jesuit priest. Posing at first as a religious reformer and a liberal in politics, he attracted many to his political movement, which was also known as Republicanism.[13] He adopted the Jesuits' system of espionage,[14] introduced Witchcraft to his followers, and developed a fraternity within his political movement that was akin to Freemasonry. After he formed his organization, with financial backing from the House of Rothschild,[15] he adopted the name *Illuminati.*

The also became known as "Free Thinkers," "The Enlightened Ones," or "The Enlightenment,"

12. Encyclopedia Britannica, 9th ed., Vol. XII, p. 706.
13. Encyclopedia of Occultism and Parapsychology, Vol. I, Shepard, p. 460.
14. Ibid., p. 460.
15. Fourth Reich of the Rich, Griffin, Emissary Publications, 1979, pp. 249, 250.

names given before Weishaupt's time to the 17th century French writers with an atheistic, anti-Christian slant.[16] In Germany, before May 1st, 1776, they were the German Rationalists, or Humanists. They, too, promoted Atheism and openly attacked Christianity and all religions as false, foolish and weird.[17]

Adam Weishaupt taught his disciples that the Illuminati are the only members of the human race who are truly enlightened and know "what it's all about." Weishaupt had his followers believing that they were to be the cream of the intelligentsia, or the only people with the mental capacity, the knowledge, the insight and understanding necessary to govern the world and bring peace.[18] However, only a few of his chosen members actually know Weishaupt personally, and he was regarded by those who had not seen him almost as a god.[19]

Gerald B. Winrod, D.D., in his booklet, "Communism Prophecy History America," compiled documentive proof of how Adam Weishaupt cleverly concealed his identity and became the most powerful figure of his day. Winrod explains how Weishaupt set in motion forces that actually destroyed millions of lives, and left his mark of evil to be felt in all future generations without even being heard of by most people. Winrod, on page 45 of his book, quotes from a letter that Adam Weishaupt wrote to an intimate friend:

> "My circumstances necessitate that I should remain hidden from most of the members as long as I live. I am obliged to do everything through five or six persons."

On another occasion he said: "...one must show how easy it would be for one clever head to direct hundreds

16. The Oxford English Dictionary, Vol. 5, 1933, p. 47.
17. Fourth Reich of the Rich, Griffin, p. 42.
18. Encyclopedia of Occultism and Parapsychology, Vol. 1, p. 460.
19. Ibid., p. 460.

of thousands of men." Again he wrote: *"I have two immediately below me into which I breathe my whole spirit, and each of these two has again two others, and so on. In this way I can set a thousand men in motion and on fire in the simplest manner, and in this way one must impart orders and operate on politics."*

Weishaupt recruited into his ranks as many young men of wealth and position as possible. Within four or five years Weishaupt's Illuminati became very powerful and even had his members directing the affairs of Germany. Weishaupt's goal was to hide the sciences of Witchcraft behind philanthropy, destroy Christianity with humanism (atheism), then set up a One World Government.

In Des Griffin's book, *Fourth Reich of the Rich*, he shows the outline plan of Weishaupt's World Revolution that he hoped to produce by these following statements:

1. Abolition of all ordered Governments
2. Abolition of Private Property
3. Abolition of all Inheritance
4. Abolition of Patriotism
5. Abolition of all Religion
6. Abolition of the Family
7. Creation of a World Government.[20]

Weishaupt, who was only 28 when he founded the Order of the Illuminati on May 1st, 1776, did not make much progress until he met a high ranking Freemason named Baron Von Knigge. Von Knigge was not only a high ranking Freemason, but he also had been admitted as a Master of most of the Secret Societies of his day. Von Knigge was, like Weishaupt and all Masters of these Secret Societies, an expert occultist.[21]

20. Fourth Reich of the Rich, Griffin, p. 54.

21. Encyclopedia of Occultism and Parapsychology, Vol. I, Shepard, p. 460.

To spread his Order and give the Illuminati higher influence in the world, and because Freemasonry is akin to Illuminism, Weishaupt connected with the Masonic Institution. He was initiated in 1777 into Freemasonry in a Lodge at Munich[22] that he planned to use to promote his world revolutionary ideas. Baron Von Knigge joined Weishaupt's Order in 1780,[23] and soon became a leader, dividing with Adam Weishaupt the control and direction of the Order. All initiates of the Illuminati were required to take an oath to secrecy and bind themselves to perpetual silence, unshakable loyalty, and submission to the Order. Like Freemasonry, only a few top men within their organization actually understood their true goals. The world accepts Freemasonry as a Great Benevolent Society, teaching the highest possible degree of morality and virtue. Since Freemasonry enjoyed prestige and honour, Adam Weishaupt and Baron Von Knigge planned a world take-over by using the Fraternal Order of Freemasonry. Their plan was to penetrate into the high levels of the Order, then take control in directing the affairs of the nations into an eventual One World Government. However, since papal Christianity was both Church and State, and had been the dominating power that Satan used to control the affairs of the world in Weishaupt's time, Satan was making ready an even worse satanical influence that would gradually unite all paganism, false Christianity and all governments of the world, under one banner.

Weishaupt's first step was, however, to get control of the International Order of Freemasonry. In order to gain control of the Order of Freemasonry, Weishaupt and Baron Von Knigge tried to sell the

22. An Encyclopedia of Freemasonry and Its Kindred Sciences, Mackey, p. 368.
23. Ibid., p. 368.

leaders of Freemasonry on the idea that their Order of the Illuminati had a higher, much older and more mysterious system than any of the higher degrees of Masonry. In its internal organization, the Order of the Illuminati was divided into three great classes:

        (1) The Nursery
        (2) Symbolic Freemasonry
        (3) The Mysteries.[24]

Adam Weishaupt's plan for world take-over was to operate under cover as long as possible, and when the gullible world finally found out it would be too late to stop them. The Illuminati was to be a Secret Society within the Secret Society of the Freemasons. And, to stay hidden from the vast population, Adam Weishaupt and his co-conspirators selected for themselves code names, such as Spartacus for Weishaupt, Von Knigge became Philo, and Herr Von Zwack was called Cato.[25]

The Illuminati also tried to hide their location as they traveled in different countries spreading their poison. They did this by using code names to communicate where they were. For instance, Ingolstadt, Germany, where their organization originated, was given the fictitious name of Eleusis; Austria was Egypt, Munich was called Athens, and Vienna was Rome. The Illuminati invented its own calendar and the names of the months were also given code names, such as Dimeh for January, and Bemeh for February.[26]

Because of Martin Luther's rejection of the Roman Catholic Church in 1517, and the corruption and strife within the Roman Catholic Church itself, the Papacy lost a great deal of its authority to dictate to the world. Before Adam Weishaupt formed his

24. Ibid., p. 368.
25. An Encyclopedia of Freemasonry and its Kindred Sciences, Mackey 33°, p. 346.
26. Ibid., p. 346.

Order of Illuminati in 1776, Free Thinking, or the Encyclopedists, were already preaching a philosophy against the tyranny and fanaticism of the Roman Catholic Church. One such voice heard in the third quarter of the 18th century was a French author, philosopher and apostle of Free Thought (Liberty) named Voltaire (1694-1778). Even though the Roman Catholic Church lost much of its power before 1798 when Pope Pius VI was dethroned,[27] Voltaire still lived in an age when the press did not exist, thought was not free; and men were not equal before the Civil Law.

Although professing belief in a Supreme Being, or a god, he denied the existence of Jesus Christ and the authority of the Bible.[28] He became a staunch opposer of papal Christianity and helped to promote the *Encyclopedis ou Dictionnaire Raisonne des Sciences, des Arts et des Metier (28 vols. 1751-17720; Supplement 5 vols. 1776-7 table analytique, 2 vols. 1780),* to which he was a contributor, and which is known to us today as the Encyclopedia.

Like Weishaupt, Voltaire, whose real name was Jean Francois Arouet,[29] was educated by the Jesuits, but later turned against Catholicism and helped promote the philosophy of Enlightenment (Illuminism) to combat papal Christianity. From the *Dictionary of Philosophy and Psychology,* Baldwin, we will read where the philosophy of the Encyclopedists and that of the Illuminists became fused into the same movement working to cause the French Revolution:

"For the Encyclopedia was more than a great dictionary of sciences, arts, and trades; it was conceived in the spirit OF THE ILLUMINATION MOVEMENT, and it carried the PRINCIPLES,

27. The Vatican and its Role in World Affairs, Pichoni, p. 88.
28. Encyclopedia Americana, Vol. 28, p. 228.
29. Ibid., p. 229.

*AS WELL AS THE RESULTS, OF THE NEW
THINKING INTO THE CULTURE OF THE
TIME, THUS IT BECAME AT ONCE A STORE-
HOUSE OF INFORMATION AND A REVOLU-
TIONARY FORCE."*
Dictionary of Philosophy and Psychology, Baldwin, The
Macmillan Company, p. 322.

There was an army of writers used by Lucifer in
the 18th century to poison the minds of the French
people against Christianity as a whole nation.
Voltaire once boastingly said: *"I am weary of hearing
people repeat that twelve men established the Christian religion. I will PROVE that one man may suffice
to overthrow it."*[30]

Actually, the ideas of the Enlightenment (Illuminati) was a continuation of the Renaissance, that
was borrowed from the Greek philosopher Plato
(427-347 BC). Weishaupt's idealism was borrowed
also from such writers in the 17th century as
Descartes and Bayle in France, Grotius in Holland,
Leibnitz in Germany, Locks in England.[31]

In the early 18th century, writers such as Newton
and Hume in England, Diderot, and D'Alembert, like
Voltaire, can all be credited with contributing to this
philosophical movement which led to the founding
of this Secret Revolutionary Society called the Illuminati.[32] In the United States, Benjamin Franklin,
who knew Voltaire, was a leading figure in the
Enlightenment. And, ironically enough, the ideas of
this movement formed the background to the
Declaration of Independence. It was our Lord,
however, that took this confusion and molded it into
a protective shield against both civil and religious
persecution.

30. The Great Controversy, White, p. 255.
31. American Peoples Encyclopedia, Vol. 8, p. 8-003.
32. Ibid., Vol. 8, p. 8-004.

Now coming back to the prophecy about the Illuminati making avowed war on the Bible (Two Witnesses), we read in Revelation 11:9-12: "*And they of the people and kindreds and tongues and nations shall see their dead bodies three days and an half, and shall not suffer their dead bodies to be put in graves. And they that dwell upon the earth shall rejoice over them, and make merry, and shall send gifts one to another; because these two prophets tormented them that dwelt on the earth. And after THREE DAYS AND AN HALF THE SPIRIT OF LIFE FROM GOD entered into them, and they stood upon their feet; and great fear fell upon them which saw them. And they heard a great voice from heaven saying unto them, Come up hither. And they ascended up in a cloud; and their enemies beheld them.*"

There may have been many minor reasons why France became a habitation of Atheists during the French Revolution with its 3½ year "Reign of Terror," however, it actually began because of Roman Catholic suppression of the Scriptures. Christ was not preached as set forth in the Gospel. It was just the opposite. Jesus was misrepresented among the vast multitudes in France, which led to Christianity being prohibited by state law. Because of the false presentation of the Gospel by the Papacy, the suppression of the Scriptures, the tyranny and fanaticism of the Papacy, an army of atheists was able to gain sympathy for their cause, and the beast that ascendeth out of the bottomless pit was able to make war on the Bible (Two Witnesses) and overcome it. Here we find the reason the Papacy lost its dictatorial power. This set the stage for not only destroying Christianity in France at that era of time, but also set the stage for the forces of France to march into Vatican City and dethrone the Pope when Napoleon came on the scene after the Revolution.

Writers have hailed the French Revolution as the dawning of a new era, but it actually was the birth of another terrible deception of the Seven Headed Dragon (Lucifer) to destroy millions of human lives. When Lucifer saw that the Papacy's power was coming to an end as predicted in Daniel 7:25, he simply raised up another movement to destroy man that would continue until the Papacy's power is restored as predicted in Revelation 13:3 which we will later study.

Now, the Illuminati movement that shall make war on the Lamb (but the Lamb shall overcome them, Revelation 17:14) is not to become world wide until the *second beast* of Revelation 13:11-17 begins to emerge and *speak as a dragon*. This, as we will learn later, is the power of Apostate Protestantism in America. But before we can understand how Illuminism, Catholicism, and Apostate Protestantism shall go forth into the world to unite them against the Real Jesus of the Bible, we need to know what name the Illuminati are operating under today.

As stated before, Adam Weishaupt connected with the Masonic Lodge in 1777. He posed at first among the Freemasons as a reformer in religion and a liberal in politics. Because Freemasonry was also anti-papal, Weishaupt's anti-papacy policies in Germany became popular immediately. Weishaupt enrolled no less than two thousand names upon the Illuminati registers in Germany. Among those were some of the most distinguished aristocrats of that country.[33]

It is quite apparent the men of the Order of Freemasonry that joined Weishaupt's Illuminati had no idea of what trap they had fallen into. Very few Masons understood what Adam Weishaupt's plans were in the beginning, as very few Masons today

33. An Encyclopedia of Freemasonry and Its Kindred Sciences, Vol. I, p. 347.

understand what their own organization teaches. Weishaupt penetrated into the Freemasonry organization with all the shrewdness and subtlety that he learned from once being a Jesuit priest.

Some historian have written that the French Revolution was not premeditated. Some will say that the French Revolution emerged only from a political crisis that coincided with an economic breakdown. This economic breakdown generated unrest and riots which even the French army could not quell. It was this, some historian will argue, that made the people of France determined to cause a social change, and overthrow their country.

What these historians say is true in part only. The parts of history some historians fail to see, or leave out, is actually what caused the people in the first place to accept this spirit (of Illuminism). As stated before, it was the suppression of the Bible, the fanatical oppression of the Roman Catholic Church, that actually generated the spark that eventually led the French people to reject Christianity, and publicly burn their Bibles. History records that the events that led up to the French Revolution were caused by anarchy. The citizens became divided into a medley of hate factions that were struggling for power, trying to exterminate each other.[34] But before this, it was the Roman Catholic Church, who slaughtered French citizens by thousands, that kindled a hatred for Christianity. The murderous character of the Papacy was seen in France. In 1572 AD Roman Catholics tried in one sweep to murder all of the Protestants in France. This is known in history as the St. Bartholomew Massacre. Within the space of one month, 60,000 Protestants are said to have been slain in France. All told there were over 75,000. The Cardinal of Lorraine gave 1000 crowns as a reward to

34. The Great Controversy, White, pp. 250, 251.

the person who brought the news to the Vatican.[35]

Here the reader may understand more clearly Revelation 11:8, *"where also our Lord was crucified." "Inasmuch as ye have done it unto one of the least of these my brethren, ye have done it unto me."* Matthew 25:40.

When the Papacy killed the Protestants in the streets of Paris, they also were destroying the Temple that Jesus dwelt in, and saith the Lord: *"YE HAVE DONE IT UNTO ME."*

During the Revolution, France was reduced to a state of moral debasement similar to that of the city of Sodom in Lot's time. She also had the same spirit of Atheism within her as did the Pharoah of Egypt in Moses' day. Both the sins of Sodom (licentiousness) and of Egypt (Atheism) France was predicted to have in Revelation 11:7,8. At the closing of the 1260 years the Two Witnesses (Old and New Testaments) were to finish their testimony.[36] And it was from here Illuminism began to emerge and overcome Christianity. History calls this movement of Illuminism (Atheism) *"The Jacobin Clubs."*[37]

The *Jacobin Clubs* in France were the aristocratic terrorists who spearheaded the French Revolution, which sent King Louis XVI, on January 21st, 1793, to the guillotine. However, most historians leave out who was really giving orders to Danton, Marat, and Robespierre, the leaders of the Jacobin Clubs. It was the Jacobin Clubs that actually abolished Christianity through the National Assembly, and established the worship of the goddess of Reason, or Liberty.

The name "Jacobin" derived from the name of the convent these aristocratic terrorists used to secretly plot the overthrow of King Louis XVI. The convent was called *Jacobin Dominican Convent.*[38]

35. Foxe's Book of Martyrs, King, p. 82.
36. The Great Controversy, White, p. 237.
37. The World Book Encyclopedia, Vol.   , p. 18.
38. Encyclopedia Americana, Vol. 15, p. 657.

They were also known as the Society of the Friends of the Constitution, and were soon organized in every important town in France. They were the most wealthy and influential people in France. They had as many as 500,000 members at the height of the influence in 1793-1794.[39]

The truth is, this aristrocratic terrorist movement called the Jacobin Club was actually French Illuminists operating under a different name.

As established earlier, Adam Weishaupt became a Mason in 1777 for the sole purpose of using that organization as a tool for boring into the high levels of government by simply replacing Freemasons who already sat in these positions.

With an inexhaustible talent for charlatanry, and a well planned system of espionage, Weishaupt's disciples infiltrated into the high levels of the governments in Germany, France, England, Belgium, Holland, Denmark, Sweden, Poland, Hungary, and Italy. However, it was Baron Von Knigge who joined the Illuminati in 1780 that gave this organization its rapid expansion, not Adam Weishaupt.

Freemasons, like all Secret Societies, choose to remain obscure and do not like to attract attention. Because the Illuminati was a Secret Society within the Secret Society of Freemasonry, even though they had penetrated into the high levels of Europe, very few indeed ever heard of them. However, shortly before the Revolution took place in France, two hard blows would land on the heads of Adam Weishaupt and his co-conspirators. The Freemasons were not long in hearing rumors about the true nature of Weishaupt's plans to capture their whole organization. When the Freemasons began to get wind of Weishaupt's true purposes, a chief council was held

39. Ibid. P. 657

to examine the nature of the Illuminati by top ranking Freemasons. A conference of Masons was held in 1782 at which time Weishaupt and Von Knigge attended.[40] But it wasn't until Weishaupt and Von Knigge had a falling out that led to Von Knigge leaving the Order, that Weishaupt began to have exposure and a threat of internal strife within the Illuminati.

A contest between Weishaupt and Von Knigge about who was to be the Rex or King of this Secret revolutionary movement was the real motive for Von Knigge leaving it. After Von Knigge left the Illuminati, the hardest blow to Weishaupt's Luciferian Conspiracy was received in 1785. One of Weishaupt's co-conspirators, named Lanze, was struck by lightning while en route from Frankfurt, Germany to deliver documents to Robespierre, the head of the Jacobin Clubs at that time. The documents that Lanze was carrying had important information about the Order of the Illuminati, and its plans of not only destroying the French government through riots and revolutions, but also governments of the world as well.[41] This is how we today have information about this *beast that ascendeth out of the bottomless pit*. All of the papers Lanze was carrying fell into the hands of the Bavarian Government, and the authorities ordered the police to raid the headquarters of the Illuminati in Germany. Adam Weishaupt had to escape for his life[42] and all documentive evidence that the Order of the Illuminati was a dangerous international terrorist group was brought to the attention of many countries in Europe. However, the warnings fell on deaf ears, as they will in our day. When the Word of God was rejected, and spiritualism took its place, France fell

40. Encyclopedia of Occultism and Parapsychology, Vol.I, Shephard, p. 460
41. Fourth Reich of the Rich, Griffin, p. 45
42. Ibid. p. 56

into a degrading worship of the goddess of Reason. This period of time in history is also known as the Age of Reason, or the Reign of Terror. And interestingly enough, the Reign of Terror lasted 3½ years, as predicted in Revelation 11:11: *"After three days and a half (prophetic years) the Spirit of life from God entered into them, (Old and New Testaments), and they stood upon their feet;"*

The beast that ascendeth out of the bottomless pit was a political power that ascended out of Witchcraft, made open, avowed war on the Bible and Christianity, caused the French Revolution, and is predicted in Scripture to continue from the French Revolution, and eventually spread to every corner of the habitable globe.

To point out how the same rebellious spirit of Nimrod and how his hatred towards the Lord of the Sabbath could be seen also in the Illuminati of the 18th century, Uriah Smith, in his book *Daniel and the Revelation* p. 285, quotes a priest of Illuminism that was a well known comedian in France at that time:

" *'God! if you exist, ... avenge your injured name. I bid you defiance. You remain silent; you dare not launch your thunders; who, after this, will believe in your existence?'* "

Daniel and the Revelation, Smith, Southern Publishing
Association, 1944, p. 285.

In the next chapter we will continue to show this gradual Luciferian Conspiracy to overthrow Christianity and all governments of the world symbolized in Scripture as the beast that ascendeth out of the bottomless pit (Illuminati), and how it can be traced through various names and guises starting from the French Revolution, to our present day.

The anarchy that was displayed in the streets of Paris through the efforts of this Antichrist movement will be seen in this country. Ellen White, in her book

Education, p. 228, saw this anarchy was soon to become a world-wide Conspiracy. She states:

"At the same time anarchy is seeking to sweep away all law, not only divine, but human. The centralization of wealth and power; the vast combinations for the enriching of the few at the expense of many; the combinations of the poorer classes for the defense of their interests and claims; the spirit of unrest, of riot and bloodshed; the world-wide dissemination of the same teachings that led to the French Revolution - All are tending to involve the whole world in a struggle similar to that which convulsed France."

CHAPTER IV

Part 1

1. The Birth of Communism

2. The History Behind The League of the Just
   (a front for the Illuminati)

3. Karl Marx writes the *Communist Manifesto*
   for The League of the Just

4. Nicholai Lenin becomes a member of the
   League of the Just, who later changed their
   name to "The League of the Communists"

5. Jacobin Clubs, The League of the Just,
   The League of the Communists and Bolshevism
   were all Illuminati fronts.

6. The plan by the modern 20th Century Illuminists
   to get control of the World's Nuclear Weapons
   through the United Nations.

In 1785, the Bavarian Government exposed Adam Weishaupt's plan to destroy Christianity and control governments. However, this was not the end of the Illuminati, as most historians have written. Weishupt's plans were only interrupted and dealt with as a dangerous revolutionary force in Germany. The other nations that the Illuminati were operating in did not heed the warning from the Bavarian Government. Just a couple of years later, the plan to destroy Christianity and World Governments was first seen in the French Revolution. This same revolutionary force reappeared again in Germany, called "The League of the Just,"[1] with branches in London, Brussels, Paris, and Switzerland.

Napoleon, when he came into power, would not tolerate the activities of the Jacobin Clubs with their independent opposition, so he completely suppressed it.[2] However, the Illuminati just operated under other names. It was under the name of "The League of the Just" that "Karl Marx" became a member. He was hired to update the writings of Adam Weishaupt, written seventy years earlier. Weishaupt died in 1830, but his revolutionary plans were carried on by a list of his successors.

In 1842 Karl Marx began to write revolutionary propaganda for the League of the Just, hoping to cause a spirit of unrest. In 1844, in collaboration with Friedrich Engels, and under the supervision of The League of the Just, Marx began to write the infamous "Manifest der Kommunistichen Partei," commonly known today as the "The Communist Manifesto," which appeared at the beginning of 1848.[3] Later, the Illuminati operating under the name

1. Masterplots Cyclopedia of World Authors, 1958, pp. 724, 725.
2. Encyclopedia Americana, Vol. 15, p. 657.
3. Encyclopedia Britannica, Vol. 2, p. 553.

of The League of the Just, changed their name to "The League of Communists".[4]

The Communists celebrate May 1st as the birth of their revolutionary movement because it was the birthday of the Illuminati, founded by Adam Weishaupt. And, it is not by chance that all Communists use the "Pentagram" (five pointed star) as one of their insigia. And, it is not by chance that the Communists use the term RED to describe their revolutionary movement. The Rothschild international banking family, who for some 200 years had a great influence on the economic and the political history of Europe, was founded by Mayer Amschel Rothschild Feb. 23, 1744 in Frankfurt. He had five sons and the family name derived from the RED SHIELD on Mayer's ancestor's house.

It was Adam Weishaupt and the House of Rothschild who started this partly religious and partly political movement[5] foretold in prophecy as the "Scarlet Coloured Beast" that shall ascend out of the bottomless pit (Spiritualism). Revelation 17:3, 8.

In the 1890's this world revolutionary movement added to its membership Vladimar Ilyich Ulyanov, who changed his name to Nicholai Lenin. As the Illuminati terrorist group in France (Jacobin Clubs) caused the fall of the government of Louis XVI, so did their later aristocractic brethren operating under the name of Bolshevism[6] cause the overthrow of the Tsar in Russia and cause the Russian Revolution in 1917.[7] It will be shown later that these Communists were financed by both European and American International Bankers.

4. Masterplots Cyclopedia of World Authors, 1958, p. 725.
5. Fourth Reich of the Rich, Griffin, p. 249
6. The Naked Communist, Skousen, p. 112.
7. Ibid. p. 112.

The ideas Lenin developed were directly from the Karl Marx Communist Manifesto, and the ideas founded in the Communist Manifesto were directly from the writings of Dr. Adam Weishaupt, who took his orders from the House of Rothschild. Gary Allen in his multimillion best seller *None Dare Call It Conspiracy*, states the following about Marx's Communist Manifesto:

> "*If you study Marx Communist Manifesto you will find that in essence Marx said the proletarian revolution would establish the Socialist dictatorship of the proletariat. To achieve the Socialist dictatorship of the proletariat, three things would have to be accomplished. 1. The elimination of all right to private property. 2. The dissolution of the family unit: and 3. Destruction of what Marx referred to as the 'opiate of the people,' 'Religion.'*"

Allan goes on to say,

> "*Karl Marx was hired by a mysterious group who called themselves 'The League of the Just Men' to write the Communist Manifesto as demagogic boob-bait to appeal to the mob. In actual fact the Communist Manifesto was in circulation for many years before Marx' name was widely enough recognized to establish his authorship for this revolutionary handbook. All Karl Marx really did was update and codify the very same revolutionary plans and principles set down seventy years earlier by Adam Weishaupt, the founder of the Order of the Illuminati in Bavaria. And, it is widely acknowledged by serious scholars of this subject that the League of the Just Men was simply an extension of the Illuminati which was forced to go underground after it was exposed by a raid in 1786 conducted by the Bavarian authorities.*"

None Dare Call It Conspiracy, Allan, Concord Press, 1971, p. 25.

Even though Allan dates the exposure of the Illuminati at another year than what we read from a Masonic book, nevertheless, it does not alter the fact that these things are historically true. Marx also called for the abolition of Capitalism, which he believed was a struggle between the bourgeoisie (the middle class) and the proletariat (the workers).[8]

Marxism tells the poor that if they would establish a dictatorship of the proletariat, which would set up a classless Communist society, everyone would live in peace, prosperity, and freedom. There would be no more need for governments, police, or armies, and all these would gradually wither away.[9] Marx said that the ruling class would never willingly give up its power, and that struggle and violence were therefore inevitable.[10]

This would naturally sound terrific to some poor struggling blacks, or to the starving in the Latin American countries. But what the Communist leaders don't tell the people is that the leaders are exempt from sharing equally the material wealth of their nation. How many Russian leaders do you see among the poverty stricken? The real motive behind Communism is not to distribute the wealth of the world equally, but the Communist Party is just a front for the super-rich as an instrument for gaining and using power. *IT IS NOT THE COMMUNISTS THAT RUN COMMUNISM. There is yet another controling power behind communism. Communism and socialism are just arms of a more devilish*

8. The World Book Encyclopedia, Vol. 4, p. 726b.
9. Ibid. p. 726b.
10. Ibid. p. 726b.

conspiracy working behind the public eye, that is not being run from Moscow or Peking, but from New York, Paris and London.

These are very serious and dangerous times. The average gullible American has absolutely no thought what is about to come upon him. Awake! Awake! This is a very serious and dangerous anti-Christian movement that has been working politically and socially since the French Revolution to destroy the sovereighty of this Nation and all nations around the world. This beast from the bottomless pit (Spiritualism) spread its poison first in Europe during the French Revolution, and from there to Russia. George Washington, even though he was a deceived Freemason, was nevertheless a loyal American, and was very aware of this International Revolutionary force to destroy all governments and religions in his own time. Des Griffin in his book *Fourth Reich of the Rich*, p. 57 explains how the Illuminati Conspiracy crept into America even when the 13 original Colonies were united:

"However, before the Colonies were united, the Constitution adopted, and our Republic established, fifteen Lodges of the Order of the Illuminati were formed in the thirteen Colonies. The Columbia Lodge of the Order of the Illuminati was established in New York City in 1785: members included Governor DeWitt Clinton, and later CLINTON ROOSEVELT (a direct ancestor of FDR), Charles Dana and Horace Greeley. The following year a Lodge was established in Virginia with which was identified THOMAS JEFFERSON. When Weishaupt's diabolical plans were exposed by the Bavarian government, JEFFERSON STRONGLY DEFENDED HIM AS AN 'ENTHUSIASTIC PHILANTHROPIST."

"Many strong warnings were issued about the activities of the Illuminati in America. On July 19th, 1798, David Pappen, President of Harvard University, issued a strong warning to the graduating class and lectured them to the influence Illuminism was having on the American scene. President Timothy Dwight of Yale University issued a similar warning.

"Also GEORGE WASHINGTON sent a letter to a G.W. Snyder in which he stated: 'It is not my intention to doubt that the doctrine of the Illuminati and the principles of Jacobinism had not spread to the United States. On the contrary, no one is more satisfied of this fact than I am.

" 'The idea I meant to convey was that I did believe the Lodges of Freemasonry in this country had, as societies, endeavored to propagate the diabolical tenets.' "

Fourth Reich of the Rich, Griffin, Emissary Publications, 1979.

Russia is a perfect example today of what the Illuminati plans are for the world. There are about 1⅓ billion persons, or about a third of the world's population, who now live under Communist rule. However, it is estimated that only 10% of the people are actually members of the Communist Party themselves.[11] Look at Russia today and its Communist brethren worldwide. The Communist Party allow no political rivals, and the voters have no real choice among candidates. The truth is that the Communist Party itself is a highly centralized government, and only its top members make important decisions. Most Communist countries are nothing less than open air concentration camps. And, contrary to Marx's predictions, their conflicts, crime and prejudices have not vanished in these Communist countries. There is just as much centralization of the wealth of a nation for the gain of a few, at the expense of the poor and middle class, in Communist

11. Ibid., p. 725.

countries as there is in non-Communist countries. There can also be seen in Communist countries the same national and racial hatred they were supposed to be free of.

Who are really pulling the strings *today* behind the Communist World Revolutionary movement? Gary Allan's statement in his book, *None Dare Call It Conspiracy,* could not state it any plainer, on page 35:

" *'Communism' is not a movement of the down-trodden masses but is a movement created, manipulated and used by power-seeking billionaires in order to gain control over the world ... first by establishing socialist governments in the various nations and then consolidating them all through a 'Great Merger,' into an ALL-POWERFUL WORLD SOCIALIST SUPER-STATE probably under the auspices of the UNITED NATIONS.''*
None Dare Call It Conspiracy, Allan, Concord Press, 1971.

It is the International Bankers who are actually pulling the strings that control the affairs of Communism, not the Communists. Russia, China, Cuba, Poland, etc. are taking their orders indirectly from the super-rich International Bankers who control the commerce of this world.

Seventy years before Karl Marx came on the scene, Weishaupt told his disciples that in order to achieve this One World Government, his conspirators would have to infiltrate every agency of the governmental affairs of the nations. They first used the Masonic Lodges as we learned earlier, to begin this task. By sitting in the top seats of all governments, the Illuminati agents could eventually guide the nations toward a *"Novus Ordo Seclorum,"* which means in Latin "A New World Order." They would accomplish this by the power of the vote which they would have while occupying positions as legislators.

However, before the people of the world would accept the *Luciferian Government* which Weishaupt, an apostle of Lucifer, hoped to eventually achieve, there would have to be a culture change within the societies of the people first, along with a spirit of unrest and riots in the air. The people of the world would have to be reduced into a godless society. Atheism was just a tool to destroy Christianity in France during the Revolution. Weishaupt and his "Inner Circle" were not ATHEISTS; they believed in a god. However, this god was not Jesus Christ, but Lucifer. Communism is just an anti-Christian, atheistic force to destroy Christianity and all world governments, by modern day Luciferians who actually control world commerce. Saith the Lord: *"For all nations have drunk of the wine of her fornication, and the kings of the earth have committed fornication with her, and the MERCHANTS OF THE EARTH are waxed rich through the abundance of her delicacies. How much she hath glorified herself, and lived deliciously, so much torment and sorrow give her: for she saith in her heart, I sit a queen, and am no widow, and shall see no sorrow. Therefore shall her plagues come in one day, death, and mourning, and famine; and she shall be utterly burned with fire: for strong is the Lord God who judgeth her. And the MERCHANTS OF THE EARTH shall weep and mourn over her; for no man buyeth their merchandise any more."* Revelation 18:3, 7, 11.

For the benefit of any skeptic, or reader who has been brainwashed into believing that this Luciferian (Illuminati-Communist-Socialistic) Conspiracy does not exist today, let us look into a warning from Winston Churchill that he wrote February 8, 1920, in the *Illustrated Sunday Herald:*

"From the days of SPARTICUS (Adam) Weishaupt to those of Karl Marx, to those of Trotsky, Bela-Kuhn, Rose Luxembourg, and Emma

Goldman, this world-wide conspiracy has been
STEADILY growing. This conspiracy has played
A DEFINITELY RECOGNIZABLE ROLE IN
THE TRAGEDY OF THE FRENCH REVOLU-
TION. It has been the mainspring of EVERY
SUBVERSIVE MOVEMENT DURING THE
19TH CENTURY; and now at last, this band of
extraordinary personalities from the underworld
of the great cities of Europe and America have
gripped the Russian people by the hair of their
heads, and have become practically the undisput-
ed masters of that enormous empire."
Quoted from The Missing Dimension in World Affairs,
Goy, p. 92.

Revelation 16:13,14 warns about the three-fold
union of the Dragon, the Beast and the False Prophet
that will unite the whole world whose names are not
written in the Lamb's book of Life, to war against
Christ and His people. The first power that will go
out into the world is symbolized as the Dragon,
Revelation 16:13. It is also symbolized as the Beast
that Ascendeth out of the Bottomless Pit. These TWO
symbols both represent Satan and his Luciferian
(Illuminati-Communism-Socialistic) Conspiracy.

Like the 18th century Illuminists of the French
Revolution, the New Age Movement (Spiritualism of
Today) is seeking to destroy Christianity by a world-
wide social transformation. Among this New Age
Movement there are teachers and office workers,
famous scientists, government officials and
lawmakers, artists and millionaires, taxi drivers and
celebrities, leaders in medicine, education, law, and
psychology, who are trying to condition the Christian world into accepting this modern version of
Nimrod's One World Government.

Marilyn Ferguson, the author of The Aquarian
Conspiracy who is a member of this Luciferian plot

herself, states the following in her book on page 26:

"*The Aquarian Conspiracy represents the Now What. We have to move into the unknown: The known has failed us too completely.*

"*Taking a broader view of history and a deeper measure of nature, The Aquarian Conspiracy is a different kind of Revolution, with different revolutionaries. It looks to the turnabout IN CONSCIOUSNESS OF A CRITICAL NUMBER OF INDIVIDUALS, ENOUGH TO BRING A RENEWAL OF SOCIETY.*"

The Aquarian Conspiracy, Marilyn Ferguson, J.P. Tarcher, Inc., 1980.

As we learned earlier, Communism derived out of an 18th century version of Babylonian Witchcraft (Illuminism), and it insisted on the forcible overthrow of all existing social conditions. Francis B. Randall, Ph.D., who has taught at both Amherst College and Columbia University, states the following about Marx in his book, The Communist Manifesto, on page 37:

"*He (Marx) insisted on the forcible overthrow of all existing social conditions with uninhibited abandon ... Let the ruling classes tremble at a communist revolution. The proletarians have nothing to lose but their chains. They have a world to win. Working men of all countries, unite! Millions have thrilled to this most memorable of all appeals that have come down to us from the Romantic Age.*"

The Communist Manifesto, Marx/Engels, edited by Francis B. Randall, Ph.D., Simon & Schuster, 1964.

As we tried to show the reader before, Communism is not a movement to help the downtrodden people of the world. But Communism is actually being run today by Capitalists, the very people who control the wealth of the world that Communism is supposedly fighting against. Very few Americans know that Karl Marx was a correspondent and political analyst for Horace Greeley, who owned the New York Times newspaper. In 1849 both Horace Greeley and Clinton Roosevelt contributed financially to the Communist League in London to assist in the publication of the *Communist Manifesto*.[12] Other contributors were the English millionaire, Cowell Stepney, and of course Friedrich Engels, who was a wealthy German. And, up until recently, two checks made out to Karl Marx by Nathan Rothschild could be seen on display at the British Museum. Lenin, Trotsky and Stalin were financed by Capitalists from America, England and Germany, to help promote the Bolsheviki Revolution in Russia.

What should a follower of Jesus of Nazareth do? Should we unite together and take up arms and defend ourselves? The answer is *NO, a thousand times NO*. This conflict is not a social, but a spiritual war. *"For we wrestle not against flesh and blood, but against principalities, against powers, against the rulers of the darkness of this world, AGAINST SPIRITUAL WICKEDNESS IN HIGH PLACES."* Ephesians 6:12.

It is foretold that Lucifer will condition the ignorant of this world into accepting a total Luciferian Rule through Spiritualism, Catholicism, and Apostate Protestantism. In the name of Peace and Love does this great delusion come. *"And with all deceivableness of unrighteousness in them that perish; because they received not the love of this truth, that they might be saved. And for this cause God shall send them strong delusion that they should believe a lie: That they all might be damned who believed not the truth, but had pleasure in unrighteousness."* 2 Thessalonians 2:10-12.

12. Wake-Up America, Preston, pp. 51, 52.

The modern Luciferian One World Government plot to enslave the whole world under socialism is attackng the world by using physical force (Communism) and by subliminal warfare coming in the name of the New Age Movement. This is nothing less than a mask for the super-rich who are really the ruling class and those who control the huge secret Society of the Illuminati.

The first Russian Marxist group was formed in 1883 in the very year of Marx's death by Lenin, who was a Russian Revolutionary exiled in Switzerland. Between 1900 and 1903 Lenin called his revolutionaries the "Bolsheviki, then later renamed themselves" Communists, after Marx's term in the Communist Manifesto.[13]

Lenin announced to the world before the overthrow of the Tsar in Russia the following: *"After Russia we will take Eastern Europe, then the masses of Asia, then we will encircle the United States which will be the last bastion of capitalism. We will not have to attack. It will fall like an overripe fruit into our hands."*[14]

Since that statement Russia, China, Mongolia, Tibet, Afghanistan, Algeria, Ethiopia, Libya, North Korea, North and South Vietnam, Czechoslovakia, Poland, Hungary, East Germany, Romania, Yugoslavia, Albania, Cuba, Chile, etc. are under Communist rule; and now Central America and Mexico are threatened with Communist guerrillas.

However, the Communist plan to overthrow the last bastion of capitalism (The United States) is to be attacked politically, socially and economically, as Lenin planned. Robert L. Preston, in his book *Wake-Up America*, states the following:

"When Nikita Khrushchev visited the United

13. The Communist Manifesto, Randall, p. 37.
14. Wake-Up America, Preston, p. 16.

States, he boasted that the Communists would bury us and that our grandchildren would live under Communist rule. He even outlined the exact manner in which they would accomplish it:

" 'You Americans are so gullible. No, you won't accept Communism outright, but we'll keep feeding you small doses of Socialism until you'll finally wake up and find you already have Communism. We won't have to fight you. We'll so weaken your economy until you'll fall like overripe fruit into our hands.'

"As outlined by Khrushchev and Lenin, there is no intention for the Communist to attack us in battle; they expect us to fall into their hands like overripe fruit. They intend to bring this about by weakening our economic structure until we are financially insolvent and by giving us more and more Socialism until we are too weak to resist the final thrust into complete Communist rule. As we review the Socialistic and economic picture in this nation today, we are forced to admit that they have once again proceeded exactly as planned."
Wake-Up America, Hawkes Publishing Inc., 3775 South 500 W., Salt Lake City, Utah 84115.

Preston goes on to quote in his book on page 18, the second point Khrushchev made that was to cause the overthrow of the United States.

"The best way to destroy the Capitalist System is to debauch the currency. By a continuing process of inflation, governments can confiscate, secretly and unobserved, an important part of the wealth of their citizens."
Wake-Up America, pp. 15-17.

There shall be wars and rumors of wars until Jesus returns. However, the world and man will not be destroyed by a world wide nuclear holocaust. The Bible makes this very clear. God's people are here and will be delivered out of this world at Christ's Second Coming. I Thessalonians 4:16. It will be Jesus who will lay this world in complete ruins, not the Communists. The threat of a world-wide nuclear war is nothing less than another Communist plot to frighten the inhabitants of the world into believing that a One World Government is the only solution for world peace. The reader must understand that Communism is not being run from Moscow, but by those who control the monetary systems of the world in London, Paris and New York. Do you really believe they would blow up each other?

As stated before, when Adam Weishaupt and the House of Rothschild formed their New Order for the Ages, or The Illuminati, they infiltrated the high levels of the nations in Europe through Freemasonry. Through this they hoped to be able to fill the top positions in the Old World Governments so they could legislate bills that would connect the countries according to their plans. Using social issues and humanitarian causes, the Illuminati of today have in their ranks untold millions promoting this same Luciferic scheme, and many in it are completely unawares. Millions upon millions of sincere people think they are doing the world a great service by joining this international Luciferian movement that's coming under a name today called "The New Age Movement."

Constance Cumbey, a Christian lawyer, got wind of this movement and spent painstaking months gathering New Age books and magazines, so she could expose it for what it really is. She states in her book, The Hidden Dangers of the Rainbow, The New Age Movement And Our Coming Age Of Barbarism, that the New Age Movement uses secret code names and symbols today, as we showed you earlier. One of the most important symbols in this modern day

Luciferian Conspiracy is, however, the rainbow. Also called the *Antahkarama*, it is used in the occult as an hypnotic devide. This modern version of the Illuminati calls the rainbow the "International Sign of Peace." But to the higher orders of this movement, it represents in symbolic language that they are building a rainbow bridge between the personality (man) and the over-soul, or the Great Universal Mind. This Great Universal Mind is *Sanat Kumara*, or Lucifer.[15] New Agers display this rainbow symbol on their cars and businesses.

After carefully investigating the publishing houses and organizations that are today promoting this modern day version of Adam Weishaupt's World Revolution, Attorney Constance Chumbey has compiled documentive proof that the New Age Movement has now a network of more than 10,000 different organizations they are working through, just in the United States and Canada.[16]

The modern day Luciferian Conspiracy to overthrow Christianity and all other religions that will not worship Lucifer is today called *THE PLAN*. It was Adam Weishaupt in the 18th century who first wrote out this Plan for a One World Luciferian Government. Then, 70 years later it was updated by Karl Marx in the 19th century. However, it was Alice Bailey whom Lucifer used to speak to the 20th century man. Alice Bailey died in 1949 leaving behind a step by step plan to destroy Christianity and all other religions and governments who will not adhere to this New Age Movement. Attorney Constance Chumbey points out in her book, *The Hidden Dangers Of The Rainbow*, how Alice Bailey, in *The Externalisation of the Hierarcy*, told New Agers to feel free to use weapons on religious groups who

15. The Hidden Dangers Of The Rainbow, Cumbey, p. 77.
16. The Hidden Dangers Of The Rainbow, Cumbey, p. 58.
17. Ibid., p. 152.

interfere in the political process of their movement. The New Age Movement plans to eliminate several billions of people from the earth's population. They say this must be done before the year 2000 if the world is to survive.[17]

The weapons that they plan to use are NUCLEAR BOMBS, gained through the promotion of a nuclear freeze and disarmament. The countries of the world are to be pressured into giving up these nuclear weapons and they are to be placed into the hands of the United Nations so they can police the world. On page 548 of her book, Alice Bailey is quoted as follows:

"As a means in the hands of the United Nations to enforce the outer forms of peace, and thus give time for teaching on peace and on the growth of goodwill to take effect. The atomic bomb does not belong to the three nations who perfected it and who own the secrets at present – the United States of America, Great Britain and Canada. It belongs to the United Nations for use (or rather let us hope, simply for threatened use) when aggressive action on the part of any nation rears its ugly head."

The Externalisation of the Hierarcy, Bailey.

The most dangerous threat for Freedom and Christianity from these modern Luciferians is coming today under the guise of WORLD PEACE.

To take control of the world, these conspirators had to get control of the world monetary systems through a Central Bank, which we shall discover they have already achieved. Now they are working night and day to condition the world governments into handing over the weapons to them and place them in the very hands of those who want this One World Luciferian Government. Coming in the name of Nuclear Freeze for Peace, or Nuclear Disarmament, it has been their greatest task to get their hands on these nuclear weapons. Alice Bailey, whom these modern Luciferians follow to the letter, states the following in her book, *The Externalisation of the Hierarchy:*

"In the preparatory period for the new world order there will be a steady and regulated disarmament. It will not be optional. No nation will be permitted to produce and organise any equiptment for destructive purposes or to infringe the security of any nation. One of the first tasks of any future peace conference will be to regulate this matter and gradually see to the disarming of the nations."

This 20th Century Luciferian prophetess told her disciples that the nations of the 20th century will eventually hand over their nuclear weapons to the United Nations. *This is their ultimate plan,* because, as the reader continues to follow the history of this One World Luciferian Government Conspiracy, we will show with documentive evidence that the *United Nations is the headquarters for the New Age Movement (Illuminati)!*

17. Ibid., p. 152.

CHAPTER IV

Part 2

1. The Papacy and the United States foretold as
   the Two Beasts found in Revelation 13th chapter

2. The One World Government Conspirators
   within High Places in the U.S.

3. The Art of Subliminal Warfare through TV,
   Magazines, Newspapers, etc.

4. The Communist plot uncovered by the
   Un-American Activities in 1947

5. Tracing early Communism (Illuminism) in early
   American History

6. More on International Banking and how
   American bankers are connected with
   the Illuminati

7. The History behind the Federal Reserve Trap

8. President Woodrow Wilson and The League
   of Nations

9. Col. Edward Mandel House and the founding
   of the Council on Foreign Relations, Inc.

10. The United Nations Headquarters for the
    One World Government Conspiracy

CHAPTER IV

Part 2

Now, let's examine the two other partly religious and partly political powers Lucifer is predicted to use to bring this final struggle between Christ and Satan to its end. In Revelation 13:5, we see again how this "First Beast" identifies with Daniel's prediction of the Papacy in Daniel 7:24, 25. Daniel stated the "Little Horn" would speak *"great words against the Most High."* And so did the Apostle John predict this, and another unmistakable fact that clearly shows us this "First Beast" is the Papacy: *"And there was given unto him a mouth speaking great things and blasphemies; and power was given unto him to continue FORTY AND TWO MONTHS."*

Here we see again this 1260 years of Papal rule. As we have already examined, 42 months in Bible prophecy equals 1260 years. Now in Revelation 13:11-17 we are shown a third partly religious and partly political power emerging in history around the time the Papacy lost its power to control Europe. We are sad to say it, but this "Second Beast" here in Revelation 13:11-17 is Protestant America. The United States is predicted from Scripture to be first a lamb-like nation; however, later it is to speak as a dragon, Revelation 13:11. Let us now examine the 13th chapter of Revelation in more detail.

Revelation the 13th chapter is divided into two parts. Verses 1 through 10 are a prophecy of not only the Papacy, but also the controlling powers of the known world in the ancient past that promoted the various astrological religions that originally derived out of the Babylonian worship of Nimrod, Cush and Semiramis.

If the reader will examine closely the "First Beast" of Revelation 13:1-10 and compare it with Daniel 7:3-8, he will see how similar the two visions are. Daniel 7:3-8 is the same prophecy John the Apostle was given almost 700 years later. Daniel saw these pagan Sun worshipping nations in sequence, while John saw the same prophecy in its full stage. Notice in Revelation 13:1,2 this First Beast is made also from parts of the animals (beasts) we read of as described in Daniel's vision. "*And the beast which I saw was like unto a LEOPARD, and his feet were as the feet of a BEAR, and his mouth as the mouth of a LION: and the DRAGON gave him HIS POWER, AND HIS SEAT, AND GREAT AUTHORITY.*" Revelation 13:2.

The Apostle John was not only given the same vision as Daniel, but he was shown even more prophetic truths. The Apostle John was shown Seven Heads among the Ten Horns, and "Another Beast" that Daniel wasn't shown. And John also saw that it is this First Beast that the "*Dragon (Satan) gave his power, seat, and great authority.*" And, it is the Beast (Papacy) about which the book of Revelation warns that will have a Mark, and will have control of commerce "*that no man might buy or sell, save he that had the mark, or the name of the Beast, or the number (666, Rev. 13:18) of his name.*"

However, it is not this first beast that will cause the whole world to receive its "Mark" or its name, or its number, 666. It is this "Second Beast" (Rev. 13:11-17) which is "*another beast*" that Daniel the prophet didn't see in his vision that will actually "*causeth the earth and them which dwell therein to worship the First Beast (Papacy), whose deadly wound was healed."* As we pointed out in history, the Papacy's dictatorial rule was taken away by the French in 1798. And in Revelation 13:3 it was predicted: *"And I saw one of his heads as it were wounded to death; and his deadly wound was healed: and all the world wondered after the beast."* The Papacy's power is predicted from Scripture to be restored!

"And I saw three unclean spirits like frogs come out of the mouth of the Dragon (Satan, Rev. 12:9), and out of the mouth of the Beast, and out of the mouth of the False Prophet." Revelation 16:13. These three Satanic powers are also symbolized in Revelation as *three beasts* (political powers), that arise from three different areas in the world. They are:

- The Beast that ascendeth out of the Bottomless Pit, Rev. 11:7, 17:3,8;
- The Beast that rises out of the Sea, Rev. 13:1, 2; and
- The Beast that comes out of the Earth, Rev. 13:11-17.

These *three unclean spirits* are predicted to perform such deceiving miracles that most of the inhabitants from the four corners of the world will believe this is the power of God. *"For they are the spirits of Devils, working miracles, which go forth unto the kings of the earth and the whole world to gather them to the battle of that great day of God Almighty."* Revelation 16:14.

As we pointed out earlier, it will be Spiritualism that will unite the whole world under a Luciferian Confederacy. And in our day Spiritualism will come in the name of *The New Age Movement (Illuminati)*, *Catholicism, and American Apostate Protestantism.*

Let us now examine by Bible prophecy and history that the Dragon and the Beast of Revelation 16:13 are symbolized here as the Illuminati and the Papacy; and let us see how it is, indeed, American Protestantism who is the False Prophet.

Like the Beast that ascendeth out of the Bottomless Pit (Illuminati), America was foretold to emerge around the time the *Two Witnesses* (Old and New Testament) were finishing their testimony (at the end of the 1260 years of Papal rule). And, like the Illuminati, Protestant America was born in the same year (1776). This will be understood by examining Revelation the 13th chapter. Both the Papacy and Protestant America are foretold in Revelation 13:1-18.

"*And I stood upon the sand of the sea, and saw a beast rise up out of the sea, having seven heads and ten horns, and upon his horns ten crowns, and upon his heads the name of blasphemy. And the beast which I saw was like unto a leopard, and his feet were as the feet of a bear, and his mouth as the mouth of a lion: and the dragon gave him his power, and his seat, and great authority. And I saw one of his heads as it were wounded to death; and his deadly wound was healed: and all the world wondered after the beast. And they worshipped the dragon which gave power unto the beast: and they worshipped the beast, saying, Who is like unto the beast? who is able to make war with him? And there was given unto him a mouth speaking great things and blasphemies; and power was given unto him to continue forty and two months. And he opened his mouth in blasphemy against God, to blaspheme his name, and his tabernacle, and them that dwell in heaven. And it was given unto him to make war with the saints, and to overcome them: and power was given him over all kindreds, and tongues and nations. And all that dwell upon the earth shall worship him, whose names are not written in the book of life of the Lamb slain from the foundation of the world. If any man have an ear, let him hear. He that leadeth into captivity shall go into captivity: he that killeth with the sword must be killed with the sword. Here is the patience and the faith of the saints.*" Revelation 13:1-10.

Revelation 13:1-10 shows the *world ruling politi-cal powers* Satan has used and is using to promote Spiritualism. Some suggest that the seven heads on the beast of Revelation 13:1 represent Egypt, Babylon, Persia, Greece, Pagan Rome, Papal Rome and the seventh head is the Papacy again, when its religious dictatorship is restored.

However, most have forgotten about another kingdom that existed before Egypt became a nation. Shortly after the flood, the first kingdom Satan used to promote Spiritualism was *Babel*. And it was at Babel that Nimrod attempted to unite the world in that day, into a One World Government. Egypt was indeed a nation that promoted Witchcraft, but Egypt was never a World Ruling Power. Babel was, and it was in control of the known world about 2,000 years before King Nebuchadnezzar ruled the known world from Babylon. Babylon was built on the ruins of Babel. So, the seven heads found on the Beast of Revelation 13:1 could also be Babel, Babylon, Persia, Greece, Pagan Rome, Papal Rome and the Papacy again restored.

Revelation 13:1-10 gives its reader a complete picture from the post flood era up until the days of this present world history. From Nimrod's Tower of Babel to the founding of the United States, history was laid out in 95 AD for the Apostle John to witness in vision.

From the Tower of Babel and down through the centuries, our Lord showed the political powers Satan would use to spread the worship of himself through Spiritualism. His worship by man started at Babel and is predicted in Scripture to be promoted from the Vatican under *a false system of Christianity*. The Papacy will be, in the near future, the head of this *New World Religion* that will unite with all Pagandom and Apostate Protestantism.

Saith the Lord: "And they worshipped the Dragon (Devil) which gave power unto the beast (Papacy): and they worshipped the beast, saying, who is like unto the beast? Who is able to make war with him?" Revelation 13:4.

During the 1260 years of Papal Rule, Satan used Catholicism to get the known world to bow before him. However, shortly before the Papacy was to receive its deadly wound (Revelation 13:3), the United States was to begin its mission in history. Here in Revelation 13:11-17 is the prophecy that predicted the power of American Protestantism that would gradually become the Prophet that will lead all the world again to accept the dictatorial rule of the Roman Catholic Church.

"And I beheld another beast coming up out of the earth; and he had two horns like a lamb, and he spake as a dragon. And he exerciseth all the power of the first beast before him, and causeth the earth and them which dwell therein to worship the first beast, whose deadly wound was healed. And he doeth great wonders, so that he maketh fire come down from heaven on the earth in the sight of men. And deceiveth them that dwell on the earth by the means of those miracles which he had power to do in the sight of the beast; saying to them that dwell on the earth, that they should make an image to the beast, which had the wound by a sword, and did live. And he had power to give life unto the image of the beast, that the image of the beast should both speak, and cause that as many as would not worship the image of the beast should be killed. And he causeth all, both small and great, rich and poor, free and bond, to receive a mark in their right hand, or in their foreheads: And that no man might buy or sell, save he that had the mark, or the name of the beast, or the number of his name." Revelation 13:11-17.

While the Papacy was losing its power in the third quarter of the 18th century, the United States as an independent Protestant Nation began to make its appearance in history. It was to emerge out of a wilderness symbolized in prophecy as Earth (Rev. 13:11). The United States in the beginning was a haven for those Protestant European people who were fortunate enough to escape the brutal Papal Inquisitions. The United States was set up to have both civil and religious freedom. However, sadly enough, the United States is predicted in Scripture to throw away its civil and religious freedoms and *"exerciseth all the power of the first beast (Papacy) before him, and causeth the earth and them which dwell therein to worship the first beast (Papacy), whose deadly wound was healed."* In other words, the United States will combine religious laws with politics, as did the Papacy when it first ruled Europe. It will force religious laws that actually derived out of Spiritualism, which the Papacy adopted from the Roman version of the religion of Astrology.

The United States is predicted in Scripture to be the False Prophet that will herald the religious dictatorship of the Pope of Rome, and cause the whole world to accept the Mark of the Beast (Papacy). Since we know now who this third power is, found in Revelation 16:13, that shall go forth with the Dragon (Illuminati) and the Beast (Papacy) unto the whole world to gather them together to battle of that great day of God Almighty, let us now examine how indeed conspirators have been working within the United States government behind the scenes, within the high places of our government and other agencies, to lead our country as it is predicted.

To comprehend how degraded our government is becoming, we need to see what the conspiracy of the Beast that ascendeth out of the Bottomless Pit

(Illuminati-Communistic-Socialistic) is working within our own country.

As we examined earlier, Adam Weishaupt, founder of the Order of the Illuminati, was a witch, and taught his followers the power of Witchcraft as a weapon to use against those who would get in their way or tried to expose them. The whole order was trained to accomplish their objectives in complete secrecy. Weishaupt himself even remained behind the scenes in his own revolutionary movement. Only his top members knew him. Using Witchcraft to brainwash his new initiates into becoming anti-Christian, Weishaupt recruited indirectly an army of international terrorists and propagandists to win others to his movement, and help in his struggle to overthrow ALL religions and ALL governments. He even had schools that were specially designed to teach Internationalism. Only a select few were chosen to attend these schools which were established in different parts of the world.

Some of the training received in Internationalism was the art of Subliminal Warfare. This takes in mind control, or mind sciences. As stated before, Weishaupt in early Illuminism hired an army of writers to write propaganda literature against Papal Christianity. For some 20 years before the French Revolution, Weishaupt degraded the morals of the French people with Atheism and with the licentious philosophies of Sodomy. And so do we see this same attack on the minds of men here in the 20th Century.

Back in the late 1940's, maybe some of you who are old enough will remember the great Communist plot that was uncovered in Hollywood, where the FBI and the House Committee on Un-American Activities exposed over 300 of Hollywood's *top stage and screen stars* as *card carrying Communists*.

Myron C. Fagan was a screen writer, producer

and director both in Hollywood and on Broadway. In 1945, at the urgent request of John T. Flynn, the author of *The Roosevelt Myth, While We Slept,* and *The True Story of Pearl Harbor,* Fagan attended a meeting in Washington, DC, where he was shown a set of microfilms and recordings of the secret meeting at Yalta attended only by Franklin Roosevelt, Alger Hiss, Harry Hopkins and Stalin, Molotov and Vishinsky, when they hatched the plot to deliver the Balkans, Eastern Europe and Berlin to Stalin. As a result of that meeting, Myron Fagan made open and avowed war on this Illuminati-Communistic-Socialistic Conspiracy, and formed an anti-Communist society called the *Cinema Educational Guild.* As a result of the work to expose Communistic propaganda in Hollywood, radio and television, in 1947 there was set up in Washington, DC the Congressional hearings that unmasked some of the most famous stars in Hollywood as *card carrying Communists.*

You may wonder why these so-called stars are allowed to continue to influence the movie screens with their presence. The answer to that is, they are working for these same international bankers who own the movie companies. As we continue, it will be shown that it is these same international bankers who control Russia, that are the same conspirators who control NBC, ABC, and CBS television networks, and many large newspapers, magazine companies, and the modern Order of the Illuminati!

When the reader understands that our media are controlled by these same international bankers, maybe he can see why the Communist activity in Hollywood is alive and well.

Man is by nature an imitator. Let an American stay in Britain for some time and when he returns, he may sound like an Englishman. Let there be a fashion change started and watch how quickly folks will attempt to imitate. By studying the life of Jesus, man learns what *truth* is *personified.* Jesus said: *"I am the way, the truth, and the life: no man cometh unto the father, but by me."* John 14:6. The more we learn about Jesus, the more we will want to become like him. However, the more our eyes take in the satanic influence of this world, the more a person can be transformed into its image.

In the ancient world Satan degraded the morals of the people and led them to commit the lowest abominations known to mankind by using Nimrod, Semiramis and Cush, who were worshipped as gods through various names and myths. Everything from cannibalism, human sacrifices, incest, sacred prostitution, homosexuality, murder, rape, self-mutilation, torture and suicide, to magic, sorcery, spell-casting, fortunetelling, necromancy, warlockery, and so on, did the gods do in the epics of their lives. Therefore, the ignorant pagans who worshipped these false gods followed in their footsteps. Now, in these modern times, its the movie stars, rock stars and athletes who have become the gods that many worship.

Do not our children or adults receive a steady diet of these same atrocities committed by these stars in the roles they portray? Even the children's cartoons are saturated with crime and violence. Are not the soap operas full of this junk? Awake! Awake! Can't the reader see the subliminal seduction by the hidden instigator of sin? Can't the reader see that there is definitely a reason behind all this crime and violence shown on TV, in movie theaters, and in magazines and newspapers?

Let's take a look again at the realm of music. Do we really need to ask where some of these rock groups get their inspiration? Take for instance Kiss, who paint their faces and leap on the stage puking blood, declaring, *"God of Rock and Roll, we'll steal*

your virgin soul." The producer Bob Ezrin described
Kiss as "symbols of unfettered evil and sensuality."
Rock magazines call them "fire-breathing demons
from Rock and Roll Hell."[1]

One of the members of Kiss, Peter Criss, boldly
declares, "I find myself evil. I believe in the Devil as
much as God. You can use either one to get things
done." Another member of the group has been
quoted as saying: "If God is hot stuff, why is he afraid
to have other gods before Him? I've always wanted to
be God."[2]

Another Rock group we should take a look at,
who have been a great influence toward Satanism, is
the Rolling Stones. Keith Richards' heroin arrest and
his statement express what they stand for: "There are
black magicians who think we are acting as unknown
agents of Lucifer."[3] Also, the songs they have made,
such as the revolutionary propaganda of "Street
Fighting Man," and the anthem of satanist "Sympathy for the Devil" or "Dancing with Mr. D" (the
Devil), bear out Richards' comment.

The lead singer of Led Zeppelin openly admits to
a fascination with black magic, and the guitarist,
Jimmy Page, owns the home of the late, infamous
Aleister Crowley, whom we studied earlier. Jimmy
Page says he has his own occult bookshop because,
he explains, "There was not one good collection of
books on the occult in London and I was tired of having to go all different places to get the books I
wanted."[4] Page was asked if he were a practicing
witch, and he answered with: "I do not worship the
Devil. But magic does intrigue me."[5]

The Bible warns that what we behold is what we

1. Rock, Bob Larson, p. 132.
2. Ibid., p. 133.
3. Ibid., p. 137.
4. Ibid., p. 135.
5. Ibid., p. 135.

220

will be changed into. King David in the Psalm 119:37 said: *"Turn my eyes from beholding vanity; and quicken thou me in thy way."* Satan from the time of Adam and Eve used every device he could foster to take the eyes off goodly things to set them upon the evil things. Shortly before the French Revolution, the Illuminati destroyed what little faith the French had in Christ by writing pamphlets to distribute among the people. Today, their anti-Christian attacks are a hundred times more subtle. They are using Hollywood, special interest groups, the Feminist Movement, Civil Rights groups, the Federal Reserve Act, Congressmen, Senators, and even Presidents to degrade and divide the people in the United States into different hate factions, as they did during the French Revolution to destroy that government and Christianity. They were known as the *Jacobin Clubs* in the 18th century in France, and today they are called *Communists.* Two weeks after the Kennedy assassination, the late FBI Chief, J. Edgar Hoover, issued this warning: *"We are at war with Communism and the sooner every red-blooded American realizes this the safer we will be."*[6]

The same poisonous propaganda that caused the French Revolution is steadily brainwashing our youth as well as the adults today. Can any born-again Christian be so blind as to doubt that the influences of Communism and the promotion of Witchcraft today are taking their toll among Americans?

Just as a sincere believer in Christ receives a *born again experience (spiritual awakening)* -- *"Therefore if any man be in Christ, he is a new creature: Old things are passed away; behold, all things become NEW."* 2 Corinthians 5:17 -- so is there a counterfeit experience of this found among witches. Just as a sinner experiences joy in his heart when he makes

6. The Death of a Nation, Stormer, p. 9.

peace with God through the sacrifice of Jesus Christ, and is baptized, and no longer wants to live a life of sin, so does a witch have a similar experience of relief when he accepts the belief found in Witchcraft that Jesus is an imposter. In many covens, before a witch can be initiated into the arts of Witchcraft, the initiate, if not born into a family of witches, must take a ceramic cross and turn it upside down, then break the cross-bar downwards. This is to show other witches that they have rejected Christianity and Jesus Christ. Today many ignorant people, who call themselves Christians, hold this sign up to show that they are for peace, when in reality it shows they have rejected Jesus. The reason the name PEACE was tagged on this evil sign is derived from the peace witches say they get after a new initiate shows his rejection of Christianity, and when he practices the arts of Witchcraft. This art of using gullible Christians to promote Witchcraft propaganda is done through *subliminal warfare*.

The Bible reveals to its reader what God is like. *"But we all with open face BEHOLDING as in a glass the glory of the Lord, ARE CHANGED INTO THE SAME IMAGE FROM GLORY TO GLORY, even as by the Spirit of the Lord."* 2 Corinthians 3:18. When the reader studies the life of Jesus Christ from the Scriptures the Holy Spirit illuminates his inner thoughts with an image that his own life will begin to imitate. God will mold little by little the character of a wicked person into reflecting the righteousness of God, which was seen in the life of Jesus. By *beholding Jesus* we become changed into His image.

It was in 1947 that America was awakened slightly from her deep sleep to see what the Communists were up to. However, America just opened her eyes a little, then fell back into a deeper sleep than before. Communists have their agents planted

In modern witchcraft, the initiate, if once a Christian, must take a ceramic cross, turn it upside down and break the cross-bar downwards to show he or she has rejected Jesus and His faith. Ignorant Christians wear this thinking it is a sign for peace. The origin of the word peace was stamped on this because, when a witch casts its spells, they get peace of mind after breaking the cross.

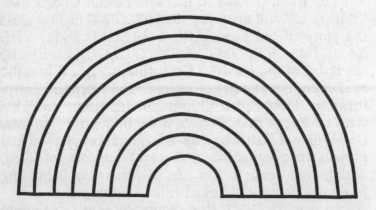

The Rainbow is the modern 1980's version of the peace sign. However, the veiled deception of this evil occult sign borrowed from God's Word, means today that the Luciferians are building a rainbow bridge between man and the over-soul who is Lucifer. See *Hidden Dangers Of The Rainbow*, Cumbey, p. 261.

in every social and political issue that is connected with the affairs of this country. Here quoted from the *Congressional Record* for the year 1947, on page 2691 we read the warning:

"The American Communists launched a furtive attack on Hollywood in 1935 by the issuance of a directive calling for a concentration in Hollywood. The orders called for action on two fronts:

1. An effort to infiltrate the labor unions.
2. To infiltrate the so-called intellectual and creative fields.

"In movie circles, Communists developed an effective defense a few years ago in meeting criticism. They would counter with the question, 'After all, what is the matter with Communism?' It was effective because many persons did not possess adequate knowledge of the subject to give an intelligent answer.

"Some producers and studio heads realize the possibility that the entire industry faces serious embarrassment because it could become a springboard for Communist activities. Communist activity in Hollywood is effective and is furthered by Communists and sympathizers using the prestige of prominent persons to serve, often unwittingly, the Communist cause.

"The Communist tactic of infiltrating LABOR UNIONS stems from the earliest TEACHINGS OF MARX, which have been reiterated by party spokesmen down through the years. They resort to all means to gain their point and often succeed in penetrating and literally TAKING OVER LABOR UNIONS BEFORE THE RANK AND FILE MEMBERS ARE AWARE OF WHAT HAS OCCURRED.

"With few exceptions the following admoni-

224

tions of LENIN have been followed: 'It is
necessary to be able to withstand all this, to agree
to any and every sacrifice, and even - if need be
-to resort to all sorts of devices, maneuvers, and il-
legal methods, to evasion and subterfuge, in order
to penetrate into the trade-unions, to remain in
them, and to carry on Communist work in them
at all cost.' "
(p. 38, Left Wing Communism, An Infantile Disorder, vol. I,
          Lenin, 1934, International Publishing Co., Inc.)

Now can the reader understand why there is so
much sex, crime, and anti-Christian propaganda
constantly seen in the theater and on television? The
average American citizen is completely unaware of
the Communist plot to program the American people
into accepting Socialism by degrading Christian
principles and exalting Sodomy, because all of the
networks of television and radio, the magazines and
newspapers are controlled by these same conspirators who are running Communism. To see that these
things are so, let us now examine the history of how
Communism began to infiltrate the American society and how the House of Rothschild connected
American New York Bankers with the Illuminati.

Now shortly before Karl Marx began to write the
Communist Manifesto, another Illuminist in America
published a book that also outlined the plans of
Adam Weishaupt. His name was Clinton Roosevelt (a
direct ancestor of Franklin D. Roosevelt). His book
was called The Science of Government Founded on
Natural Law. In it Roosevelt had some of the same
philosophy shown in Adam Weishaupt's writings,
"that the men of the Illuminati are to be regarded as
the most perfect and enlightened of men."[7] And in his
book, Roosevelt outlined the plans of the Illuminati
for the regimentation of ALL MANKIND. In other
words, enslavement of the vast populations of the

7. Fourth Reich of the Rich, Griffin, p. 64.

world. To accomplish this, the whole world was to eventually be reduced to what we studied earlier during the French Revolution.

Des Griffin quotes a statement made by Clinton Roosevelt about how Roosevelt felt about our Constitution: a *"leaky vessel which was hastily put together when we left the British flag."*[8] He also stated his atheistic and blasphemous feelings toward our Creator in his book by saying: *"There is no God, of justice to order things aright, if there be a God, he is a malicious and revengeful being, who created us for misery."*

Clinton Roosevelt published his book in 1841. Before this Illuminati propaganda was published to poison the minds of Americans, another Illuminist played maybe even more of a part in spreading poison to degrade the morals of the American people. This Illuminist was sent to the United States from England, like a Christian missionary is sent to a foreign land to preach the Gospel of Christ. She arrived in New York in 1818 and later in 1828-29 held a series of lectures among American Illuminists. Now remember, the word *Communist* was not used before by Illuminists to describe this movement until Karl Marx wrote the *Communist Manifesto* in 1844-48. But, here we will learn where the word *Communist* actually derived from and what these Luciferians' real plans are for America.

In Des Griffin's book, *Fourth Reich of the Rich,* he states the following:

"In 1829, American Illuminists sponsored a series of lectures in New York by English Illuminist Frances 'Fanny' Wright. She advocated the entire Weishauptian program of her auxiliary of the Order of the Illuminati including COMMUNISM MADE MORE PALATABLE BY THE LABEL OF 'EQUAL OPPORTUNITY AND

8. Ibid., p. 64.

EQUAL RIGHTS, ATHEISM, EMANCIPATION OF WOMEN AND FREE LOVE.' Those present were informed that the Illuminati intended to *UNITE THE NIHILIST AND ATHEIST GROUPS WITH ALL OTHER SUBVERSIVE ORGANIZATIONS INTO AN INTERNATIONAL ORGANIZATION TO BE KNOWN AS COMMUNISM.* This new destructive force was to be used by the Illuminati to foment future *WARS AND REVOLUTIONS.* Clinton Roosevelt (a direct ancestor of FDR), Charles Dana and Horace Greeley were appointed a committee to raise funds for this new undertaking."

Fourth Reich of the Rich, Griffin, Emissary Publications, 1979, p. 62.

So you see, the Communist movement, as a tool to foment future wars and revolutions by the Illuminati, was actually formed here in the United States! Frances "Fanny" Wright's revolutionary aims for the United States could be seen in a tract she wrote called *Views of Society and Manners in America.* The London *Quarterly Review* said of her book: "*A most ridiculous and extravagant panegyric on the government and people of the U.S. accompanied by the grossest and most detestable calumnies against the country.*"[9]

In the mid 1800's Albert Pike emerged to join this Luciferian Conspiracy. As we learned earlier, Albert Pike became the most recognized leader and author of Freemasonry.

He was also the head of an order that promoted the exaltation of Lucifer who were called the *Palladists,* which most Christian Masons never knew about. In 1834 Giuseppi Mazzine, the Italian revolutionary who was appointed by the Illuminati to be its director after Adam Weishaupt died, appointed

9. The Peoples Almanac #2, Wallechinsky/Wallace, Bantam Books, Inc. 1978, pp. 1339, 1340.

Albert Pike to head the operations of the Illuminati in the United States.[10] Eventually, Mazzini and Pike divided betweem them the work that was to be done to carry on this One World Government Conspiracy planned earlier by Adam Weishaupt.

Pike took control of the THEOSOPHICAL SIDE of, their operations, while Mazzini was in charge of the POLITICAL SIDE of the Order. To further their goals to destroy the Christian religion and to promote a Luciferian One World Government, Pike as the head of the Ancient and Accepted Scottish Rite of Freemasonry, organized another Order of Freemasonry called the *"new and reformed Palladian Rite."* He named this after the Luciferian Order of which he also was the head, then he established this Order of Freemasonry with Three Supreme Councils in the world. They were in Charleston, SC, Rome, Italy, and the third in Berlin, Germany. The promotion of the worship of Lucifer was then openly laid out to these Freemasons by instructions issued by him on July 14, 1889, to 23 Supreme Councils of Freemasonry in the world.

Now in order that the reader may understand what Pike said to these 23 Supreme Councils, the reader must remember what we earlier learned about in the modern beliefs found in Witchcraft. Modern day witches say they do not worship Satan. They believe Satan and Lucifer are not the same god, as Christians believe. Satan, to modern day witches, is just a Christian invention to scare people into being good. However, higher witches and Doctors of Occultism believe Lucifer is really the Good God, while they say it is Jesus Christ who is the Evil One. Des Griffin quotes Lady Queenborough's book, *Occult Theocrasy*, that records Pikes own words: *"That*

10. Fourth Reich of the Rich, Griffin, p. 65
11. Ibid. p. 69.

which we must say to the crowd is "We worship a God, but it is the GOD one adores without superstition.

"To you, Sovereign Grand Instructors General, we say this, THAT YOU MAY REPEAT IT TO THE BRETHREN OF THE 32nd, 31st, 30th degrees: The Masonic religion should be, by all of us initiates of the high degrees, maintainjed in the purity of THE LUCIFERIAN DOCTRINE."

"IF LUCIFER WERE NOT GOD, WOULD ADONAY (the Christian God) whose deeds prove his cruely, perfidy, and hatred of man, barbarism and repulsion for science, would Adonay and his priests calumniate him?"

"YES, LUCIFER IS GOD, AND UNFORTUNATELY ADONAY IS ALSO GOD. FOR THE ETERNAL LAW IS THAT THERE IS NO LIGHT WITHOUT SHADE, NO BEAUTY WITHOUT UGLINESS, NO WHITE WITHOUT BLACK. FOR THE ABSOLUTE CAN ONLY EXIST AS TWO GODS: DARKNESS BEING NECESSARY TO LIGHT TO SERVE AS ITS FOIL AS THE PEDESTAL IS NECESSARY TO THE STATUE, AND THE BRAKE TO THE LOCOMOTIVE..."

"THE DOCTRINE OF SATAISM IS A HERESY; AND THE TRUE AND PURE PHILOSOPHIC RELIGION 'IS THE BELIEF IN LUCIFER,' THE EQUAL OF ADONAY; BUT LUCIFER, GOD OF LIGHT AND GOD OF GOOD, IS STRUGGLING FOR HUMANITY AGAINST ADONAY, THE GOD OF DARKNESS AND EVIL."

(La Femme et L' enfant dans La Franc-Maconnerie Universelle, by A.C. De La Rive, p. 588; and Occult Theocrasy by Lady Queenborough, pp. 220, 221) Quoted from Fourth Reich of the Rich, Griffin, pp. 70, 71.

Here is another shocking quote from this Apostle of Lucifer that all sincere Christians or Non-Christians everywhere better become aware of. Pike, in a letter dated August 15, 1871, (which until recently was on display in the British Museum Library in London) gave Mazzini details of the Luciferian plan for the world conquest. In this letter he outlined the plans FOR THREE WORLD WARS. Pike said during the THIRD WORLD WAR:

"WE SHALL UNLEASH THE NIHILIST AND ATHEISTS, AND WE SHALL PROVOKE A FORMIDABLE SOCIAL CATACLYSM WHICH IN ALL ITS HORROR WILL SHOW CLEARLY TO THE NATIONS THE EFFECT OF AB-SOLUTE ATHEISM, ORIGIN OF SAVAGRY AND OF THE MOST BLOODY TURMOIL. THEN EVERYWHERE, THE CITIZENS, OBLIG-ED TO DEFEND THEMSELVES AGAINST THE MINORITY OF REVOLUTIONARIES, WILL EX-TERMINATE THOSE DESTROYERS OF CIVILIZATION, AND THE MULTITUDE, DISILLUSIONED WITH CHRISTIANITY, WHOSE DEISTIC SPIRITS WILL FROM THAT MOMENT BE WITHOUT COMPASS (DIREC-TION), ANXIOUS FOR AN IDEAL, BUT WITHOUT KNOWING WHERE TO RENDER ITS ADORATION, WILL RECEIVE THE PURE LIGHT THROUGH THE UNIVERSAL MANI-FESTATION OF THE PURE DOCTRINE OF LUCIFER, BROUGHT FINALLY OUT IN THE PUBLIC VIEW, A MANIFESTATION WHICH WILL RESULT FROM THE GENERAL REAC-TIONARY MOVEMENT WHICH WILL FOLLOW THE DESTRUCTION OF CHRIS-TIANITY AND ATHEISM. BOTH CONQUERED AND EXTERMINATED AT THE SAME TIME."

Quoted in Fourth Reich of the Rich, Griffin, pp. 71, 72.

Now can the reader see who is behind this Charles Manson Family, and motorcycle gangs, some Rock groups, Hollywood and Television, high interest rates, Feminist movements, civil rights organizations, and Labor Unions that are degrading the American people into different hate factions akin to that of the French Revolution? The Bible predicted this revolutionary force as the beast that ascendeth out of the bottomless pit. But, we live in a time where we can examine this movement inwardly because History says its been working behind the scenes to bring these plans around since the French Revolution. We can trace their footprints in history, to show where they began and where they lead and who they are.

To plainly state it, all the footprints from Adam Weishaupt's time to our time will lead us to the doors of a *ring of international bankers*, who control the worlds wealth, and have the same beliefs as Albert Pike. Under them, is a network of industrialist, scientists, military and political leaders, educationalists, economists and entertainers.

It is a well known fact that International Bankers have financed nations to fight against each other. Where do you think the countries get their money to buy tanks, guns, uniforms, etc., to arm their nations for war? They borrow from international bankers. International Bankers have financed both sides of countries at war with each other. They care not who wins because, while the nations are borrowing huge amounts of money to kill each other, international bankers make huge amounts of money from the interest charges they make the nations pay. They also have the power to control the out come of the war by simply cutting off the flow of money they lend. So under the threat of war, international bankers have used their power to gain or increase control over governments. By keeping a nation in debt to them they are in a position to demand a voice in the government affairs of that nation.

However, another goal which they have already achieved is to control all the world's Monetary Systems. Here we will learn how American bankers connected with the Rothschilds and the History behind the Federal Reserve Trap.

Gary Allan, in his book *None Dare Call It Conspiracy*, points out that in Karl Marx Communist Manifesto, one of the planks written for world conquest was to get control of the Monetary Systems. Gary says:

"Lenin later said that the establishment of a CENTRAL BANK WAS NINETY PERCENT OF COMMUNIZING A COUNTRY. Such conspirators knew that you cannot take control of a nation without military force unless that nation has a central bank through which you can control its economy."

None Dare Call It Conspiracy Allan, Concord Press, 1971, pp. 41, 42.

It was on May 1st, 1776 that Adam Weishaupt backed and led by the House of Rothschild, formed the International Revolutionary force called the Illuminati which later became known as Communism. Now, the revolutionary slogan for the Illuminati in Latin, was *"NOVUS ORDO SECLORIUM,"* which means *"A NEW ORDER FOR THE AGES,"* which comes from the philosophies of Astrology.

As we saw earlier, the insignia on the back of a dollar bill with the ALL-SEEING-EYE, was a Witchcraft sign found among the Masons, which the Illuminati was a part of shortly after the Americans signed the Declaration of Independence, on July 4th, 1776. Americans are made to believe that the Roman numerals MDCCLXXVI on the pyramid, which add to 1776, is to celebrate Independence Day of July 4th, 1776. But reader, nothing could be further from the truth about this matter. This occult sign with its slogan "NOVUS ORDO SECLORUM" is to commemorate the founding of the Illuminati on May 1st, 1776, not the fourth of July. And, it is not by chance that the EAGLE which was a symbol for Lucifer to the ancients, and was known as the Phoenix, is now used as a symbol of the office of the President of the United States, which according to Bible Prophecy, will "SPEAK AS A DRAGON." Revelations 13:11.

To show some more *subliminal warfare of the devil by his people,* let us look at the number 13 to see its importance to these conspirators. The number 13 to witches is a most powerful magical number in practicing warlockry. As established earlier, Witch covens today have usually 13 members in number, but do vary. When witches cast spells to injure people or cure them, 13 witches stand within the pentagon, (the center of the five pointed star), and call on spirit guides (familar spirits Deut. 18:11) which are in reality demons, and the witches control them to do their bidding. The demon appears in the center of the Hexagram (the six pointed star), which the deceived modern Jew calls the Star of David.

Reader, now take a very close look on the back of your One Dollar Federal Reserve Note. Not only is the Phoenix (EAGLE) displayed here, but look closely at the stars over the eagle's head. Notice there are 13 stars. Look how they are arranged. It is not by chance that these 13 stars from the HEXAGRAM which by the way, is the most EVIL SIGN IN WITCHCRAFT. Americans are made to believe that these 13 stars represent the 13 original colonies.[12] However, if the reader will again look closer into this great seal of the

12. The Daughters of the American Revolution Magazine, Hall, July 1982, p. 485.

The All-Seeing Eye and the Fenex, or Eagle have been Lucifer's symbols from the birth of Witchcraft. The seal showing the pyramid with the All-Seeing Eye, with its slogan, "Novus Ordo Seclorum," was placed there under F.D.R. administration. Roosevelt was a Freemason himself and it was he and Eisenhower who handed over Eastern Europe to the Communists. Lenin prophesied the Communists would take Eastern Europe after Russia.

United States, he will discover that those who designed this seal did not display this magical number 13 by accident. Note the number of times 13 is used.

1. The Hexagram formed by 13 Pentagrams (stars)
2. The Eagle Breast Shield has 13 stripes.
3. There are 13 Berries on the olive branch in the eagle's right talon.
4. There are 13 arrows in the eagle's left talon.
5. There are 13 leaves on the olive branch.

But for the record, the reason again for the witchcraft signs found on the back of the One Dollar Federal Reserve Note is because the six men who had a part in its design were Benjamin Franklin, John Adams, Thomas Jefferson, Francis Hopkinson (also the designer of the flag), Charles Thomson, and William Barton.[13]

As stated earlier, more than 50 of the signatories of the Declaration of Independence were earlier Masons or Rosicrucians and were identified with the esoteric sciences (the occult). So you see, it is not hard to understand why the Federal Reserve displays witchcraft signs on their notes, because, believe it or not, the Federal Reserve itself, is comprised of 12 member banks and one Federal Reserve Board - 13 in all. The reader will be shocked to know that the Federal Reserve is not a U.S. run institution. Now, let's trace its footprints to see where they lead.

Again, in the mid 1800's another German Illuminist was sent on a mission from the House of Rothschild to accomplish a goal of this New Order For the Ages. His name was Jacob Henry Schiff (1847-1920). He came to New York first for the sole purpose of getting control of the United States monetary system. He eventually became the head of the banking firm of Kuhn, Loeb & Company. He bought Kuhn & Loeb out later with Rothschild money.

13. The Daughters of the American Revolution Magazine, Hall, July 1982, p. 485.

He also became the director in many important corporations, including the New York City National Bank, the Equitable Life Assurance Society, and the Union Pacific Railroad.[14]

Using charity as a front to hide his Illuminati One World Government activities, Jacob Schiff became one of the most important successors of Albert Pike in leading the United States towards anarchy. As stated by Lenin earlier, one of the first goals of the communists is to get control of all monetary systems of the world. And this was to be Jacob Schiff's first achievement. On December 22, 1913, began one of the worst acts the communists accomplished that pushed America towards the doom it was to experience in Albert Pike's plan for world conquest. Here we will really see how the Bible is so correct in stating how we are at war with *"spiritual wickedness in high places"* Ephesians 6:12.

A Republican, Senator Nelson Aldrich proposed a National Reserve Association in 1911 consisting of a Central Bank, fifteen branches, and a top board controled by the nation's leading bankers (which was then dominated by J.P. Morgan) of whom we will study more of in a moment. But Aldrich's proposal never passed. However, the Illuminati conspirators landed one of their first men to become a President of the United States. His name was Woodrow Wilson. We will also look into the life of Wilson and what part he played in this conspiracy in a moment. However, before we examine how actually our Presidents become canidates for the office, we should understand another acheivement that Jacob Schiff accomplished in the United States. This was connecting the bankers of America, J.P. Morgan, Paul Warburg, and the Rockerfellers into this Luciferian Conspiracy. Gary Allan in his book *"None Dare Call It Conspiracy"*

14. The American Peoples Encyclopedia, Vol. 17, The Spencer Press, Inc. 1953, p. 17-328.

states how the American big bankers formed a confederacy with Jacob Schiff, who was actually working as agent for the House of Rothschild:

"*Paul Warburg married Nina Loeb, daughter of Solomon Loeb of Kuhn Loeb and Company, America's most powerful international banking firm. Brother Felix married Frieda Schiff, daughter of Jacob Schiff, the ruling power behind Kuhn, Loeb.*" Stephen Birmingham writes in his authoritative *Our Crowd*: "*In the eighteenth century the Schiffs and Rothschilds shared a double house*" in Frankfurt. Schiff reportedly bought his partnership in Kuhn and Loeb with Rothschild money. Both Paul and Felix Warburg became partners in Kuhn, Loeb and Company.

"*None Dare Call It Conspiracy*" Allan, Concord Press, 1971, p.45.

Senator Nelson Aldrich, whose daughter married John D. Rockfeller Jr., together with Paul Warburg and other internationist bankers set-up a secret meeting at Jekyll Island Georgia, to make plans to get control of America's Banking Systems by establishing a central bank. Some of the invited guests were Henry P. Davidson of J.P. Morgan and Company; Frank A. Vanderlip, President of the Rockefeller-owned National City Bank; Assistant Secretary of the U.S. Treasury; A. Piatt Andrew and Benjamin Strong of Morgan Bankers Trust Company.[15]

It was stressed during this secret meeting that in order to get Congress to accept this Central Bank Scheme, the name "*Central Bank*" must be avoided at all cost. Out of the Jekyll Island meeting came the Aldrich Bill. But, the centralization of the American Banks never passed through Congress. However, these conspirators just fell back and regrouped again

15. None Dare Call It Conspiracy, Allan, pp. 46, 47.

again and re-named the Central Bank Conspiracy, "*The Federal Reserve Act*," to make it sound more like a U.S. Government run agency. And, to see to it that it would pass through Congress this time they landed their very first president in office. His name was Woodrow Wilson. Jacob Schiff, Bernard Baruch, Henry Morgenthau, Thomas Fortune Ryan, and *New York Times* Publisher Adolph Ochs, all contributed heavily to finance the Wilson Campaign.[16]

When Wilson tried to get this Central Bank called the "*Federal Reserve System*" to pass through Congress, he chose Rep. Carter Glass to propose this Federal Reserve Act instead of Aldrich. And in December while Congress desired to adjourn for Christmas, the Federal Reserve Act was passed by a vote of 298 to 60 in the House and the Senate by a majority.

As it was during the French Revolution, so is it today. The Illluminists or Communists have penetrated into the high levels of American Politics, and the High levels of its governmental institutions. Be not deceived! They have their top men posing as Congressmen, Senators, even Presidents, FBI and CIA agents, as military officers, and even as clergymen.

The power of the Illumnati is money. And they use their money to gain control in the Religious, Political, Economical, Educational, Medical, Military, and Social areas that deal with society as a whole. And during the "*Russian Revolution*," it was under the name of "*Bolshevism*" that the Illuminati penetrated in these same areas and caused the overthrow of Czarism in Russia.

Des Griffin in his book "*Fourth Reich of the Rich*," has compiled some very important facts about

16. Ibid. pp. 47, 48.

who were working behind the scenes in the Russian Revolution:

"*After being thrown out of France and Spain, Leon Trotsky and his family arrived in New York aboard the steamer Monserrat on January 13, 1917. Although he was never known to have a job, the Trotskys lived in a fashionable apartment and traveled around in a chauffeured limousine. For some time the source of his wealth was unknown.*

"*Trotsky left New York aboard the S.S. Kristianiafjord bound for Petrograd to organize the Bolshevik phase of the Russian Revolution. When the ship docked at Halifax, Nova Scotia, on April 3, 1917, the Trotsky party was detained by Canadian authorties under instructions received from the British Admiralty in London.*

"*Within hours, great pressure was brought to bear on Canadian authorities by high officals in both Washington and London to recently declassified by the Canadian government, reveal that the authorities knew that Trotsky's group were 'Socialists leaving (America) for the purpose of starting revolution against the present Russian government...' (Wall Street and the Bolshevik Revolution, by Antony G. Sutton, Arlington House publishers 1974, p. 28). Trotsky and his group were quickly released.*"

The Fourth Reich of the Rich, Emissary Publications, 1979, p. 89.

Des Griffin goes on to show where the money came from that was needed for the Russian Revolution: "*President Woodrow Wilson was the fairy godmother (presumably under instructions from "Col. House and his backers") who provided Trotsky with a passport to return to Russia to carry forward the revolution. This American passport was accompanied by a Russian entry permit and a British transit visa. Jennings C. Wise, in Woodrow Wilson: Disciple of Revolution, makes the pertinent comment, "History must never forget that Woodrow Wilson, despite the efforts of the British police, made it possible for Leon Trotsky to enter Russia with an American passport (Sutton, p. 25).*

"In April, 1917, Lenin and a party of 32 Russian revolutionaries, mostly Bolsheviks, journeyed by train from Switzerland across Germany through Sweden to Petrograd, Russia. They were on their way to join Leon Trotsky to complete the revolution. Their trans-Germany transit was approved, facilitated and financed by the General Staff" unknown to the Kaiser (p. 39). At this time Max Warburg, the brother of Paul and Felix Warburg, leading instruments in shackling the "Federal" Reserve System on the American nation, was high up in German intelligence. Max was also the head of the Rothschild/Warburg bank in Frankfurt. VERY INTERESTING! Can anyone doubt that the international bankers were running the whole show from behind the scenes?"
Fourth Reich of the Rich," Griffin, Emissary Publications, 1979, pp. 89-91.

It was confirmed by the New York Journal American of February 3, 1949, that Jacob Schiff gave 20 million in gold to help the final triumph of Bolshevism in Russia.[17]

Now we need to take a deep look into the American politics and learn how this same Luciferian threat is planning and working behind the scene in the United States, as they succeeded in doing to the Russian people. Jacob Schiff, again acting from orders of the House of Rothschild, planned an

17. Fourth Reich of the Rich, Griffin, p. 91.

an organization akin to that of the Jacobin Clubs and the Bolsheviks in Russia. These aristocratic terrorists would penetrate into American politics as their brethren did before them in France and Russia. Woodrow Wilson was the sole property of Jacob Schiff and J.P. Morgan and other internationalist bankers. But the man who was really running things in the White House was the mysterious "Col." Edward Mandel House during Wilson's term in office.

Col. Edward House, who was a British-educated son of a representative of England's financial interest in the American South, wrote a revolutionary book which he admitted to later, that revealed plans to overthrow the government of the United States. The book was called *Philip Dru: Administrator*, and it was symbolically written to also show the detailed plans for the creation of a One World Totalitarian Government.

It was House and the internationalist bankers who promoted Wilson as the Presidential candidate. Woodrow Wilson, who was the 28th President of the US, served two terms as President from March 4th, 1913 to March 4th, 1921. But it was House who converted Wilson to accept the principles of the centralization of the US Monetary System. It was House that helped promote the Presidential candidacy of Franklin D. Roosevelt.[18] It was Franklin D. Roosevelt who gave the Communists East Germany and eastern Europe.

And it was Edward M. House, under the watchful eye of Jacob Schiff, who was under the watchful eye of the HEAD of this international conspiracy (the House of Rothschild of London and Paris), that established in 1921 what their earlier comrades established, to overthrow the governments of France and Russia. Called the Jacobin Clubs in France in the

18. Colliers Encyclopedia, Vol. 9, 1961, p. 571.

18th century, this aristocratic revolutionary movement today in America is called THE COUNCIL ON FOREIGN RELATIONS, INC. and its off-shoot is the TRILATERAL COMMISSION. The Council on Foreign Relations, Inc. is the political side of the Illuminati today. They have produced Congressmen, Senators and even Presidents, that they have used to pass laws that have little by little led America into becoming a Socialist country.

The Trilateral Commission is an international organization founded by David Rockefeller, who also had a part in founding the Council On Foreign Relations, Inc., and who is the chairman of the board.[19] The Trilateral Commission is the Illuminati's attempt to unite Western Europe's Common Market, Japan, Canada, and the United States, into an economic and political confederacy. What they couldn't do through the political side of the Illuminati (Council On Foreign Relations, Inc.), they are trying now through the economic approach.

The first attempt in the 20th century to unite the whole world into a One World Luciferian slave unit was tried in history by these super-rich conspirators at the close of World War I. President Woodrow Wilson on January 8th, 1918 laid out a 14 point plan to Congress for lasting peace.[20] Within this package of world peace was neatly hidden a plan for these conpirators to get all nations of the world to give up their sovereignty. It was labeled as "The League of Nations."

These modern money changers used World War I to make tons of money and as a tool to frighten the war-torn people of the world at that time into believing if all the governments of the world would unite into a One World Government, this would stop all

19. Council On Foreign Relations, Inc., Annual Report 1979-1980, p. 2.
20. The Peoples Almanac, Wallechinsky, p. 449.

wars between nations, and would achieve world peace and security.

The League of Nations headquarters was in Geneva, Switzerland, and it was during World War I that our own President Woodrow Wilson in 1918 began to draw the United States citizens, along with the rest of the world, into accepting this sham. Eventually, with the help of "Col." Edward Mandell House, 63 nations joined the League, although the total membership at one time never exceeded 58. However, President Wilson was dumbfounded when he was unable to obtain the two-thirds vote in the US Senate required for ratification of a treaty, and the United States never joined The League of Nations.

This caught these Conspirators completely off guard because surely, they thought, the United States would fall for this sham, for it was the President of the United States who was promoting it.

Now when the Conspirators saw that their One World Government couldn't be achieved using the name The League of Nations, Col. House, under the direction of Jacob Schiff, formed an aristocratic secret organization called the Council On Foreign Relations, Inc. This private Secret Society is to produce enough Congressmen, Senators, and Statesmen, etc., so the next attempt to incorporate the US into a One World Government will not fail, because of the voting power they hope to have. But reader, remember, *this is not a United States Government run establishment.* Here from their own publication, *Council On Foreign Relations, Inc., Annual Report 1979-1980,* which is controlled by David Rockefeller, we read the following on page 5:

"The Twenty-one Americans, who, together with British counterparts, founded in Paris in 1919 'The Institute of International Affairs,' were a diverse group that included Col. Edward M.

House, Herbert Hoover, Gen. Tasker Bliss, Christian Herter, and such scholars as Charles Seymour, later president of Yale, Professors Archibald Cary Coolidge of Harvard and James T. Shotwell of Columbia. In 1921 their American branch of the Institute MERGED WITH A LARGER, EXISTING GROUP OF NEW YORK BUSINESS AND PROFESSIONAL MEN TO FORM THE COUNCIL ON FOREIGN RELATIONS, INC."

We are living today during their second attempt for their *NOVUS ORDO SECLORUM*, the New World Order. The Council On Foreign Relations, Inc. is only the Illuminati front working in the United States for world government; their brethren in England, as we have already read, are The Institute of International Affairs. Another super-rich group for Internationalism which the IRS approved, is a so-called charitable organization called The American Friends of Bilderbergers. The Bilderberg movement, like the Jacobin Clubs in France, chose their name from the name of the meeting place where they held their first meeting. In this case, it was the Bilderberg Hotel in Oosterbeek, Holland in May of 1954.

Like the Jacobin Clubs, Bolsheviks, and the Council On Foreign Relations, Inc., The Bilderbergers are an aristocratic Secret Society for the super-rich. It is made up from the world of international banking, political circles, and business and professional people. They hold top-secret meetings annually to promote Internationalism.

The chairman of this Secret Society of the elite is one Prince Bernard of the Netherlands, royal consort of Queen Juliana, who is reported to be the richest woman in the world. Queen Juliana and Lord Rothschild are the principal stockholders of Shell Oil Company, while the Rockefellers control Standard

Oil. The Bilderbergers are also known as "The 500."

Des Griffin states some names of the invited guests to the Bilderbergers annual meeting in his book, *Fourth Reich of the Rich,* page 118:

"A lot can be learned from noting the names of the people who attend these clandestine annual meetings: David and Nelson Rockefeller, Emilio Collado, Executive Vice President of Exxon Corporation, Giovanni Agnelli, owner of the Fiat car company, Robert Strange McNamara, President of the World bank, Heinz (Henry) Kissinger, Gerald Ford, Senator Mathias, Britan's Prime Minister James Callaghan AND his "conservative" counterpart Margaret Thatcher, Rothschild puppet President Valery Giscard D'Estang of France, and many other people in similar positions in various nations."

Now, according to the Council On Foreign Relations, Inc. *Annual Report 1979-1980,* Kissinger, Mathias and a host of other political American figures are members of the Council. Howard Baker, George Ball, Harold Brown, Ellsworth Bunker, Donald Bush, Hodding Carter, Douglas Dillon, Arthur Goldberg, Alexander Haig, Jacob Javits, David LIttle, Henry Cabot Lodge, George McGovern, Robert McNamara, Walter Mondale, Donald Regan, Dean Rusk, Adlai Stevenson III, and Andrew Young are just a few names listed in their annual report, as members of this Secret Society.

Back in the days of Wilson, the headquarters for this international New World Order was The League of Nations. Today this masterpiece of deceptions is called the *United Nations.* Many of the same nations that were duped by their leaders into joining The League of Nations were duped again into joining the United Nations.[21]

21. The World Book Encyclopedia, Vol. 20, p. 24.

The UN, like The League of Nations, was set up after the world experienced the horrors of war, in hopes that this time, the war-torn people of the United States would join. The League of Nations really only differed in two ways from the United Nations of today. Instead of its headquarters being located in Geneva, Switzerland, this time the conspirators placed it in New York City. Who donated the money to buy the land and the building materials to unite the nations? It was John D. Rockefeller who sank 18½ million as a gift to the UN, to buy 18 acres of land along the East River in New York, where it is located today.[22]

Gary Allen, in his multi-million best seller, *None Dare Call It Conspiracy*, states the following about who actually laid the foundations to this modern day Tower of Babel,

> "At least FORTY-SEVEN C.F.R. (Council On Foreign Relations, Inc.) members were among the American delegates to the founding of the United Nations in San Francisco in 1945. Members of the CFR group indluded Harold Stassen, John J. McCloy, Owen Lattimore (called by the Senate Internal Security Subcommittee a 'conscious articulate instrument of the Soviet conspiracy'), Alger Hiss (Communist spy), Philip Jessup, Harry Dexter White (Communist agent), Nelson Rockefeller, John Foster Dulles, John Carter Vincent (security risk), and Dean Acheson."
>
> *None Dare Call It Conspiracy*, Allan, Concord Press, 1971, p. 86.

As we learned earlier from the pen of the modern Luciferian prophetess, Alice Bailey, the most diabolical scheme to bring about a One World Religion and a One World Government shall be perpetrated through the medium of the United Nations sham. The ultimate

22. Ibid., p. 40.

goal today in the One World Luciferian Government Conspiracy is to take the weapons away from the citizens of the world so they will have no problem exterminating those who will not bow to their god. This is to be done by conditioning the gullible world into accepting the phony peace plan which is to set up the United Nations as the policemen of the world. Under this plan, the United Nations would discipline any nation that would try to start a war, by threatening that nation with nuclear weapons, which the nations were to hand over to them.

However, as we warned before, the real motive behind this scheme is to use these weapons to cleanse the world of the billions of people who will not adhere to their wishes.

Not one in 1000 citizens of America who adhere to the principles of Jesus of Nazareth are aware of what is about to fall upon them. Not one in 1000 American citizens, even non-Christians, have any knowledge of how organizations like the National Rifle Association and their Institute for Legislative Action have kept the Luciferians from accomplishing their world take-over plans. It has been the members of the National Rifle Association and their Institute for Legislative Action who have been battling with such gun-law strategists as the American Civil Liberties Union, which, by the way, was the legal organization that used Congress to abolish prayer and Bible study in public schools. They also acted as counsel for the American Nazi Party, and they helped promote the right for a teacher to teach the principles of evolution.[23]

However, gun-law supporters such as the American Civil Liberties Union and the National Coalition to Ban Handguns suffered a major set-back in their plans to call for an immediate handgun

23. Encyclopedia Americana, Grolier International, Inc., 1980, pp. 680, 681.

prohibition. This would have eventually led to a prohibition of all firearms under a bill called Proposition 15, if passed. If it had been made law in California, this would have opened the door for handgun abolition efforts across the country. Instead, because of the National Rifle Association's Institute for Legislative Action, this gun-law bill was defeated by a margin of nearly 2 to 1. Another Constitutional amendment in New Hampshire, making clear the individual right to keep and bear arms, was passed by 72 percent of the voters. Such defeats of ardent supporters of gun-laws has only been a set-back. These Luciferians never quit. Patriotic Americans must become aware of the issues of the day, so that they can gain knowledge of how to fight for their rights. We are at war, but this is a spiritual battle, not a physical one. We are not to raise our 30.06 at these conspirators, but our voice in government!

24. American Hunter, February 1983, National Rifle Association, p. 44.

CONCLUSION

1. The Communistic Trap to use Christianity to destroy Christianity through The World Council of Churches.

2. Signs today that show the Coming Merger of Communism (Illuminism), Catholicism, and Apostate Protestantism.

3. The Coming World-wide "Reign of Terror."

4. The Seal of the Living God on their Foreheads.

5. Jesus Christ, who was, is, and is to come.

6. A Sign given by Christ to Show the Earth and its inhabitants that Jesus Christ is the Creator.

7. What the Mark of the Beast (Papacy) is.

8. The Papacy is branded with the number 666

9. Come out of her, My People.

10. Jesus Christ will destroy Lucifer and all his people.

11. The Universal Product Code

CONCLUSION

"And I saw another angel fly in the midst of heaven, having the everlasting Gospel to preach unto them that dwell on the earth, and to every nation, and kindred, and tongue, and people, Saying with a loud voice, Fear God, and give glory to him; for the hour of his judgment is come: and worship him that made heaven, and earth, and the sea, and the fountains of waters. And there followed another angel, saying, Babylon is fallen, is fallen, that great city, because she made all nations drink of the wine of the wrath of her fornication. And the third angel followed them, saying with a loud voice, If any man worship the beast and his image, and receive his mark in his forehead, or in his hand, the same shall drink of the wine of the wrath of God, which is poured out without mixture into the cup of his indignation; and he shall be tormented with fire and brimstone in the presence of the holy angels, and in the presence of the Lamb:" Revelation 14:6-10.

The Bible expresses that the whole world has been deceived into false systems of religions which were invented by Lucifer. The Scriptures admonish us to turn to our Creator "and worship him that made heaven, and earth, and the sea, and the fountains of waters." Revelation 14:7.

We have not reached this period of time yet when the United States will speak as a dragon, and how he "exerciseth all the power of the first beast before him (Papacy), and causeth the earth and them which dwell therein to worship the first beast, whose deadly wound was healed." Revelation 13:11,12. But we are hurrying toward the fulfillment of these predictions. Hardly a day goes by that the reader will not see something in the US about the great work the Pope is doing in the world. Constantly, the Papacy is being exalted directly or indirectly before Americans as a Great Religious Movement working in the world for the benefit of mankind. In some Protestant circles, it is almost considered blasphemy to even mention anything against the Papacy or her Pope. She has painted a picture of herself today as a religious movement that has respect to all religions. However, let her again become powerful and dictatorial, and the same murderous character that slaughtered the French people who did not obey her authority will again be demonstrated.

It was because of her idolatry that the Protestants refused to be connected with her during the Dark Ages. In the Bible, the doctrines she adopted from Sun worship and forced people to obey or die, are called the Wine of her fornication. Revelation 17:2,4.

The United States is predicted from the Scriptures to exercise all the power of the First Beast (Papacy). In other words, the US will also become a religious dictatorship that will force the idolatry of the Papacy on its citizens and cause the other nations of the world to follow its example. It will be the *Protestants* in America, not the Papacy itself, but the *Protestants*, that will reinstate the Papacy with its Pope, in another religious tyranny even worse than during the first 1260 years it cast the Truth to the ground. It has been foretold and it shall come to pass.

But, the reader may question, how could this ever happen in the US? In our Constitution we are protected from any religious movement forcing religious laws on people which force citizens to obey religious opinions and beliefs. *The goal of all three of these powers foretold in Scripture "that go out into the world to gather them together whose names are not written in the Lamb's book of life" will be to change*

our *Constitution by simply calling for an amendment
or Constitutional convention.* As stated before, these
three powers as symbolized in Scripture are:
- Dragon - Beast from the Bottomless Pit
  (Communism)
- Beast - First Beast of Revelation 13:1 (Catholicism)
- False Prophet - Second Beast of Revelation 13:11-17
  (American Protestantism)

They are ever working separately behind the public
eye in high places within our government to change,
and eventually try to throw out, our Constitution. Be
not deceived, the Papacy has planted their agents in
our government just like the Communists have. They
too have had Congressmen, Senators, and even a
President that have been inventing laws along with
the Communists, that have little by little been chisel-
ing away our Constitution. Remember, Adam
Weishaupt, the real author of the *Communist
Manifesto,* learned to infiltrate governments by once
being a Jesuit priest himself. The Jesuits are the
Gestapo of the Roman Catholic Church. If the reader
needs something to show what the Papacy's real in-
tentions are for America, here is a bit of information
right from their own publication, that should alert
any loyal American, Christian or non-Christian:

*"Protestantism is just as wrong now as it was
in 1517. It is the duty incumbent on us as Catholics to 'spread the word' and make America
Catholic ... Father Isaac Hecker founded the
Paulist Fathers for the express purpose of making
America Catholic. They are still at it and doing a
fine job of it. It is the goal of every bishop, priest
and religious order in the country. No Catholic
can settle, with good conscience, for a policy of
appeasement, or even mere co-existence with a
non-Catholic community."*

Our Sunday Visitor, July 31, 1960 - Quoted from
Preparation for the Final Crisis, Chaij,
Pacific Press Publishing Association, 1966, p. 177.

But the reader still may question how the Papacy could unite with Communism, along with the Protestants, into a New World Order when the Papacy appears to be so set against it? This may quickly be answered by just briefly looking into the modern philosophy of both Catholicism world-wide, and Protestantism in these modern times. In John Stormer's book, *The Death of a Nation*, he brings out how Catholicism, Protestantism and Communism are today finding mutual ground:

"*The fight against communism, J. Edgar Hoover has said, '... is economic, social, psychological, diplomatic and strategic - but above all IT IS SPIRITUAL.'*

"*America is losing the economic, social, diplomatic and strategic battles with communism because the traditional spiritual leaders of the nation - the churches and the clergy - are largely committed, knowingly or unknowingly, to the communist side.*

"*This is a serious charge - but careful investigation shows that churches and men who call themselves 'Christian' are deeply divided today.*"
The Death of a Nation, Stormer, Liberty Bell Press, 1968, p. 90.

In the beginning of the study of the origin of Communism, which derived out of Witchcraft, we stated that one of the *ultimate goals* of the Illuminati was to destroy all religions, including Christianity. It may seem to be a contradiction to state that Communism and Catholicism and Protestantism will unite under one banner after stating Communism wants to destroy Christianity. However, Communism, as stated before, is not being run by Communists, but by the Luciferians, who control the wealth of the world. They want to cause another "Reign of Terror," and this time *the anarchy is to be world-wide.* Communism, Catholicism, and Protestantism are ALL just tools of the Devil which he is using to eventually destroy the Real Religion of the Bible, and attempt to make Lucifer the only god of this world.

Using Catholicism, Protestantism, and Communism, the Luciferians hope to throw the world into complete mayhem, so in the end, the people of the world who survive this coming Holocaust will become disillusioned with both Christianity and Communism, and just as during the French Revolution, blame Christianity and Christ as the reasons for the world's problems. Earlier, Albert Pike made this very clear. This is no nursery rhyme or part in a play we have been presenting before you, these things are for real, and deadly serious. This is Satan's last effort to take complete control of this world. Jesus Himself predicted what will happen in the last days we live:

"And woe unto them that are with child, and to them that give suck in those days! But pray ye that your flight be not in the winter, neither on the Sabbath day: For then shall be Great Tribulation, SUCH AS WAS NOT SINCE THE BEGINNING OF THE WORLD TO THIS TIME, NO, NOR EVER SHALL BE. AND EXCEPT THOSE DAYS SHOULD BE SHORTENED, THERE SHOULD NO FLESH BE SAVED: BUT FOR THE ELECT'S SAKE THOSE DAYS SHALL BE SHORTENED."
Matthew 24:19-22.

To continue to show how these *three unclean spirits* will gather the people of the world into a great battle against its Real Creator, let's now look at how Communism has penetrated into Protestantism. International bankers have made a ton of money financing nations to buy weapons to kill each other. Any concerned Christian who has any insight into Bible prophecy can see that the Korean and Vietnam Wars,

like the World Wars, were just a money making venture by these international bankers who are controlling American foreign policy. The United States
could have flattened the whole nation of North Vietnam without sending one soldier to walk its territory.
Without using the nuclear bomb, the US Naval Fleet
or the US Air Force could have stopped the Communist aggression in Vietnam many years before it
ended. One doesn't have to be a military officer to
say that. But the fact is, the military leaders were
under orders not to end the war. The long, meaning-
less Vietnam war only accomplished three things.
First, it proved to be a bonanza for the super-rich. Second, it destroyed over 50 thousand American men
and women. And third, it helped destroy the morale
of many Americans.

What many Americans do not realize is that the
Communists have been using Christianity to spread
Communism by posing as missionaries, and great
humanitarians, while at the same time overthrowing
countries by riot and revolution. In the name of
Peace they have destroyed many.

To put it bluntly, the Communists have been
working through Protestant organizations and civil
rights groups to spread their movement. What appeared at first to be a Protestant Christian organization is now a political monster coming in the name
of Christianity. It is one of the biggest Communist
traps next to the United Nations. And like the United
Nations, it too had Communist elements behind its
founding.

We are pointing to the organization which calls
itself The World Council of Churches, and its off-
shoot called The National Council of Churches. It was
the World Council of Churches that helped Vietnam
fall completely into the Communists' hands by using
its members to pressure the US into stopping its

bombing of North Vietnam. Stormer goes on to state in his book, *The Death of a Nation*, what the World Council of Churches did to prolong the war:

> "American efforts to prevent communism from enslaving the people of South Vietnam has been attacked and condemned by major church leaders and organizations. Since 1966, the World Council of Churches, of which most major U.S. Protestant denominations are a part, has regularly denounced American efforts to halt communism's spread. In February 1966, for example, the Central Committee of the World Council meeting in Geneva, Switzerland ... called upon the United States to halt its bombing of North Vietnam, pull its troops out of South Vietnam, and 'review and modify' its policy of trying to contain communism." St. Louis Post Dispatch, February 16, 1966.

Quoted in *Death of a Nation*, Stormer, Liberty Bell Press, 1968, pp. 90, 91.

Stormer wrote his book while the Vietnam war was still going on. And as we now know, the United States did stop its bombing of North Vietnam and did pull out of South Vietnam leaving millions of dollars of military equipment as a gift to the Communists to give to other Communists to help with their efforts in spreading riot and revolution in other countries such as Central America. The World Council of Churches was formally constituted at Amsterdam on August 23, 1948[1] for the sole purpose of religious ecumenicity for the New World Order of the super-rich.

Even though the Roman Catholic Church keeps itself at a short distance from being a member of this Protestant movement, the Roman Catholic Church for years has been advocating not only a religious ecumenical merger, but also a social one as well. She has been showing for the past few decades how she

1. The Oxford Dictionary of the Christian Church, Cross, p. 1477.

will merge with the Dragon (Illuminati-Communistic
-Socialistic Movement) and her herald, the False Prophet (Apostate Protestantism), as it was predicted
almost 2,000 years ago in the book of Revelation
13:11-17; 16:13,14. John A. Stormer has also compiled information from an official publication of the
Catholic Church, showing how today the Roman
Church is beginning to merge with Communism:

"*John C. Bennett is a leader in the World and
National Councils of Churches. As head of an important seminary he is responsible for training
young ministers. He frequently appears on television to give the 'Christian' point of view on major
issues. Yet, he cannot bring himself to condemn a
Godless force which has brutally slaughtered
40-million Chinese. His words show he is not a
naive, uninformed man. He knows the communists used brainwashing, mass murder, and
dictatorship in bringing communism to China.
Even so, he refuses to reject these 'means'
because they are being used to achieve what he
believes is a good end.*

"*Bennett is not alone in his views. The World
Council of Churches Conference on the Church
and Society heard Red China described as ...
'THE NEW SAVIOUR OF THE POOR NATIONS
OF THE WORLD.' - AP, The News and Observer,
Raleigh, N.C. July 17, 1966.*

"*SIMILAR VIEWS ARE EXPRESSED IN
CATHOLIC CIRCLES. Msgr. Charles Owen Rice,
in his column in the October 6, 1966 Pittsburgh
Catholic, official publication of the diocese of Pitt-
sburgh, PA., used almost the same words as John
C. Bennett. Msgr. Rice wrote:*

"*'It may sound strange coming from a
Catholic priest, but I am convinced we should
pray for the survival of the present government*

of China ... The present government, even though Communist, has brought order to its vast nation, order and admirable measures of internal peace.

" 'Mao Tse-tung and his followers have changed China utterly, and the change has been for the better ... To be sure he has established and maintained tight control, and has insisted on an austere program. He incessantly propagandizes. He, alas, uses hate as a weapon for control and motivation. Many are the mistakes of Mao and his coterie, but the evidence is that the men now ruling from Peking desire the welfare of the people of China ...'

"While Msgr. Rice was writing these words Red Guards were roaming China carrying out a wave of terror in which at least five Catholic priests were buried alive and thousands of people were tortured and slain. His words reveal an apparent awareness of such terror campaigns and his approval of them. He said: '... terribly slow progress was badly dislocated by over communization and the Great Leap Forward. It is again, probably, being hampered by the current Red Guard campaign.

" 'However, the Red Guard campaign is not foolishness ... The masses of China must sacrifice for the sake of the nation ... Any development of a superior class to ride on the shoulders of the masses must be rooted out with PERIODIC RUTHLESSNESS IF PEKING'S PROGRAM IS TO HAVE ANY CHANCE OF SUCCESS. PEKING ALSO MUST CONTINUE THE VIRTUALLY HOPELESS ATTEMPT TO KEEP THE REVOLUTIONARY FERVOR ALIVE.

" 'WE SHOULD LOOK ON THIS WITH A CERTAIN SYMPATHY AND TOLERANCE ... ACTUALLY WE HAVE TO MIX ADMIRATION

WITH OUR SYMPATHY FOR THE MIRACLE OF MANAGEMENT AND MASS MANIPULATION THAT PEKING HAS ACCOMPLISHED.'

"With men who think like John C. Bennett and Msgr. Rice providing the leadership, the General Board of the National Council of Churches voted 90 to 3 on February 23, 1966 to advocate of the Red Chinese butchers to the United Nations - UPI, Philadelphia Evening Bulletin, Mar. 15, 1966." The Death of a Nation, Stormer, Liberty Bell Press, 1968, pp. 93, 94.

Communism, The Papacy, and the Apostate Protestant Churches will unite shortly into one movement as the Scriptures have predicted, with the office of the Pope directing the affairs of this New World Order. But before the ordinary people will accept this New World Order, there will come a spirit of world-wide revolution that will be seen everywhere, especially in the streets of the cities of the United States. The riots of the 1960's were only a shadow of what's coming. All this anarchy is to frighten the world into believing that a new world order is the only solution to avoid the entire destruction of the human race.

However, before the whole world will be thrown into complete anarchy our Lord's last day message is to go out into the world. This last day message is given as we have read in Revelation 14:6-10. This last day message is to go out to every kindred, nation and tongue and people before God allows Satan to throw the world into a holocaust which has never been witnessed in the history of this world. In Revelation 18:1-5 our Lord is calling His people out of Babylon which represents the coming confederacy of a One World Religion and One World Government that has left God out as it was in the days of Nimrod. The time allowed by God to keep in check the universal destruction among all nations is symbolized in Revelation 7:1-3. "*And after these things I saw four angels standing on the four corners of the earth, holding the four winds of the earth, that the wind should not blow on the earth, nor on the sea, nor on any tree. And I saw another angel ascending from the east, having THE SEAL OF THE LIVING GOD: and he cried with a loud voice to the four angels, to whom it was given to hurt the earth and the sea, Saying, Hurt not the earth, neither the sea, nor the trees, till we have SEALED THE SERVANTS OF GOD IN THEIR FOREHEADS.*"

Not only will man cause destruction in this coming holocaust, but nature herself will be thrown out of order. Jesus foretold in Luke 21:10-13, 25,26: "*Then said he unto them, Nation shall rise against nation, and kingdom against kingdom. And GREAT EARTHQUAKES shall be in divers places, and FAMINES, and PESTILENCES; and FEARFUL SIGHTS AND GREAT SIGNS SHALL THERE BE FROM HEAVEN. But BEFORE ALL THESE, they shall lay their hands on you, and persecute you, delivering you up to the synagogues and into prisons, being brought before kings and rulers for my name's sake. And it shall turn to you for a testimony. And there shall be SIGNS IN THE SUN, AND IN THE MOON, AND IN THE STARS: AND UPON THE EARTH DISTRESS OF NATIONS, WITH PERPLEXITY; THE SEA AND WAVES ROARING; MEN'S HEARTS FAILING THEM FOR FEAR, AND FOR LOOKING AFTER THOSE THINGS WHICH ARE COMING ON THE EARTH: FOR THE POWERS OF HEAVEN SHALL BE SHAKEN.*"

All this is to happen shortly before Jesus comes again. "*And then shall they see the Son of man coming in a cloud with power and great glory. And when these things come to pass, then look up, and lift up your heads; for your redemption draweth nigh.*" Luke 21:27,28.

Those who are alive in these last days who are to

go through this coming great tribulation must be *sealed in their foreheads with the seal of the Living God.* The Scriptures have predicted that the majority of the earth's inhabitants will accept the *Mark of the Beast,* for the Protestants of the United States will *"causeth all, both small and great, rich and poor, free and bond, to receive a mark in their right hand, or in their foreheads."* Revelation 13:16.

There is a *Seal of God* and a *Mark of the Beast* (Papacy). It will be these two principles that will separate those who will obey God or Lucifer. As we studied throughout this book, Satan has always used camouflages and religious rites that teach just the opposite of what the Lord says in Scripture, to turn people to him instead, through a network of false gods and false doctrines. Sun worship was and still is the biggest rival of True Christianity. *In order to understand what the Seal of God is, the reader must understand just who was Jesus Christ.* In the book, *Beware Its Coming - The Antichrist 666,* published by Workers For God, Inc., it is brought out for the ordinary reader very clearly:

"Before the birth of the real incarnate of God, the Seed that will bruise the serpent's head, the real Bright and Morning Star, the real God-Man, was to make His appearance on the behalf of man, Satan's messiah had already been preached and worshipped throughout the world, counterfeiting the religious rites passed down to God's people by the Patriarchs. Satan tried to destroy the True Faith by false gods, and when the written word was given, Satan hoped the learned men of the world would look to Christ as just another pagan messiah. When the Greatest Advent in man's history came into the world for the salvation of the human race: 'He is despised and rejected of men; a man of sorrows, and acquainted

with grief: And we hid as it were our faces from him; he was despised, and we esteemed him not. Surely he hath borne our griefs and carried our sorrows: Yet we did esteem him stricken, smitten of God, and afflicted. But he was wounded for our transgressions, he was bruised for our iniquities: The chastisement of our peace was upon him; and with his stripes we are healed.' Isaiah 53:3-5.

"In the ancient world, Satan deceived millions with the darkness of pagan Sun worship. In these modern days Satan has taken on a brighter look, it's called Christianity. Instead of using the name Baal, which means Lord or Master, he is coming in the name of Jesus.

" 'But when ye shall see the abomination of desolation, spoken of by Daniel the prophet, standing where it ought not, (let him that readeth understand) then let them that be in Juda flee to the mountains: And let him that is on the housetop not go down into the house, neither enter therein, to take any thing out of his house. And let him that is in the field not turn back again for to take up his garment. But woe to them that are with child and to them that give suck in those days.' Mark 13:14-17.

"One thousand years before the first advent of our Lord, David likened the people of God to Sheep, and our Lord to a GOOD SHEPHERD. David was a shepherd as a boy, who protected his sheep from the evil beasts around them. David, just a boy, killed a lion and a bear that took a lamb out of his flock. See I Samuel 17:34-37. David knew as the shepherd of the field protected his sheep from the evils of the world, so does the Good Shepherd in Heaven watch over His Flock. Just as the shepherd of the field could call his sheep by name, and his sheep knowing his voice would follow, so will the people of the Lord's Flock hear His voice from the Scriptures and do the things which He commands us. One millennium before God became a Man in Christ, David wrote:

" 'The Lord is my shepherd; I shall not want. He maketh me to lie down in green pastures: He leadeth me beside the still waters. He restoreth my soul: He leadeth me in the paths of righteousness for his name's sake. Yea, though I walk through the valley of the shadow of death, I will fear no evil: For thou art with me: Thy rod and thy staff, they comfort me. Thou preparest a table before me in the presence of mine enemies: Thou anointest my head with oil; my cup runneth over. Surely goodness and mercy shall follow me all the days of my life: And I will dwell in the house of the Lord forever.' Psalm 23.

"At a later time, Jesus said:

" 'I am the Good Shepherd, and know my sheep, and am known of mine. My sheep hear my voice, and I know them, and they follow me.' John 10:14,27.

"In these final days of earth's history, there are multitudes of Christian churches, pastors, priests, Bible instructors, laymen, using television, radio, magazines, newspapers, and tracts proclaiming the Gospel of Christ; however, there is much religious confusion. But if the seeker would forget about what churches have to say, and find the Lord of the Bible, and seek to do His will: 'Then shall ye return, and discern between the righteous and the wicked, between him that serveth God and him that serveth him not.' Malachi 3:18.

" 'Thus saith the Lord the King of Israel, and his redeemer the Lord of Hosts; I am the first, and

I am the last, and beside me there is no god. And, behold, I come quickly, and my reward is with me, to give every man according as his work shall be. I am Alpha and Omega, the beginning and the end, the first and the last. I Jesus have sent mine angel to testify unto you these things in the churches. I am the root and the offspring of David, and the bright and morning star. And the spirit and the bride say come ... and whosoever will, let him take the water of life freely.' Isaiah 44:6; Revelation 22:12, 12, 16, 17."

Quoted from *Beware It's Coming - The Antichrist 666*, W.F.G., Inc., 1982, pp. 107, 108 (by permission). If the reader would like to study more into the deceptions with which Satan has fooled both pagans and Christians alike, may we recommend you get yourself a copy of *Beware It's Coming - The Antichrist 666.* It proves through archaeology and history that Sun Worship indeed began with Nimrod, and that the *Roman Catholic Church doctrines are from paganism and not from the Bible. They prove this by a complete study of Catholicism using their own publications.* This book, *Beware It's Coming - The Antichrist 666,* is one of the most complete studies about the Antichrist and that mysterious number 666 that has ever been published. If the reader cannot find a copy in a Book and Bible House, you may order a copy through us from the back of this book.

Indeed, very few who call themselves Christians realize that it was Jesus Himself who created this Earth. Jesus is the God of the Old Testament which spoke through the Old Testament Prophets. It was Jesus who told Eve that *"the day that thou eatest thereof thou shalt surely die."* Genesis 2:17. Paul, describing Jesus to the Ephesians, tried to make them understand, by saying: *"And to make all men see what is the fellowship of the mystery, which from the beginning of the world hath been hid in God, who created all things by Jesus Christ."* Ephesians 3:9. Again Paul, describing who Jesus was to Timothy, said: "And without controversy great is the mystery of godliness: God was manifest in the flesh, justified in the Spirit, seen of angels, preached unto the Gentiles, believed on in the world, received up into glory." I Timothy 3:16.

Jesus Himself said: "I and the Father are one." John 10:30. We are very much aware how some churches deny that Jesus was God and the existence of the Holy Trinity. But the Bible says: "For there are three that bear record in heaven, the Father, the Word, and the Holy Ghost: And these three are one." I John 5:7.

Jesus is the Word Of God incarnated. Revelation 19:11-13. John saw Jesus in a vision and said: "And I saw heaven opened, and behold a white horse; and he that sat upon him was called Faithful and True, and in righteousness he doth judge and make war. His eyes were as a flame of fire, and on his head were many crowns; and he had a name written, that no man knew, but he himself. And he was clothed with a vesture dipped in blood: and his name is called THE WORD OF GOD."

The Apostle John described Jesus as the Word Of God that created the whole universe: "In the beginning was the Word, and the Word was with God, and the Word was God. The same was in the beginning with God. All things were made by him; and without him was not any thing made that was made. And the Word was made flesh and dwelt among us (and we beheld his glory, the glory as of the only begotten of the Father), full of grace and truth." John 1:1-3, 14.

Jesus Christ was God manifested in the Flesh. It was Jesus who was the creative force of the Godhead that said, "Let there be light." Genesis 1:3. "In whom we have redemption through his blood, even the forgiveness of sins: Who is the image of the invisible God, the firstborn of every creature: For by him were all things *created, that are in heaven, and that are in earth, visible and invisible, whether they be thrones, or dominions, or principalities, or powers: All things were created by him and for him."* Colossians 1:14-16. The Child that Isaiah the Prophet said that was to be born of a virgin (Isaiah 7:14) also said *"his name shall be called Wonderful, Counsellor, The Mighty God, The Everlasting Father, the Prince of Peace."* Isaiah 9:6.

It was Jesus who gave Moses the *Ten Commandments.* And it was Jesus who said in the Fourth Commandment, Exodus 20:8-11:

"REMEMBER THE SABBATH DAY, TO KEEP IT HOLY. Six days shalt thou labour and do all thy work: But the SEVENTH DAY (Saturday) is the SABBATH OF THE LORD THY GOD: in it thou shalt not do any work, thou, nor thy son, nor thy daughter, nor thy manservant, nor thy maidservant, nor thy cattle, nor the stranger that is within thy gates: FOR IN SIX DAYS THE LORD MADE HEAVEN AND EARTH, THE SEA, AND ALL THAT IN THEM IS, AND RESTED THE SEVENTH DAY: WHEREFORE THE LORD BLESSED THE SABBATH DAY, AND HALLOWED IT."

The *seventh day Sabbath* was given to man to help him remember that it was Christ himself who created the heaven and earth in six days and rested on the *seventh day* from all of His works that he had made. Multitudes of Protestant Doctors of Divinity, Pastors, Teachers, etc., will tell us that the *seventh day Sabbath was only given to the Jews to observe.* However, this is as false as the worship of the Sungod. Jesus gave the *seventh day Sabbath* at Creation which was over 2,000 years before the Jews came into history. In Genesis 2:1-3 we read: *"Thus the heavens and the earth were finished, and all the host of them. And on the seventh day God (Christ)* ended his work which he had made; and he rested on the seventh day from all his work which he had made. And God blessed the seventh day, and sanctified it: Because that in it he had rested from all his work which God created and made."

The seventh day Sabbath recognizes Jesus Christ as creator of this world. Sunday observance is not from the Bible, but from the astroloical worship of the Sun-God. Sunday is the first day of the week, not the seventh day. From the Encyclopedia of Religious Knowledge, Vol. IV, Schaff, Funk & Wagnalls Company, 1894, P. 2259, we read the following: "Sunday (Dies solis, of the Roman Calendar, 'Day of the Sun,' because it was dedicated to the Sun), the first day of the week, was adopted by the early Christians as a day of worship." On the same page of this Encyclopedia, we read the following: "No regulations for its observance are laid down in the new testament, nor, indeed, is its observance even enjoined;"

As we studied earlier, in the worship of the Sun-God, every thing that was first was dedicated to the Sun-God and so was the first day of the week. This is Satan's counterfeit to our Lord's day. According to Funk & Wagnalls Encyclopedia of Religious Knowledge, Sunday was substituted for the seventh day Sabbath given at creation by Christ himself by early Christian men, not by the one who instituted the Sabbath. Sunday observance was instituted by men, not by Christ or his apostles. We are fully aware that there are Protestant Pastors and Teachers telling the congregations that the original day of worship (The Seventh Day) was changed to commemorate the resurrection of Christ, however, that sounds good, but their is no such commandment in either the Old or the New Testament commanding Christians to observe the pagan day of Sunday. Absolutely Not!

On the contrary, Jesus Himself warns about tampering with the Word of God as we saw earlier in Revelation 22:18, 19. Man is not to change or add anything to Sacred Scripture. *"Add thou not unto his words, lest he reprove thee, and thou be found a liar."* Proverbs 30:6.

Many are those who tell others that it was Jesus who changed the Sabbath from Saturday to Sunday, but the Bible says *"I am the Lord, I change not;"...* *"Jesus Christ the same yesterday, and to day, and for ever."...* *"Therefore the son of man is Lord also of the Sabbath day."* Malachi 3:6, Hebrews 13:8, Mark 2:28.

Jesus is our example. He came down from Heaven to show His people how to live and the right road that will lead to eternal life. *"Then spake Jesus again unto them, saying, I am the light of the world: he that followeth me shall not walk in darkness, but shall have the light of life."* John 8:12. If we claim to be Christians we claim also to be His followers. *"He that saith he abideth in him ought himself also so to walk, even as he walked."* I John 2:6. In other words, if you say you are Christian, you are to walk in Christ's footprints.

"And he came to Nazareth, where he had been brought up: and, as his custom was, he went into the synagogue on the Sabbath day, and stood up for to read." Luke 4:16. Jesus kept the Seventh Day Sabbath holy, not the pagan day of the Sun-God which is the first day of the week, which is even called Sun-Day, the day of the Sun-God, who in reality was Lucifer. It was Satan who changed the Sabbath into Sunday, not Christ or His apostles. This was also foretold. Daniel the Prophet in the seventh chapter of Daniel predicted four acts that the Little Horn would do against God in Daniel 7:25: *"And he shall speak great words against the most High, and shall wear out the*

saints of the most High, and think to change times and laws: and they shall be given into his hand until a time and times and the dividing of time."

As we stated before, the Little Horn of Daniel 7:8, 23, 24, and the First Beast of Revelation 13:1-10 are symbols of the Papacy. Daniel the Prophet foretold in more detail what the Papacy was to do against the Most High, while John in the book of Revelation 13:1-10, 18 saw a similar vision of this anti-Christian power, but was given a clue that would absolutely identify it as a deception of Satan's, for it would be branded with Satan's number 666. We will see more of this in a moment.

We have already seen how the Papacy has fulfilled everything in history which Daniel foretold about it except one of the four points of Daniel 7:25: *"and think to change times and laws."* Here, from the Roman Catholic Church's own publication, is really who is responsible for tampering with God's Law that has caused millions to trample it underfoot. *"The Catholic Church for over one thousand years before the existence of a Protestant, by virtue of her divine mission, changed the day from Saturday to Sunday."* Catholic Mirror, Sept., 1983.

From another Roman Catholic publication, we again read the following: *"Of course the Catholic Church claims that the change was her act...And the act is a Mark of her ecclesiastical authority in religious things."* H. F. Thomas, Chancellor of Cardinal Gibbons.

From another Roman Catholic publication called, *Plain Talk for Protestants*, p. 213 we read the following: *"The observance of Sunday by the Protestants is an homage they pay in spite of themselves to the Authority of the Catholic Church."*

The Roman Catholic Church does not hide the fact that it was her church that is responsible for throwing away the Commandment to keep Holy the Seventh Day as it is set forth in the Fourth Commandment found in the Ten Commandments. (Exodus 20:8-11). In the book *Unfolding the Revelation*, Roy Allan Anderson, D.D. it states the following:

> "Whatever the Mark of the Beast is, it must be something clear and definite. God's unmingled wrath would not be reserved as a punishment for an unknown offense. Furthermore, the mark of the beast must be in contradistinction to the 'seal' or mark of God. His seal, the sign of His creative power, as we have already noted, is God's rest day, or the true Sabbath. It follows that the seal or mark of this universal apostasy would be man's rest day, or the false day of worship."

Unfolding the Revelation, Anderson, Pacific Press Publishing Association, 1974, p. 155.

As we have already observed, too, throughout this book that those who deal in Witchcraft have always had their secret signs to let other occultist know who they are, so does the Lord of the Sabbath let His people know that they have the right God: "And hallow my Sabbaths; and they shall be a (SIGN) between me and you, that ye may know that I am the Lord your God." Ezekiel 20:20.

Sunday is the (MARK) of the beast (Papacy). The seventh day Sabbath is the (SEAL) of God. The mark of the beast and the seal of God, are not a literal mark on the forehead as multitudes have said. Lucifer is at war with God over the control of the mind of man. The *Mark of the Beast* is applied when Sunday-Keepers by law force the observance of Sunday as a day of rest. Today they are called BLUE LAWS. The Sabbath and the false Sabbath, Sunday, will shortly bring the line of distinction between those who will settle in their minds which of the two powers they will obey, the Roman Catholic Church, or the Christ of the Bible. Looking to the end of the world Jesus said to those who will go through this Great Tribulation: *"But pray ye that your flight be not in the winter, neither on the Sabbath day."* The end of the world has not yet come. And Jesus tells us to pray that our flight to the wilderness during the coming holocaust be not in the winter *or on the Sabbath Day,* showing Jesus stills holds man responsible today for keeping the Sabbath Day holy.

In Revelation 14:6-11 is Christ's *last* warning to the world. In it, He is calling His people to turn away from the Papacy and *worship Him* who created the Heaven, Earth, and the Sea, and the fountains of waters. When you observe the Sabbath *(Seventh Day)* as it is set forth in the Ten Commandments, you are showing that you recognize Jesus Christ as the Creator. When you observe Sunday, you are showing you obedience to Rome. It was Satan who used the Roman Catholic Church to change, and tuck away the original day of worship, to Sunday, which derived out of Sun-worship. And, *"Know ye not, that to whom ye yield yourselves servants to obey, his servants ye are to whom ye obey;"* Romans 6:16 (first part).

In ancient times, Kings would use a *seal* to authorize all their important documents. A seal is a badge of authority. A seal not only shows the king's authority, but also his territory, and his name. When a worshipper of Christ observes the Sabbath of the Bible, he shows that he recognizes Christ's authority, His ownership of this world, and that there is *"none other name under heaven given among men, whereby we must be saved."* Acts 4:12.

The False Sunday Sabbath will be the tool that will unite the merchants and the labor unions which are controlled by The Illuminati, to join the Protestants in a joint effort to force through legislation the observance of Sunday, which will bring persecution on those who do not recognize it.

The God of the Bible is calling to Him a people who will follow Him all the way and will help restore the Seventh Day Sabbath back to its rightful place. Even in the New Heaven and New Earth, God's true people will be observing the Seventh Day Sabbath. Isaiah the Prophet foretold this in Isaiah 66:22, 23: "For as the new heavens and the new earth, which I will make, shall remain before me, saith the Lord, so shall your seed and your name remain. And it shall come to pass that from one new moon to another, and from one Sabbath to another, shall all flesh come to worship before me, saith the Lord."

The Lord of the Sabbath is calling His people who have been deceived by the Papacy, whether they are members of the Catholic Church or are Protestants who have been taught to observe Sunday, to come back to the doctrines of the Bible and come out of Babylon the great, which is a symbol of all churches that teach doctrines that derived out of Sun-worship.

The Bible makes very clear that the THREE UNCLEAN SPIRITS or the three powers that go forth to gather the world against God will combine their forces under one banner. It will be the Principle of Sunday legislation that will be the factor that will become the issue, that they will find common ground which will unite them under one banner. "These have one mind, and shall give their power and strength unto the Beast." Revelation 17:13.

Once a believer finds out about the Papacy's apostasy, and how they have been duped into believing in a system of false Christianity, the Lord will demand his or her loyalty to Him. As we showed from Scripture earlier, our Lord accepts our worship even if we are in error, if we are worshipping him with knowledge we have received. But when our ignorance has been exposed, we are to turn from error and darkness, to Truth and Light. Sunday worship is a invention of Satan himself and it is the *Mark* (*Sign*) of apostasy while the Seventh Day Sabbath is a *Seal* (*Sign*) that we are the property of God. Won't you take your stand to restore the ancient day of rest that recognizes Jesus as the Creator?

During the 1260 years of the Papal apostasy, the Scriptures foretold that Babylon the Great, the Mother of Harlots, would move its seat from Babylon to eventually end up in Vatican City. However, Babylon the Great is not only the Papacy, it is all religions that teach these same doctrines we have studied throughout this book. The Lord makes it very plain that he has people still in Babylon and he is calling them out! This Great False Religious System is also predicted from Scripture to be destroyed, and those who do not take their stand to come over to the Lord's side will also receive their reward. *"And after these things I saw another angel come down from heaven, having great power, and the earth was lightened with his glory. And he cried mightily with a strong voice, saying, Babylon the great is fallen, is fallen, and is become the habitation of devils, and the hold of every foul spirit, and a cage of every unclean and hateful bird. For all nations have drunk of the wine of the wrath of her fornication, and the kings of the earth have committed fornication with her, and the merchants of the earth are waxed rich through the abundance of her delicacies. And I heard another voice from heaven, saying, Come out of her, my people, that ye be not partakers of her sins, and that ye receive not of her plagues.'* Revelation 18:1-4.

The line that will show who are really on God's side and who are just pretending, will be clearly seen in those who make an all out effort to follow Jesus all the way. The Christian has been duped by the Devil and conditioned by the Devil to observe Sunday as a day of rest. The whole world schedules its activities either around Sunday or Friday (the Moslem Sabbath), while the real day of worship (*the Seventh Day Sabbath*) has been neatly tucked away as a whole. Revelation 14, which warns about receiving the *Mark of the Beast*, in the same chapter also goes on to show those who are not deceived and have recognized how to avoid being deceived. *"Here is the patience of the saints: Here are they that keep the commandments of God, and the faith of Jesus."* Revelation 14:12.

In another area of this last book of the Bible, it clearly shows our Lord's True Church and how the Dragon (Devil) has made open avowed war on her. In Revelation 12:17 we read: *"And the Dragon was wroth with the woman, and went to make war with the remnant of her seed, which keep the commandments of God, and have the testimony of Jesus Christ."*

Reader, that's all TEN, not just nine of them. *"For whosoever shall keep the whole law, and yet offend in one point, he is guilty of all. For he that said, Do not commit adultery, said also, Do not kill. Now if thou commit no adultery, yet if thou kill, thou art become a transgessor of the law."* James 2:10, 11.

Once saved, always saved, is as false as Sunday worship. Jesus makes this very plain in Matthew 7:21-23: *"Not every one that saith unto me Lord, Lord, shall enter into the kingdom of heaven; but he that doeth the will of my Father which is in Heaven. Many will say to me in that day, Lord, Lord, have we not prophesied in thy name? And in thy name have cast out devils? And in thy name done many wonderful works? And then will I profess unto them, I never knew you: Depart from me, ye that work inquity."*

Even to people who call themselves Christians, who can cast out devils, speak in tongues, foretell the future, or perform healing miracles, our Lord says: "*To the law and to the testimony: If they speak not according to this word, it is because there is no light in them. He that saith I know Him, and keepeth not his commandments, is a liar, and the truth is not in him. He that turneth away his ear from hearing the law, even, his prayer shall be abomination.*" Isaiah 8:20, I John 2:4, Proverbs 28-9.

Even though the reader may have trampled underfoot the Seventh Day Sabbath *which recognizes Christ as creator,* our Lord is still holding back the winds of destruction so that those who are still in Babylon may have a chance to flee out of it before it receives its plagues. God promises a blessing on those who make their stand for Him in Isaiah 58:13-14.

"If thou will turn away thy foot from the Sabbath, from doing thy pleasure on my Holy Day, and call the Sabbath a delight, the holy of the Lord, honourable, and shalt honour Him, not doing thine own ways, nor finding thine own pleasure, nor speaking thine own words: Then shalt thou delight thyself in the Lord; and I will cause thee to ride upon the high places of the earth, and feed thee with the heritage of Jacob thy father: For the mouth of the Lord hath spoken it."

Now to show the reader that there is no mistake in identifying this Beast where Satan's seat is (Revelation 13:1, 2), who even boasts about changing God's Law, "*Here is Wisdom. Let him that hath understanding count the number of the beast: for it is the nmber of a man; and his number is Six hundred threescore and six.*" Revelation 13:18.

The Beast here is the Papacy as we have already seen. Our Lord made it very plain that this religious power will also be branded with Satan's number. Our Lord does not leave His people in darkness about this. In *Unfolding The Revelation*, by Roy Allan Anderson, he has compiled some very interesting facts that show how the Papacy is branded with this number of doom.

Let us now see how the Papacy itself and the name of it's Pope today, add to 666. Here found on page 130 of Anderson's *Unfolding The Revelation* is the location of this Beast's residence. Here in Greek with its numerical values, is "HĒ LATINĒ BASILEIA," which means in Greek with its transliterations, "THE LATIN KINGDOM."[2]

```
H Ē    L A T I N Ē      B A S I L E I A
0 8    30 1 300 10 50 8   2 1 200 10 30 5 10 1  = 666
```

The name "LATIN" is derived from the earlier Romans, centuries before the age of the Papacy. It was the name of the Sun-god who the early Romans worshipped. Hence the Romans, to identify themselves with their Sun-god, adopted their god's name. They called themselves "LATINS."

Here is a name that shows in what country this religious power has its church. Here again in Greek with its transliterations and numerical values is "ITALIKA EKKLĒSIA" which means in Greek, "ITALIAN CHURCH."[3]

```
I T A L I K A        E K K L Ē S I A
10 300 1 30 10 20 1   5 20 20 30 8 200 10 1  = 666
```

The Papacy not only adopted the pagan rites of the early Roman Sun worshippers, but the sacred language of the pagan Romans. LATEINOS is the

2. Unfolding the Revelation, Anderson, p. 130.

3. Ibid., p. 130.

Greek spelling for Roman Sun-god (Latin). It also means, "Latin-speaking Man," or "Latin Man." Here is Latin-speaking man (LATEINOS):[4]

L A T E I N O S
30 1 300 5 10 50 70 200 = 666

Now here from a Roman Catholic authorized publication, the official name of the office of the Pope: *"The Title of the Pope of Rome is VICARIUS FILII DEI and if you take the letters of his title which represent Latin numerals (printed large) and add them together they come to 666."* Our Sunday Visitor, Nov. 15, 1914. Quoted from *Beware Its Coming - The Antichrist 666*, W.F.G., Inc., p. 143.

Here is VICARIUS FILII DEI which means in Latin "VICAR OF THE SON OF GOD," added in Roman Numerals:[5]

V I C A R I U S   F I L I I   D E I
5 1 100 0 0 0 1 5 0   0 1 50 1 1   500 0 1 = 666

Since the publication of Roy Allan Anderson's *Unfolding the Revelation*, and *The Antichrist 666*, there have been elected two new Popes. And, a new dynasty to what the Papacy claims to be the succession of Peter. There have been in numerous newspapers and magazines claiming Pope John Paul to be "Christ in the Flesh," which is blasphemy. And ironically enough, if you write John Paul Vicar of God in LATIN, and add it up in Roman Numerals, you get:

J U A N   P A U L O   V I C E   D E O
0 5 0 0   0 0 5 50 0   5 1 100 0   500 0 0 = 666

4. Ibid., p. 131.

The book of Revelation predicts that all powers
of this world, including the Illuminati and Apostate
Protestantism, will make the Papacy the absolute
authority in the near future. It may appear that the
Papacy is at odds with Communism, however,
through the sure word of prophecy they will unite. It
may sound confusing to some, but that's actually
why the Divine Language in Revelation 17:5 calls it
*Mystery, Babylon the Great, the Mother of Harlots
and Abominations of the Earth.* Babylon means confusion, and this term applied here in Revelation 17:5
means *the great spiritual confusion of the world.*
Babylon the Great is pictured in Revelation 17 as sitting on a scarlet (red) color Beast that ascends from
the Bottomless Pit (Spiritualism), which symbolized
the Illuminati-Communistic-Socialistic movement
today. This shows that this Political Power is also to
become world-wide. However, it will be the Papacy
that is to be the Head of this last Political Power
again shortly before the Second Coming of Jesus
Christ.

The Beast that ascendeth out of the Bottomless
Pit has *eight powers*, and we have already seen that
heads on a Beast in Bible prophecy represents the
controlling powers. It is still unclear what powers
for sure are the eight powers mentioned in Revelation 17:9-11 and it is dangerous to be dogmatic when
it comes to unfulfilled prophecy. However, we can
know for sure who the first five are, because they
have already passsed in history. Says the Bible: "And
there are seven kings: FIVE ARE FALLEN, and one is,
and the other is not yet come; and when he cometh, he
must continue a short space. And the beast that was,
and is not, even he is the EIGHTH, and is of the seven,
and goeth into perdition."

The first five heads here suggests: Babylon,
Persia, Greece, Pagan Rome, and Papal Rome. It is

the *sixth and seventh head* where most who have studied deep into the Mystery of Godliness have still a problem solving because we have not reached in history as yet when the Papacy is fully restored. However, we can be positive in saying that the *eighth power represents the confederacy of Communism, Apostate Protestantism and the Roman Catholic Church.*

There are, however, some suggestions of who the sixth and seventh heads are. One Bible Commentary suggests the following about the Eight Powers found on the Beast that ascendeth out of the Bottomless Pit: *"According to this pattern of interpretation the powers represented by the first five heads would be Babylon, Persia, Greece, The Roman Empire, and the Papacy. The Sixth and Seventh Heads might be Revolutionary France and the United States, or the United States and a restored Papacy."* S.D.A. Bible Commentary, Vol. 7, p. 855.

So, the eight powers may be:

Babylon	Papacy
Persia	Illuminati (Communism)
Greece	United States (Apostate Protestantism)
Rome	Papacy, United States, Communism

Before we close there is another important issue of the day we need to seriously examine. Attorney Constance Cumbey, while investigating "The New Age Movement," exposed another goal of these One World Luciferian Government conspirators. They will call for a "World Food Authority."[6]

Although we do not agree at all with Constance Cumbey's interpretation of Revelation the 13th and 17th chapters, however, we do believe that there is a wealth of valuable information for concerned Christians and non-Christians alike, found in her book that will help a seeker of truth avoid being

6. Hidden Dangers of the Rainbow, Cumbey, p. 257.

another victim of this world-wide conspiracy. We suggest the reader obtain a copy of *The Hidden Dangers of the Rainbow*, by Constance Cumbey.

We are very much aware of the many different interpretations given throughout Christendom about who this Second Beast is in Revelation 13:11-17 and how this Mark of the Beast shall keep the true followers of Jesus of Nazareth from buying and selling. One of the most popular interpretations found in the 1980's on this subject tells us that this Second Beast of Revelation 13:11-17 is not a political power (U.S.), but it is supposed to be a man who is a Jew from the tribe of Dan and a master of Satanic magic. He will proclaim that the "First Beast" (which has been interpreted also as a man, not a political power) is the Antichrist and it will be this "False Prophet" (Second Beast, Rev. 13:11-17) that will cause the whole world to worship the First Beast (man who is the Antichrist), because he will claim to be God.[7] This "Second Beast," according to Hal Linsey, is the "False Prophet" (man) who will force the worship of this "First Beast" (man), who will be a Roman dictator. And this, according to Lindsey, is the Antichrist.

Now, this last world dictator, according to Mary Stewart Relfe, Ph.D., will control the world's buying and selling through the Universal Product Code that is found now on the back of the items you buy at your favorite supermarket. Mary Steward Relfe states in her book, *The New Money System 666*, on page 206, what she thinks is the Mark of the Beast:

"The Mark of the Beast, the only unpardonable sin specifically named in the Bible, and the only sin for which God metes out a named 4-fold punishment is:

7. The Late Great Planet Earth, Linsey, pp. 111, 112.

1. Receiving of one's own volition the Mark (brand) in the right hand or forehead; which I believe will be a bar code facsimile incorporating a concealed use of '666,' unintelligible to the eye, which will entitle one to all the benefits of "Man's Great Society," in exchange for:

2. Worship of the Beast (Man) who claims to be God; and

3. Worship of his image."

This would sound very interesting to the casual seeker who would like to know what this most solemn warning really means. However, those who are learned in the areas of Bible prophecy and have studied deep into Jewish symbolism, know that what Relfe and Linsey stated about the "Two Beasts" found in Revelation the 13th chapter (as being two men), breaks every law of good Biblical scholarship. A Beast, in Bible prophecy, is a symbol of a "political power," not an individual man. Daniel the Prophet was clearly shown this (Daniel 7:17, 23, 24). Like the names Baal and Bel, multitudes also get the Number of the Beast (666) and the Mark of the Beast confused as being the same thing. They are NOT the same thing. There are five different warnings from our Lord concerning identifying with this Beast (who is the Papacy).

1. Worship of the Beast
2. Worship the image of the Beast
3. Receive the Mark of the Beast
4. Or have the Name of the Beast
5. Or the Number of his Name (666)

The Mark of the Beast is not the Universal Product Code. It is a settling in your mind of whom you will obey. The "First Beast" found in Revelation 13:1-10 is symbolized here as the Papacy and all the pagan nations before it that promoted Spiritualism. The Mark of the Beast is forced observance of the

False Sabbath, Sunday. The Roman Catholic Church is responsible today in causing the majority of Protestant Churches to trample underfoot the original Day of Rest (Seventh Day Sabbath). Sunday worship is not a Commandment from the Bible, but a commandment found on the pages of most astrological heathen religions.

It was Lucifer, *"The Shining One,"* whom the ignorant Sun worshippers bowed to and so is it today. The Sun is just a camouflage the Devil hides behind to get the people of the world to turn their backs to the Real Creator. And so is it with the observance of Sunday. Sunday tradition is an invention of Satan himself. Jesus of Nazareth said He is the *"Lord of the Sabbath,"* not Sunday. See Mark 2:27, 28. However, nobody has received the Mark of the Beast as yet. The Universal forced Sunday observance law is still in the near future. There shall be multitudes of Sunday observers who died in Christ in Heaven. The controversy between Sunday and the Seventh Day Sabbath is an issue that will be settled in these latter times. Just before Jesus of Nazareth comes for his people, all the doctrines that were lost during the 1260 year Papal apostasy will be presented before those who call themselves Christians. When the truth about the Seventh Day Sabbath is brought out in the light, multitudes of sincere Sunday keepers will begin to ask their religious leaders where in the Word of God is the Commandment to observe Sunday! This will stir up a controversy in both Christianity and in the Pagan Religions. While worldly Christians try to find excuses to ignore the call for Sabbath reform, a small group of sincere Christians from all faiths will hear what the Spirit is saying unto the churches and will obey the call from God to:

"Remember the Sabbath day to keep it holy. Six days shalt thou labour, and do all thy work: But the Seventh Day is the Sabbath of the Lord thy God: In it thou shalt not do any work, thou, nor thy son, nor thy daughter, thy manservant, nor thy maidservant, nor thy cattle, nor thy stranger that is within thy gates: For in six days the Lord made Heaven and Earth, the Sea, and all that in them is, and rested the Seventh day: Wherefore the Lord blessed the Sabbath day, and hallowed it." Exodus 20:8-11

Sunday worship is part of the wine of her fornication (False Doctrines) that has made the whole world intoxicated with false religions. Witchcraft (Spiritualism), the powerful force of Lucifer's might, will reach its peak shortly. The Father of Lies will pour out every conceivable sign and lying wonder to gather the ignorant against those who will not sanction Sunday. *"Babylon the Great"* of Revelation the 17th chapter is a symbol of all the religions of the world united together under a New World Religion. This New World Religion which will have both Roman Catholic and Protestant movements, will unite with Spiritualism. This New Age Movement calling for a New World Religion will also call for a Universal Day of Rest. This day will be Sunday. And it will soon be a criminal offense with the pain of death, if not sanctioned. It has been foretold and it will come to pass.

We should not ignore however, what Mary Stewart Relfe, Ph.D., is trying to show her readers. The Bible clearly states that the true followers of Jesus of Nazareth will suffer persecution in these closing days. *"And that no man might buy or sell, save he that had the Mark, or the Name of the Beast, or the Number of his Name."* (666) Revelation 13:17.

Even though Mary Stewart Relfe, Ph.D., has the Universal Product Code mixed up as being the Mark of the Beast, nevertheless, the Bible makes it very plain that the followers of Jesus of Nazareth will not be able to buy or sell either, unless they accept the Number (666) of the Beast. We should not ignore this universal plan to introduce a World Wide Credit Card, or Money Card, with its International Code as being 666. We thank Mary Stewart Relfe for her efforts in trying to make sleeping Christians to become aware and behold what Satan is doing today. Like Constance Cumbey's, *The Hidden Dangers of the Rainbow*, we recommend the reader possess a copy of Mary Stewart Relfe's Book, *The New Money System*.

Whether or not World Commerce will be conducted by a cashless system for exchanging goods by using a Universal Credit Card still remains to be seen. However, the sad truth about this whole Antichrist movement is that the Bible predicts that most people living in these latter days will be deceived and lost by it.

Why will multitudes of Christians be deceived? Again, the Scriptures remind us: *"My people are destroyed for lack of knowledge. Because thou hast rejected knowledge, I will also reject thee, that thou shalt be no priest to me seeing thou hast forgotton the law of thy God, I will also forget thy children."* Hosea 4:6.

We must know the issues for ourselves. We must have a firm knowledge and belief in Jesus Christ and His Holy Scriptures!! The religion of Astrology is predicting a Utopian World Government will be established in the New Age of Aquarius. Lucifer and his people are trying to condition the world to unite together so peace and safety will come. In the name of Peace and Love does this great delusion go forth. However, Paul the Apostle of Jesus of Nazareth foretold: *"For when they shall say Peace and Safety, then sudden destruction cometh upon them, as travail upon a woman with child; and they shall not escape. But ye, brethren, are not in darkness, that that day should overtake you as a thief. Ye are all the children of light: We are not of the night, nor of darkness."* I Thessalonians 5:3-5.

There will never be peace in this present evil world until Satan, His angels, and his people are destroyed by Jesus of Nazareth. Terrible will it be for those in this world who rejected the Love of Jesus. Revelation 6:15 foretells how those who reject Jesus of Nazareth will feel at his Second Coming. *"And the kings of the earth, and the great men, and the rich men, and the chief captains, and the mighty men, and every bondman, and every free man, hid themselves in the dens and in the rocks of the mountains: And said to the mountains and rocks, Fall on us, and hide us from the face of Him that sitteth on the throne, and from the wrath of the Lord. For the great day of His wrath is come; and who shall be able to stand?"*

Jesus will not set up His kingdom in this present evil world. Jesus plainly states: *"My kingdom is not of this world: If my kingdom were of this world, then would my servants fight, that I should not be delivered to the Jews: But now is my kingdom not from hence."* John 18:36.

It will be Lucifer himself, personating Jesus, that will deceive the very elect if possible into believing that long looked for Kingdom of God has come upon the earth. Lucifer himself will personate Jesus of Nazareth just before the real Christ comes with all His angels. This has been foretold and it will come to pass.

There is hardly a Christian Church today that hasn't already been deceived by the false doctrine of a 1000 year reign of Christ on earth. The 1000 year reign of Christ is foretold in Revelation 20:1-10. Jesus of Nazareth will not meet His people on this earth. We are to meet Him in the Air. I Thessalonians 4:16, 17. The 1000 year reign is in Heaven, not on earth.

What are we to do to escape the sudden destruction that will surely come upon the world? First, make sure you have made peace with God through Jesus of Nazareth. *"And take heed to yourselves, lest at any time your hearts be overcharged with surfeiting, and drunkeness, and cares of this life, and so that day come upon you unawares. For as a snare shall it come on all them that dwell on the face of the whole earth. Watch ye therefore, and pray always, that ye may be accounted worthy to escape all these things that shall come to pass, and to stand before the Son of Man."* Luke 21:34, 36.

"Likewise also as it was in the days of Lot; they did eat, they drank, they bought, they sold, they planted, they builded; But the same day that Lot went out of Sodom it rained fire and brimstone from Heaven, and destroyed them all. Even thus shall it be in the day when the Son of Man is revealed." Luke 17:28-30.

The cities of Sodom and Gomorrah were only a shadow in ancient times of how the whole world was predicted from Scriptures to become. Our Lord is just as surely calling His people out of the cities and heavily populated areas today, as He called Lot and his family out. We are to flee the cities!! We are to get out in the rural areas where a plot of land can be used to grow our own food. The cities and heavily populated areas will be thrown into a world-wide Reign of Terror. The cities will become blood baths. The Ark of safety for Christians is to buy a piece of land as far away from the cities and heavily populated areas as possible. Those who are like Lot's wife that cannot give up worldy pleasures will also fall victim as the heathen, if they do not listen.

Our Lord's council for us today is found in the prophesies of Isaiah 26: 20-21.

"Come, my people, enter thou into thy chambers, and shut thy doors about thee: Hide thyself as it were for a little moment, until the indignation be overpast. For, behold, the Lord cometh out of His place to punish the inhabitants of the earth for their iniquity: The earth also shall disclose her blood, and shall no more cover her slain."

We are living in the last era of the earth's history. It will end with Jesus' Second Coming. *"And to you who are troubled rest with us, when the Lord Jesus shall be revealed from Heaven with his mighty angels. In flaming fire taking vengeance on them that know not God, and that obey not the Gospel of our Lord Jesus Christ: Who shall be punished with everlasting destruction from the presence of the Lord, and from the glory of His power"*: II Thessalonians 1:7-9.

"Seek ye the Lord while He may be found, call ye upon Him while He is near: Let the wicked forsake his way, and the unrighteous man his thoughts: And let him return unto the Lord, and He will have mercy upon him; And to our God, for He will abundantly pardon." Isaiah 55:6, 7.

FURTHER STUDY

1. *The World Book Encyclopedia*, Vol. 11, The World Book — Childcraft, 1979.
2. *Encyclopedia Britannica*, Vol. 6, Encyclopedia Britannica, Inc., 1915.
3. *The American Heritage Dictionary of the English Language*, American Heritage Publishers, 1969.
4. *The Two Babylons*, Hislop, Loiseaux Brothers Inc., Neptune, NJ.
5. *Young's Analytical Concordance*, Young, William B. Eerdman's Publishing Company, 1970.
6. *The Compleat Astrologer*, Parker, McGraw Hill Book Company, 1971.
7. *The Golden Bough*, Frazer, McMillan Company Inc., 1928.
8. *Beware It's Coming — The Antichrist 666*, W.F.G. Inc., 1980.
9. *Funk and Wagnall's Standard Dictionary of Folklore, Mythology and Legend*, T.W. Crowell.
10. *Harper's Dictionary of Classical Literature and Antiquities*, Peck, Cooper Square Publishing, 1965.
11. *Encyclopedia Britannica* 14th edition, Encyclopedia Britannica, Inc.
12. *Josephus Complete Works*, Kregel Publications, 1978.
13. *Encyclopedia Americana*, Americana Corporation, 1980.
14. *Astrology*, McCaffery, Charles Scribner's Sons, 1942.
15. *The Mythology of All Races*, Hollumberg, Cooper Square Pub., Inc. 1964.
16. *City of God*, Everyman's Library, 1973.
17. *New College Edition, The American Heritage Dictionary*, Houghton Mifflin Company, Boston, 1981.
18. *Webster's New Twentieth Century Dictionary Unabridged*, William Collins Pub., Inc.
19. *Mexican and Central American Mythology*, Nicholson, Paul Hamlyn Group Limited, 1969.
20. *Man, Myth and Magic, An Illustrated Encyclopedia of the Supernatural*, Cavendish, BPC Pub. Ltd., 1970.
21. *Collier's Encyclopedia*, Macmillan Educational Corporation, 1980.
22. *Encyclopedia of the Unexplained: Magic, Occultism and Parapsychology*, Cavendish, Rainbird Reference Books Ltd., 1974.
23. *The Catholic Encylopedia*, Broderick, Thomas Nelson Inc., Pub., 1975.
24. *The American People's Encyclopedia*, Spencer Press, Inc., 1953.

25. The Encyclopedia of Religious Knowledge, Shaff, Funk & Wagnalls Company, 1844.

26. Encyclopedia of Religion and Ethics, Hastings, Charles Scribner's Sons.

27. Anacalypsis, Vol. 2, Higgins, Longman, 1836.

28. The Religion of Ancient Egypt and Babylonians, Sayce, T & T Clark, 1902.

29. Arkansas Democrat Family Weekly, September 12, 1982.

30. Discipleship in the New Age, Bailey, Lucis Pub. Co., 1944.

31. Bulfinch's Mythology, Bulfinch, Doubleday & Company, Inc., 1968.

32. The Book of the Dragon, Allen/Griffiths, Orbis Pub. Limited, 1979.

33. The Book of Talismans, Amulets and Zodiacal Gems, Pavitt, Tower Books, 1914.

34. The Aquarian Gospel of Jesus the Christ, Levi, De Vorss & Co. Pub., 1935.

35. Dance and Drama in Bali, De Loote, Oxford University Press, 1973.

36. Student's Encyclopedia, Halsey, Crowell Educational Corporation, 1971.

37. The Encyclopedia Americana, Americana Corporation, 1947.

38. The Encyclopedia Britannica, Cambridge, England University Press, 1910.

39. Encyclopedia of Occultism and Parapsychology, Shepard, Gale Research Company, 1978.

40. Rosicrucian Questions and Answers with Complete History, Lewis, Rosicrucian Press.

41. Secret Societies, Mackenzie, Holt, Rinehart and Winston, 1967.

42. Morals and Dogma, Pike, The Supreme Council of the Southern Jurisdiction of Freemasonry, 1871.

43. The Masonic Report, McQuaig, McQuaig.

44. Occult Illustrated Dictionary, Day, Kay & Ward, 1976.

45. Life Forces: A Contemporary Guide to the Cult and Occult, Stewart, Andrews and McMeel, Inc., 1980.

46. Helter Skelter, Bugliosi, Bantam Books, 1974.

47. Dictionary of Symbols and Imagery, Vries, North-Holland Pub. Co.

48. Magick in Theory and Practice, Crowley, Castle Books.

49. The Death of a Nation, Stormer, Liberty Bell Press, 1968.

50. San Antonio Light, February 1, 1982.

51. *Drawing Down the Moon*, Adler, Viking Press, 1979.
52. *Hand Book of Secret Organizations*, Whalen, The Bruce Pub. Co., 1966.
53. *Unfolding the Revelation*, Anderson, Pacific Press Association, 1978.
54. *Communism In Prophecy History America*, Winrod, Defenders Pub., 1946.
55. *Encyclopedia Americana*, Americana Corporation, 1980.
56. *Encyclopedia Britannica*, 9th edition, Henry Allan & Co.
57. *Fourth Reich of the Rich*, Emissary Publications, 1979.
58. *An Encyclopedia of Freemasonry and Its Kindred Sciences*, Mackey, The Masonic History Company, 1921.
59. *The Vatican and Its Role in World Affairs*, Pichon, Dutton, 1950.
60. *The Great Controversy*, White, Pacific Press Pub. Association, 1939.
61. *Foxe's Book of Martyrs*, King, Fleming H. Revell Co., 1976.
62. *Cyclopedia of World Authors*, Magill, Harper & Brothers, 1958.
63. *The Naked Communist*, Skousen, Reviewer, 1962.
64. *The Late Great Planet Earth*, Lindsey, Zondervan, Pub., 1970.
65. *The New Money System 666*, Ministries, Inc., 1982.
66. *Rock*, Larson, Tyndale, 1980.
67. *The People Almanac*, Wallechinsky, Bantam Books, Inc., 1978.
68. *The Daughters of the American Revolution Magazine*, Hall, July 1982.
69. *None Dare Call It Conspiracy*, Allan, Concord Press, 1971.
70. *Dictionary of American History*, Charles Scribner's Sons, 1976.
71. *Congressional Record*, 1947.
72. *Council On Foreign Relations, Inc., Annual Report*, 1979-80.
73. *The Oxford Dictionary of the Christian Church*, Cross, Oxford University Press, 1974.
74. *The Aquarian Conspiracy*, Ferguson, J.P. Tarcher, Inc., 1980.
75. *The Communist Manifesto*, Randall, Simon & Schuster, 1964.
76. *Wake Up America*, Preston, Hawkes Publishing, Inc., 1972.
77. *Encyclopaedia of Religion and Ethics*, Hastings, Charles Scribner's Sons, 1910-34.

78. *Discipleship in the New Age*, Bailey, Lucis Trust, 1971.

79. *The Externalisation of the Hierarchy*, Bailey, Lucis Trust, 1968.

80. *The Compleat Astrologer*, Parker, McGraw-Hill Book Company, 1971.

81. *The Godfathers*, Chick Publications, 1982.

82. *Daniel and the Revelation*, Smith, Southern Publishing Association.

83. *Education*, White, Ellen G. White Publications, 1952.

84. *The Illustrated Sunday Herald*, February 8, 1920.

85. *The Hidden Dangers of the Rainbow*, Cumbey, Huntington House, Inc., 1983.

86. *Encyclopedia Americana*, Grolier International, Inc., 1980.

87. *American Hunter*, February 1983, National Rifle Association.

88. *Preparation of the Final Crisis*, Chaij, Pacific Press Publishing Association, 1966.

INDEX

289

Other books by TEACH Services, Inc.

Absolutely Vegetarian   *Lorine Tadej* .... $ 8.95
A complete guide to maintaining a strict vegetarian lifestyle. A way to reach your ideal weight and maintain it, as long as you live.

Activated Charcoal   *David Cooney* .... $ 7.95
This publication represents an attempt to gather together most of what has been reported to date on the use of activated charcoal as an oral antidote and as a remedy for other ailments.

Adam's Table   *Reggi Burnett* .... $ 8.95
A cookbook to help the user obtain optimum healthier and happier lifestyle through changes in their cooking style. Originated from Adam's Table Restaurant in Albuquerque, NM.

American Democracy   *R. S. McClanahan* $18.95
Will its maintenance be a 21st century reality? An overview of an evolving Constitutional "Achilles' Heel".

An Adventure in Cooking   *Joanne Chitwood Nowack* $12.95
This book has been compiled especially to teach young people, in a step-by-step, progressive way, the art of vegetarian cookery. Cooking is a real art, and very practical one too, since we need to eat every day.

Angel At My Side   *Bob Hoyt*............................. $ 8.95
The author, a pastor, Bible worker, and Literature evangelists, tells of his experiences with angels, dogs, guns, horses, floods, skunks, life threatening hazards, and a heart-wrenching deathbed vigil.

The Antichrist 666   *William Josiah Sutton*.................. $ 8.95
Positive proof for Bible Believing People: Who the beast is; Who his image is; What the mark of the beast is; How to count the number of the beast. Edited by Roy Allan Anderson, D.D.

The Anti-Christ Exposed   *Dan Jarrard*................... $ 5.95
A biblical and historical study of the counterfeit religious system which is against God and His people.

The Art of Massage   *J. H. Kellogg* $12.95
A practical manual for the student, the nurse and the practitioner.

Aunt Joanne's Plays   *Joanne Johnson* .... $ 9.95
This collection gives alternative Christmas themes to work with rather than just the regular Joseph and Mary or Wise Men themes.

Aunt Joanne's Skits   *Joanne Johnson* .... $ 9.95
A collection of skits that children can act out, training them to not only hear, but see the results of Biblical morals.

Caring Kitchen Recipes   *Gloria Lawson* $12.95
Specializes in recipes for better health that features: whole grains, vegetarian, dairy-free and nourishing dessert recipes.

The Celtic Church in Britain *Leslie Hardinge* .... $ 8.95
This is an authoritative study of the beliefs and practice of the Celtic
Church which at the same time holds much interest for the non-specialist,
containing as it does fascinating descriptions of the life of the early Celtic
Christians in their monastic walled villages modelled on the Old Testa-
ment cities of refuge. Their elaborate penitential discipline was based on
Old Testament compensatory regulations. Obedience to the Scriptures
led them to establish a remarkable theocracy based on the laws of the
Pentateuch and including the keeping of the Seventh-day Sabbath.

Children's Bible Lessons *Bessie White* .... $ 3.95
These seven Children's Bible Lessons are prepared for use during
Evangelistic Meetings, Bible seminars, Vacation Bible Schools, or at the
Church's discretion.

Christian Apparel *Allen & Patti Barnes* .... $ 4.95
This book is an appeal to Seventh-day Adventist to establish a new
standard—not the customs of society or of the church, but the words of
Scripture, and the every specific instructions which God has so bounti-
fully given through the Spirit of Prophecy.

Convert's Catechism *Peter Geiermann* .... $ 2.50
The quoted statement on changing solemnity from Saturday to Sunday
can be found in this reproduction.

Divine Philosophy & Science of Health & Healing *G. Paulien* . $19.95
All of the principles of the Bible and the Spirit of Prophecy are designed
to allow us to function in perfect harmony with God Himself. This book
discusses the methods and means of healthful living. It deals with going
back to First Things, and relying by faith upon the substances which God
has established for our benefit.

Don't Drink Your Milk *Frank Oski, MD* .... $ 7.95
Dr. Oski, the head of Pediatrics at Johns Hopkins University School of
Medicine, gives the frightening new medical facts about the world's most
overrated nutrient.

Dove of Gold *Leslie Hardinge* .... $ 7.95
This book approaches the vast subject of the Holy Spirit viewing His
functions through illustrations He himself has selected as vehicles for the
revelation of His character and work. As one observes the related aspects
of the nature and function of the natural object used as a symbol, the work
of the Holy Spirit will become clearer, and His disposition of concern
and affection much more appealing.

Earthly Life of Jesus *Ken LeBrun* $19.95
Biblical accounts of each event in Christ's earthly life carefully arranged
together from the KJV Bible. Words of Jesus in red with full index.

The Elijah People *Ken LeBrun* .... $ 1.00
Those who, in the spirit and power of Elijah, take part in this final work
of reform, will be those who, like Elijah, will be taken to heaven seeing
death. Let us be among them.

Fire Bell in the Night   *Ralph Moss* . . . . $ 5.95
News items and stories from both the secular press and from religious newspapers, along with journals and articles by secular and religious authors will be linked with Bible prophecy to reveal a most startling scenario in just the last few years, and to lay a case to expose an undreamed of enemy who is rapidly winning the confidence of most of this world's inhabitants.

From Eden to Eden   *J. H. Waggoner* . . . . $ 9.95
A most interesting study of the more important historic and prophetic portions of the Scriptures.

Garlic—Nature's Perfect Prescription   *C. Gary Hullquist, M.D.* $ 9.95
Garlic, the Lily of Legend, has today become the focus of modern medical research. Recognized for thousands of years for its amazing curative powers, this bulb is today not only known for its potent bouquet but is drawing the attention of the scientific world as a potential antibiotic, anticancer, antioxidant, anti-aging, anti-inflammatory…the lost goes on and on.

God's DNA for Pure Religion   *Ernest H. J. Steed* . . . . $ 5.95
This book presents a key formula to measure truth and error, the genuine or the counterfeit, so essential in today's world of confusion.

God's Justice—Administered in Love   *Dick Beman* . . . . $ 5.95
You can learn the secret of how to stand firm in the Judgment, without being afraid, and yet maintain a healthy, respectful fear of God.

Gospel In Creation   *E. J. Waggoner* . . . . $ 6.95
This book directs our wandering gaze to the open pages of God's created works as the expression of the gospel, the power of God to save from sin. Facsimile Reprint.

Healing By God's Natural Methods   *Al. Wolfsen* . . . . $ 4.95
Al. Wolfsen has taught hundreds of sick people how to use only simple, non-poisonous remedies.

Healthful Living   *Ellen G. White* $10.95
Wherever this book has been received, it has been recognized as a veritable storehouse of seed thoughts relating to the great practical themes with which it deals. Facsimile Reprint.

Healthy Food Choices   *Leona R. Alderson* $14.95
Some special features include: guidelines for menu planning, breakfast suggestions, ideas for brown bag lunches, and much more!

Helps to Bible Study   *J. L. Shuler* . . . . $ 2.95
A Bible marking system which contains Bible studies covering twenty-eight topics including "The Second Coming," "The Seal of the Living God," "Bible Temperance," and "Christian in Dress." It is simple and practical in its approach, and will benefit all ages.

Holy Spirit Seminar   *Harold Penninger* . . . . $ 7.95
A collection of Holy Spirit Seminars for study, inspiration, etc.

Hoofbeats in Time   *W. G. Moore* . . . . $ 6.95
The title is an allusion to one of the 4 major prophecies of Revelation—
the Four Horsemen of Apocalypse. These horsemen hold fascinating
predictions concerning the world we live in, events both in the past and
the future to come.

Hydrotherapy—Simple Treatments   *Thomas/Dail* . . . . $ 8.95
Help your body overcome common diseases using hydrotherapy and
simple home treatments.

In Heavenly Places Now!   *Richard Parent* . . . . $ 5.95
A devotional study of the sanctuary service which seeks to focus our
attention on our High Priest, Jesus Christ, who ever lives to make
intercession for us.

Incredible Edibles   *Eriann Hullquist* . . . . $ 7.95
Some "health" meals taste bland, some are hard to make, others require
strange or hard to find ingredients. Eriann has developed a simple method
of meal preparation where each recipe looks good and tastes great.

Judgment?? Whose Judgment?   *Robert Frazier* . . . . $ 6.95
Is God really on trial and being judged? This book explores this question
and others.

The Justified Walk   *Frank Phillips* . . . . $ 8.95
Before you can rightly tackle a problem, you must first be able to clearly
understand its nature. Before you can discuss it with others, you must
first define your terms. In this book Elder Phillips makes clear how the
plan of salvation works in our daily lives. Faith, Grace, Sin, Justification,
Sanctification and Righteousness are made real and tangible.

Lessons On Faith   *Jones & Waggoner* . . . . $ 6.95
This is a compilation of articles and sermons given in the 1890's by Jones
and Waggoner on Righteousness By Faith.

Let the Holy Spirit Speak   *Garrie Fraser Williams* . . . . $ 4.95
A remarkable new book that is not just a study guide but a unique resource
of Bible study methods and small group information.

Miracles At The Door   *Don Draper* . . . . $ 8.95
Reading this will encourage the reader and show them how God still
works miracles even in this modern world we live in.

Mystical Medicine   *Warren Peters* . . . . $ 7.95
Many people today have come to believe that our modern, technological
system of health care in the Western world isn't proving to be the great
boon that it was once thought to be. Frustrated and disillusioned people
are turning to "more natural" methods of treatment. As we become aware
of the intimate connection between the physical, mental and spiritual
aspects of our nature, we are flocking to holistic medicine by the
thousands.

Living Fountains or Broken Cisterns   *E. A. Sutherland*. $12.95
This book tells how we should set up our education systems to follow the heavenly blueprint. The goal is to have the best Christian schools in the world.

National Sunday Law   *A. T. Jones* . . . . $ 7.95
This book is a report of an argument made concerning the national Sunday bill that was introduced by Senator Blair in the fiftieth Congress.

Nature's Banquet   *Living Springs*. $12.95
Cooking is an Art and a Science. You will find that the art and science of cooking is especially enjoyable when using natural foods and when learning to be a vegetarian cook. The art of food preparation will give you the opportunity to exercise your enlightened preference and your personality to create attractive, delicious and nutritious meals. The science of cooking involves techniques and properties of food which affect its successful preparation.

Nutrition Workshop Guide   *Eriann Hullquist* . . . . 10 for $ 9.95
Chock full of nutritional recipes, as well as lots of helpful nutritional tips for special situations, such as road trips, fast foods, etc.

Now!   *Merikay McLeod* . . . . $ .99
This book written by a 17 year old girl, graphically portrays a possible end-time scenario. It is a heart warming and thrilling account of God's protection and care of His people, and the trials, triumphs, and joy that lie ahead for them.

Pioneer Stories   *Arthur W. Spalding* . . . . $ 9.95
It is good for children to know what their fathers and mothers did; for sometimes that makes a pattern of what the children should do. Especially is this true if the children are set to finish the work their parents began. And that is the reason why this book is written, to tell the children of the pioneers in the second advent movement the beginnings of that movement, and reasons why they are to carry it on.

Place of Herbs in Rational Therapy   *D. E. Robinson* . . . . $ .90
Quotations relative to the use of herbs in therapy from D. E. Robinson, who was the secretary to Mrs. White.

Power of Prayer   *E. G. White* . . . . $ 7.95
Prayer is our connection with God—our strength, our bridge to heaven! As we pray, the Holy Spirit Himself unites in our petitions and "maketh intercession for us." We are not alone in our battle of life; all heaven is on our side!

Preparation For Translation   *Milton Crane* . . . . $ 7.95
This book is about YOUR preparation for translation. It is about YOUR plans to live without a mediator after probation closes. It is about God's plans for YOUR overcoming temptation NOW in anticipation of those events. It is about His plans for the renewing of YOUR mind through the final atonement ministry of Jesus. Spanish editions—$8.95.

Principles To Live By   *Mel Rees* . . . . $ 4.95
Dominion calls for individual decision and action—therefore, God gave man guiding principles to live by.

Quick-n-Easy Natural Recipes   *Lorrie Knutsen* . . . . $ 2.95
Every recipe has five or fewer ingredients and most take only minutes to prepare. Now you can enjoy simple, natural recipes without the drudgery!

Raw Food Treatment of Cancer   *Kristine Nolfi* . . . . $ 3.95
This book tells of the importance of raw vegetables in the diet of healing and general good health. Dr. Nolfi was a physician in Denmark for over 50 years.

Returning Back to Eden   *Betty-Ann Peters* . . . . $ 9.95
These recipes have been taste-tested by the world-wide travelers that have visited the Back to Eden Restaurant & Bakery in Minocqua, WI.

Right of the People   *A. T. Jones* $11.95
This work, first printed in 1895, showed the relation that should exist between the church and state at the present time, as proved by Holy Writ and the historical evidence of twenty-five centuries

Rome's Challenge   *Catholic Mirror* . . . . $ .99
"The pages of this brochure unfold to the reader one of the most glaringly conceivable contradictions existing between the practice and theory of the Protestant world, and unsusceptible of any rational solution, the theory claiming the Bible alone as the teacher.

Rural Economy   *Ken LeBrun* . . . . $ 2.50
"All that God's Word commands, we are to obey. All that it promises, we may claim. The life which it enjoins is the life that, through its power, we are to live."—Education, p. 188, 189.

The Sabbath   *M. L. Andreasen* . . . . $ 9.95
Attacks upon the Sabbath throughout the ages have been numerous and persistent, and they have all been grounded upon human reasoning as as against the command of God. Men can see no reason why any other day than one commanded by God is not just as good. Men cannot see why one day in seven is not just as good as the seventh day. The answer, of course, is that the difference lies in God's command. It is at this point that man's reason sets aside a positive command of God. It is not merely a question of this or that day, but the greater question of obedience to God's command.

The Savior Guides—Bible Stories for Children   *Alberta Wiggins* $ 8.95
The illustrations in this book assist the teacher to make this learning experience a delight for the young learners because it is compiled of drawings from among their peers and to furnish a complete lesson plan for the teacher who has limited time for preparation.

Sin Shall Not Have Dominion Over You Charles Fitch . . . . $ 6.95
Fitch clarifies his position on sanctification and holiness by answering
three questions: 1) Has God made provisions to save His people from
their sins? 2) If so, can Christians avail themselves of it in this life? and
3) In what way may this provision become available? He uses the Bible
as his only source to answer these questions.

Spurious Books of the Bible *Gar Baybrook* . . . . $ 9.95
Compare the so-called Lost Books of the Bible with proven Scripture.
Most have flagrant errors, some are tainted with pagan beliefs, while
others are quite subtle in their claims.

Steps To Christ Study Guide *Gail Bremner* . . . . $ 2.95
This study guide is designed to encourage the youth, and the young at
heart, to understand and experience more fully a living relationship with
Jesus.

Story of Daniel the Prophet *S. N. Haskell* $11.95
This book especially applicable to our day: points out the immediate
future and in its simplicity will attract many who might not be inclined
to read deep, argumentative works. Facsimile Reprint.

Story of the Seer of Patmos *S. N. Haskell* $12.95
The Book of Revelation pronounces a blessing upon everyone who reads
it or hears it. This books gives the historic SDA view. Facsimile Reprint.

Stress: Taming the Tyrant *Richard Neil* . . . . $ 8.95
Stress is an inevitable part of our 20th century lifestyle. Under the proper
circumstances stress can be uplifting as well as depressing. It can either
help us grow our hasten or death. Find out how to control, manage and
modify stress.

Studies in Daniel and Revelation *Kraid Ashbaugh* . . . . $ 4.95
A convenient handbook containing paraphrases of EG White's com-
ments after each verse in the books of Daniel & Revelation.

Studies in the Book of Hebrews *E. J. Waggoner* . . . . $ 6.95
A series of studies given at the General Conference of 1897. The Bible
studies that Elder Waggoner gave each day, are presented as live and full
of hope for each Bible student today.

Subtle Challenge to God's Authority *Milton Crane* . . . . $ 5.50
Satan's deceptions are many and subtle. He has concentrated his attack
on God's authority.

Such A Cloud of Witnesses *Milton Crane* . . . . $ 4.95
You are called to be a witness for or against the government of God. Will
your testimony help God or aid His enemy?

375 Meatless Recipes–CENTURY 21 *Ethel Nelson, MD* . . . . . . $ 7.95
This book will help you learn how to feed your family in such a way that
they will enjoy eating the foods that nutritionists tell us are an absolute
must if we are going to make it into the twenty-first century.

Truth Triumphant *B. G. Wilkinson* $12.95
   The history of God's true Church from Ireland, to the Waldenses, the struggle to preserve the Bible and the pure doctrine of the apostles is disclosed. Facsimile Reprint.

Understanding the Body Organs *Celeste Lee* . . . . $ 7.95
   Simply and concisely explains how the body organs function and how they relate to one another. Also includes the eight laws of health, explaining each one and sharing many benefits that will be derived from following the entire plan.

Victory and Self-Mastery *J. N. Tindall* . . . . $ 5.95
   How Christ maintained a sinless character in a fallen, sinful, human nature. Facsimile Reprint.

Warning in Daniel 12 *Marian Berry* $14.95
   A study of the twelfth chapter of Daniel. It is warning we shall all need to understand before the end of time.

Who Killed Candida? *Vicki Glassburn* $17.95
   Although diet is an important part of getting well, even the best food and supplements are undermined if you continue to unknowingly support yeast growth! The author will show you how making simple lifestyle choices can actually STOP THE YEAST SUPPORT CYCLE that other Candida programs do not address.

Whole Foods For Whole People *Lucy Fuller* $10.95
   Whole Foods For Whole People is not just a cookbook, but a manual to teach people how they can live a longer, healthier lifestyle by using the natural resources which surround us.

The Word Was Made Flesh *Ralph Larson* . . . . $ 8.95
   This book is on the human nature of Christ, with a limited, rather specialized objective. Dr. Larson does not deal directly with the whole issue of Christ's human nature. He traces the understanding of this aspect of Christology within the Seventh-day Adventist church from 1852–1952, providing a fairly comprehensive survey of historical data.

To order any of the above titles, see your local bookstore.

However, if you are unable to locate any title, call 518/358-3652.

The Antichrsit 666
BOOK 1

William Josiah Sutton
Positive proof for Bible Believing People: Who the beast is; Who his image is; What the mark of the beast is; How to count the number of the beast. Edited by Roy Allan Anderson, D.D.

The Illuminati 666
BOOK 2

William Josiah Sutton
Find out about the Illuminati, its startling history, and how powerful it has become. Includes a study of the origins of false religions, and the forms they are taking today. Introduction by Roy Allan Anderson, D.D.

New World Order 666
BOOK 3

William Josiah Sutton
In *New World Order 666*, the author shows with amazing clarity and with great accuracy in certain apocalyptic passages of the Bible who will usher it in, the coalitions involved and the part played by the United States of America.

Published by TEACH Services, Inc.
Available at your local bookstore or call 518/358-3652